An Author and His Image

The Collected Short Pieces

J. P. DONLEAVY

VIKING

VIKING

Published by the Penguin Group
Penguin Books Ltd, 27 Wrights Lane, London w 8 5 tz, England
Penguin Books USA Inc., 375 Hudson Street, New York, New York 10014, USA
Penguin Books Australia Ltd, Ringwood, Victoria, Australia
Penguin Books Canada Ltd, 10 Alcorn Avenue, Toronto, Ontario, Canada m 4 v 3 b 2
Penguin Books (NZ) Ltd, 182 – 190 Wairau Road, Auckland 10, New Zealand

Penguin Books Ltd, Registered Offices: Harmondsworth, Middlesex, England

This collection first published 1997
10 9 8 7 6 5 4 3 2 1
First edition

Copyright © J. P. Donleavy, 1976, 1977, 1978, 1983, 1984, 1985, 1986, 1987,
1988, 1989, 1991, 1992, 1994, 1995, 1996, 1997

The moral right of the author has been asserted

Set in 11/13½ pt Monotype Ehrhardt
Typeset by Rowland Phototypesetting Ltd, Bury St Edmunds, Suffolk
Made and printed in England by Clays Ltd, St Ives plc

A CIP catalogue record for this book is available from the British Library

isbn 0-670-80193-3

Contents

Introduction   Why Do I Write   ix

PART 1   The Writer and His Art

An Author and His Image   3
Tools and Traumas of the Writing Trade   11
An Essay in Contemplation of Writing the Second
  Volume of *The History of the Ginger Man*   23
Shaun Beary – A Portrait of the Playwright as a Man   32

PART 2   People and Places

My Own Romantic Bronx   37
An Expatriate View of America   51
Rat Holes and Magic Places   71
To London from Mullingar   73
Come to Cong Where the Glamour is Still Glowing   78

PART 3   What a Sport

Georgian Cricket or Whither Goes Those Wickets   87
Sexual Exercises for Women   93
Whither Goeth Those Racquets and Riches at
  Wimbledon   97
Dublin Horse Show   110
Donleavy is Better Than McEnroe   115
The Manly Art of Knocking Senseless   119

PART 4   Life, Death and Affairs of the Heart

Whither Goeth That Bullet   127
Sentimental Journey – My Favourite Hotel   136
My First Love   146
Pasha of Heartbreak House   151
Love Letters Straight to the Heart   157

PART 5   Gone But Not Forgotten

W. B. Yeats Commemoration   165
Christmas Recollections – for Better or Worse   166
Remembrance of a Pain Past   173
The Funeral of Denny Cordell   178
The Funeral of the General   183

PART 6   Castles and Mansions, Conduct and Etiquette

An Open Letter to Those of the Nobility Befuddled
    by Clutter   189
Ghosts and Dolls in Donegal   192
Upon Conduct Becoming and Unbecoming
    a Philanderer   201
Nothing Looks Better Than a Harris Tweed Jacket
    and Faded Blue Jeans on a Sunday   223

PART 7   Dear Old Dublin

Trinity Quatercentenary   235
The Dublin Ghosts Remembered on Bloomsday   239
Night Out in Dublin   245
The Bloom of a City   249
The De Alfonce Bank   257

PART 8   Introductions and Reviews on
Other Authors

Review of Selina Hastings's Biography of Evelyn Waugh   261
Introduction to John Ryan's *Remembering How We Stood*   268
Review of John de St Jorre's *The Good Ship Venus*   274
A Voyage to the Swiftian City – an Introduction to
   Gulliver's Travels   277
A Bit More Blarney about the Emerald Isle   283

PART 9   Ireland, Then and Now

The Water of Life   291
The Second Revolution – the Modern Enthral of
   the New Ireland   295
A Book of Irish Quotations   301
The Boy is Back in Town   304
Pasha of Heartbreak House Seeks Companion   310

Introduction
Why Do I Write

I don't imagine my reasons for writing could differ greatly from those of any other author. But since I have been writing now for about forty five years, the answer to the question 'Why do I write' seems difficult to dig out of a long past.

Having been a painter before becoming an author taught me that the written word travelled further and reached deeper and into more minds than a painting, and was also something, once published, no amount of tearing up or a boot through a canvas could destroy or stop. Also there is the satisfaction that the written word could willy nilly penetrate and annoy people in the privacy of their own homes. And the greater justice could be done as their immediate resentments might anger them enough to put dents in their more valuable pieces of antique furniture. Or words instead touch their sensibilities so that they know they listen to a kindred soul.

But I'm sure the basic reason why one writes must originate and still lurk in one's vanity. Which, as a testament to one's existence, might flower in the bliss of fame and fortune. The reason also can be found in wanting to shake one's tiny fist against a monstrous and indifferent world and speak words about that world one felt should be spoken and that no one else dared speak, especially to a world cautioning with punishment that such words should not be spoken. But as much as the conscious reason to write, the unconscious reasons must be equally as strong, and one such reason must be the mating instinct. To let kindred spirits in the world know as soon as possible that one had a beautiful if occasionally obscene mind. And to make known, if not flaunt, the uniqueness of one's identity. Which, too, comes contradictorily out of the awareness of one's own insignificance.

If the reasons above are why I began to write, that asks, too, another question. Why does one continue to write. And here is, if not a profound, at least an eminently sensible answer. I'm sure that at no time in my life has it ever been lost upon me that scribbling down whatever came into one's day dreaming mind and later constructing and embellishing it, and then selling it, and turning one's worst moments into money, is a damn nice way to make a living. Of course, too, one way or another, you live what you write. Suffering the same pain, embarrassment, sorrow and joy. Even being involved in the same mystery and love that speaks on your pages. And in the reflected romantic glory of that world of written life, you endure better your own lived life. And you not only preserve the past, but help defy death in the present.

During those forty five years there has always been a particular pleasure in publishing these short pieces and sketches in various newspapers and periodicals worldwide knowing that they would reach a public who were not normally book readers and for a moment or two one would penetrate vicariously into their lives. But as they say, periodicals and newspapers wrap fish, keep vagrants warm and help light fires. However, one keeps faith that books preserve their pages better between covers and these pieces separately written over these past twenty one years can now keep each other company.

J. P. Donleavy
Mullingar, 1996

PART I

The Writer and His Art

An Author and His Image

An author is always unconsciously fighting for an image and when he gets one, consciously fighting against it. But an image is often the most important endowment he can have. And a novelist usually has made his long before someone meets him. By his picture on a book jacket, or in a newspaper, for drunkenly socking a headwaiter on the jaw, or just by rumours that he is recently being released from the institution.

But most times folk see him as the autobiographical hero of what he's written. When you find yourself faced, as I might be, by avid readers of *A Singular Man*, thinking that I am reclusive, rich, lonely and sad but with a private part two feet long. Or by readers of *The Onion Eaters*, wondering if I'm in my damp Irish castle, overwhelmed by uninvited guests, plaster and other matters falling from the ceiling, rats nibbling at my shoelaces, as I sit in front of a turf fire bemused by my three testicles. And when you're the author of *The Ginger Man* and folk had warning I was coming, especially to their house, the furniture would be secretly screwed down, the drink locked up, and the key hidden to one's host's wife's chastity belt.

However, the author starts out with no image at all except his burning sincerity, determination and dedication, and perhaps an occasional fist shook in a scorning relative's face that by God he's going to be rich and famous. A legend in his lifetime. The author of a paragraph that school children have to memorize or not get into college. His female readers tucked up in corners of the world on lonely beds, reliving the words of that writer reclusively somewhere who has such a beautiful or such an extremely dirty mind. To whom such sad and obscene things must have happened. And that they, had they known him, those years ago, would have realized, that as he scooped up his fudge sundae at the local candy store, that even the way he held his spoon reeked with destiny.

So an author really begins with an image of himself. As a lonely ignored hero to a private public he carries around in his mind. Who clap, cheer and encourage. To get him through the unknown years. And speak an unspoken answer to all the voices saying, who do you think you are. Proust or something. He thinks he is Balzac. Because he owes for last month's rent and yesterday's hashish. His close friends plant careful seeds of despair in his open hearted yearning for recognition. By someone. Preferably sitting on an editorial throne of judgement, surrounded by unabridged dictionaries. But instead this someone happens to be the best known literary gossip writer on the biggest serious newspaper. Who, as he dismisses one more pompous best selling novelist just flown into town, ends his column saying he has just read a manuscript of promise delivered by hand to his club. A young man obviously writing under duress, just north of 233rd Street in the Bronx, and especially deserving of a Foundation grant. And on this dream the author hibernates.

Till the unbelievable one day he wakes up for good when he is finally published. The book does not soar into the stratosphere. That's the place where people think you sit overlooking the Plaza Fountain taking noonday breakfast with the waiter plugging in the phone to take your calls from the Coast with your Louis Roederer and scrambled eggs. But alas for this author a major silence of five years descends. Of distant minor little voices saying to one another, hey you ought to read this book.

And one day you meet one of these voices. Which says are you really him, just standing here in your moccasins in the supermarket on Columbus Avenue and West 70th Street, with two cans of frozen orange juice, powdered coffee, salami and jar of stuffed olives. I mean gee isn't everyone dying to know you. Aren't you crowded out of your mind with tour dates and seminars. I mean holy cow don't you know who you are.

With this previous incident you rush one hundred and ten yards home to sit and think. Squeaking in the wicker chair in your begrimed bay window. Three solid hours next to an unringing phone. My God I was recognized. Someone knew me. And I saw her ashen faced tell her husband as I left. And they watched me carrying the specially reduced bargains. They're going to think I haven't got a pot to piss in. That my book which didn't sell, didn't sell. And now the people who didn't buy it will never buy it. The writer blundering into his first taste of fame. And at a loss as to what props to carry or what demeanour to wear.

But the one he unconsciously or consciously tries to wear is the one which sells books. And it's not easy to know which image does that. But the experimental struggle to find out is immense. If it calls for mounting a horse top hatted and pink coated and chasing a fox across New Jersey most authors would risk their necks, followed closely by their tweed suited publishers commandeering an ambulance, photographers in attendance. But what the author really wants is not to be out there, face flushed, hustling in the market place. But to be seen quietly, just recognizable by candlelight, solemnly dining with an adoring stunning woman, with the word whispered through the swank hotel's lobby, he's in there, boy just look at those white chamois gloves he wears to eat his lobster.

But in the hurrying world no image lasts for long. And the practice of private elegance becomes little comforting with book emporiums returning books to the publisher. The author in his economic rejection sets out to commune with nature. Next publishing season he will sell his deep sincerity acquired contemplating in an uninhabited mountain range in Utah. He's only bitten once by a rattlesnake, poisoned twice by ivy and chased three times by a grizzly bear. And eighteen months and one wife later we see him on his next book jacket. Standing in front of his isolated mountainside cabin. Built with local logs with his own two bare hands. Smoke curling from the chimney. His most recent wife a Bryn Mawr graduate holding her homemade jar of wild blackberry jam in the doorway. Both grinning with the outdoor purity of it all.

Her name is Martha. She summers at the Vineyard. Her father is an investment banker. She was born and bred in Boston. And she's the initial M in the most recent novel's dedication. To M, who stood by. She hunts to hounds. Her bowler hatted image sweeps the fashion magazines. As she momentarily lies prostrate on the literary altar of sacrifice. And deeply interested and profoundly influenced by the Far East. There are photographs to prove it. Of her newly shaved head and the saffron nightdress she wears for evening cocktails. Until just recently. She tried on a pair of horns. When she discovered the Hopi Indians.

Not much of the author's image is seen these days. But his wife is frequently quoted in her interviews about the god damn trouble she's having with her husband's meddling in her first novel. At which she works feverishly while, she complains, he spends his days, feet propped up on their tropical fish tank, the television blaring with a six pack of beer by his chair reading movie magazines while proclaiming his admiration for ditch digging Austrian women. Because at long last the neighbourhood loners and the smart kids in the colleges are beginning to read his books and the royalties are trickling in.

The fan letters come. Some of adulation. Others disconcerted because not one of their friends has ever heard of you. One offers you the rights to his life story. Enclosing a photograph but wants it understood that it is not a homosexual proposition. Profits split fifty fifty because the balance between comedy and tragedy in your work is so achingly true to life. The author takes comfort that he has sprinkled a little magic in these distant lives. That makes their voices speak back. And know that your own voice has been heard. Even by a young woman who's read everything you've written. She sees in you a sad dispossessed heart like her own. Ready to take gymnastic advantage of her measurements,

37-27-37. She presently resides in an elegant mental institution, listening to Brahms as she writes. She thinks you are a bit of a phoney but someday she'd like to meet you, drink champagne and read Pushkin together.

By now the author's first book is acclaimed. His second reprinted. His third adapted for the stage and produced on Broadway. And to keep the pot simmering his image is overhauled. He was now the most famous non selling, unknown best selling underground author in the world. Little legends begin appearing on the copyright page. Seventh printing. Ninth printing. Literary gossips whisper, hoping it isn't true, hey this guy must be getting rich. The critics are waiting. For his fourth book. To pan this affluent author who served no public penance for his growing sales and fame. Who now had a secretary waiting, legs crossed, pencil poised in case he wanted to sue someone. His second law suit will soon be going to court. Someone's named a restaurant after one of his books. His horse kicked an anti blood sport enthusiast. And the legal bills flood in.

Somehow the author blames the reflection of his heartfelt words that lie wounded on the page. Which make him look like a pushover. Publishers say look at all that serious adoration he's getting, what the hell does he need to reserve all his subsidiary rights for, too. Anyway our warranty clause will make him pay for all our costs in that last legal action. On the next book jacket the writer insists to be seen scowling. His two eyes staring out from the page say I'll get you yet, you son of a bitch. He also wanted to be photographed with a sub machine gun across his knees so his former wife Martha and her lawyers would get the message. That nobody is going to take half his royalties plus his Mercedes shooting brake, Connecticut country house and sixteen Arab horses.

But members of his own profession. They see him on easy street. Able to buy first class plane tickets and champagne for the dazzling girl that sits next to him on the way to Mexico. To whom he's thought to gallantly say, my car's meeting me at the airport can I give you a lift. And in case you want to see my private island my yacht is getting up steam to sail.

But there is another contingent who have a different picture of you. And they don't like your image one damn bit. They live in nice little white houses. With nice little watered green lawns. With wives who comb their hair back straight and wear earrings on Saturday nights when other wives just like them with two children, four and six, come to dinner. Their husbands have cosy dens with pipe racks and paperbacks where they dissect you. And while keeping your name off the bulletin boards, make sure you get the dismissed reputation they think you deserve. These are the academics. They are sure you cannot do without them. Because they are certain you want desperately to hear that word masterpiece. And they might just, if only you'd answer their letters, be on the verge of saying it. But for the time being they must reserve judgement because they understand you can't spell and do not know who wrote *The Decameron*.

So the author's image as it glows, or glowers, waxes briefly and wanes again. A strange star in a familiar solar system. Until people sidle up at the cocktail party, look him carefully up and mostly down. Desperately wanting to remind you. That all you are is just a human being. But what are you working on now. The question means don't think you can afford to rest your laurels on those other old hat books you wrote. The author affects a departing stance, that he's just a micro second in town from his East Hampton summer house. Their eyes narrow, they pluck the stuffed olive off the toothpick and chew while their eyes mist over with a genuine concern for your career. Which always means do you think you've shot your bolt. Which in turn means does the author think he is still capable of sexual intercourse.

Suddenly the time's come yet again for the author to present yet another image. Of his bulging bicep when he's been shaking hands with prize fighters. Or even demonstrating how fast and hard he can hit with a right hook. He comes mornings in the altogether skipping rope out of his bedroom. The new wife Helga from the Cincinnati proletariat and a graduate of Ohio State, keeps the shades down so the neighbours won't see what a nut she thinks he's making out of himself. But he's telling the world that if someone gets hit in one of his books, the punch might have come delivered from the still powerful muscles of the author. Who has plenty of uppercuts and right hooks left. And even at the advanced age of forty six can go two consecutive rounds in the ring. With any other two fisted writer you care to mention.

By such machinations the author hopes to keep his public guessing. And despite his headline dissipations he is still far from needing handouts on the geriatric come back trail. Nor had he yet been driven, as they'd all like to see him go, to the light chocolate coloured walls of the boarding house room. From whence he hobbles unshaven to sell blood every time a manuscript returns special delivery and rejected by a publisher.

But still now, creeping into latter middle age, there's an image left, carefully cultivated and lurking behind each novel the writer published. And that is the novel, not yet ready, that he never published. Which, when he did, would turn the tide, already beginning to slowly wash the author right out of one *Who's Who* after another. This is the big book. The one the author has always secretly been working on. Kept behind bars in packing cases in the basement of the Federal Reserve Bank at 33 Liberty Street. The major work, the deeply serious one for which the author had all the warm up publications. Behind a door weighing ninety tons, it sits there in the subterranean vault, five hundred thousand words safe from critics and beyond the chequebook blandishments of publishers. Any moment now, the last orgy of work upon it will be begun. When finally published, journalists will take off their typewriter covers and say, here at long last, after all those awful pot boilers, the germ of promise sown so many years ago now blossoms to make us tremble in our tracks with the rumble of printing presses.

9

But the author ends as he began. If ever he did begin. Pained in isolation. Pained by glad facing among the cocktails. Further away than ever from the kindred souls to whom he sent the songs he sings. Alone. Again locked up in his own tiny world. Haunted a little by the ricochets of all the accumulated images. Fading as they come back to tempt yet another change. And hope to sell another book. But you know no matter what you do the world will always finally turn its face away. Back into all its own troubled lives. Busy to be seen with a new pair of shoes and heard with another author's name. Forgetting what you wanted them to see. Silent with what you wanted them to say. And empty with what you wanted them to feel.

Except somewhere you know there will be a voice. At least once asking. Hey what happened to that guy, did he die, you know the one, who wrote that book, can't remember his name but he was as famous as hell. That was the author. And that was his image.

1978

Tools and Traumas of the Writing Trade

One late summer sunny day during a long London afternoon perambulation and while innocently looking in the window of an old established cheese shop, the definition of what writing is all about hit me. Writing is turning one's worst moments into money. And money is one of the motives for becoming a writer. The others are leisure and money, women and money, fame and money, and sometimes just money all alone by itself.

And to the young dreaming writer money portrays itself as a blazing blue beautiful world set on a gently nodding horizon complete with a twelve metre racing yawl. Under his captain's hat, the author as sailor, a gentle breeze, two published novels and a currently running West End stage production behind him, he stands in the rear cockpit, binoculars at the ready, searching the evening shore ahead where on some mysterious promontory a faintly lighted dining table is being laid ready for his appearance. And he appears. And out of the flowery landscaped darkness folk rush to him and say, their eyes glistening, gee your conversation is even more beautiful than your book, and gosh, you're even better looking than your photograph.

And as a youthful American, such dreams are dreamed sitting at one's kitchen table over the milk and peanut butter during the years of high school while Ma is saying, 'Haven't you done your homework yet, Junior.' 'But Ma, I'm going to be a famous writer and a millionaire.' Ma says, 'Drink your milk and go and do your homework. How do you ever expect to get a job with the Asbestos Company.' A few minutes later when no one is looking, Junior has closed his biology book and sneaks out into the summer evening for an illicit smoke with friends. Walking along the maple shaded street, finding that no one else believes his dream yet saying behind a shaking fist, 'I'll make one hundred thousand dollars with my first best seller and then they'll be sorry.'

And so the budding writer, among his uncaring sceptical cronies and invariably hostile family, learns that being a writer is antisocial, anticommunity, because it's not a job, and that the natural reaction of the immediate working society around him is to destroy or drive out the bad apple in its midst. Who would want to be a millionaire without first filling out an application form. Or who would forsake an afternoon's tennis to lonely reconnoitre in the local cemetery. And now when he meets with his friends and they say, 'Hey, what are you really going to be when you grow up' and all one can say is, 'Rich', and they say, 'How' and you say, 'I'm going to be a dentist', the writer has picked up a useful tool in his survival, cunning.

As the high school years go by, the first steps towards the great dream ahead are taken when the poems get written. The girls say, 'That's really beautiful, but you copied it out of a book.' The boys say, 'Gee you're a Shakespeare.' College approaches. The four years of indoctrination for the corporation. Or the grooming of a literate mind till it's full of the most recently accepted critical opinions that can be safely repeated for graduation. This is where the young writer founders. And toys with his maiden trauma. As he offers his scribblings for appraisal, he's told, 'Get your degree first, your security, then think of becoming a writer.' And during this testing time the road ahead fatefully forks, when you can no longer think or dream of becoming a writer, you must be a writer. Or else get shunted off on an English course in literature to the conniving assassinating world of criticism, grants and fellowships, rarely to return to that of writing.

But collegiate or not, one more indoctrination is inevitable. And most traumatic of all. The nice girl turns up. She likes you because you have a beautiful sensitive mind. You're so good at judging people, so good at turning the world into visions. She says, 'You would look so handsome making decisions behind a desk. Just what they're looking for on Madison Avenue. And then we could move to Scarsdale or Sunningdale out of all this filthy mess.' And so, if you haven't told her to go to hell, and she's still stealing from the supermarket, one day sometime later a little baby is born. Along with the infant screams and sleepless nights, the relentless sledgehammer of responsibility lands. You get to recognize the tiptoe to the apartment door of the rent collector and the disguised voices of the terminators of gas and electricity. Plus the soft uncomforting words of the bank, 'But you've got no regular job or collateral for a loan.'

And so we come to the first indispensable tool of the writer. Money. And by money is meant capital. For only with capital can come independence and the long term purchase of time. The writer's most important ingredient. Time to wake up in the morning haunted with the anxiety that the money is running out. Time to sit at the typewriter putting down that first page, haunted by the anxiety that one will never write a second. And finally time to realize that you may need a year, or two or three. When surely by that time you'll be in the asbestos plant or the poorhouse.

On your first pages the struggle may go on for weeks. The sentences trying to find life. That can begin to weave a story that lives. Which in turn can lend you confidence to continue on. Spelling out the words you clutch from your brain. And that conjure on the page a meaning you want to mean. Until suddenly, one day, a chord is struck. It will have a strange reverberating music. But when you hear it you'll know you're on your way. Able now to further brazen through the chronic prevailing ignominy. And at last sure, when no one else is, that you're a writer.

And what did you do for money. Only God knows. And it would embarrass him. But now you have a desk, a typewriter, carbon paper, a wife screaming why don't you get a job. You also have the vague but burning presumption that you have written something that someone else might want to read. And also make your Ma and Pa drop dead with shame. Plus a slew of relatives who will also tell them I told you so. But all this brings into function the second most important tool of the writer, a suicidal and ruthless nerve. It's a trait which makes your friends a trifle shifty eyed and much uncomfortable. And with it there comes the slow but sure alienation, a stepping back and apartness from the world around you. For the born writer this has happened years ago, when his girl friend or later mother in law said he had a dirty disgusting mind. Or when, for his evil influence on other students, he was expelled from high school or kicked out of college. And leaving all your old neighbourhood friends to whisper, 'He isn't the same George we used to know when he told us he was going to be a dentist.'

And along with this alienation an author finds his next best all purpose tool is that of an empty head. From which learning and knowledge, the two greatest enemies of a working writer, have been eliminated. Which alas will provoke an oft heard refrain about you, 'Holy cow, not only can't he spell but he's illiterate too.' But your business now is to see and hear both in yourself and in the world around you. Especially involving the incidents which caused you the most acute embarrassment. These, your uninhibited observations and feelings, are the building bricks and cement. Variously styled by others as malicious rumour and falsehood. They accumulate and get mixed in dreams, conversations and drunken brawls. And get coloured by despairs and joys and tempered by passing time and morbid hangovers. To finally unearth during the long bouts of lonely despair as the threads which bind and weave your story.

But hopefully, and amid protests from those nearest and dearest that 'My God that's not literature that's libel', this narrative as it unfolds becomes a novel. And the writer has found that the everyday tools he has needed have not been a university course in English, journalism or writing, but the accumulated gossip, hearsay and scandal circulating among his more steadfast cronies, a thousand or more dollars or pounds, a typewriter, a disciplined use of it for three or four hours a day, the finishing of a page, the rewriting of it, watching each sentence catch fire and bring to life another and that another, until one day arrives. The writer reaches over on his desk and pinches between thumb and forefinger a stack of paper. He lifts it and it has weight. He punches holes, threads through ribbon, or nuts and bolts, puts on a cardboard cover, and suddenly he's got a manuscript. This is where the traumas begin.

All the old friends in search of their life's safety are gone on their ways to higher degrees. Or to steady or not so steady jobs mending tracks on the railroad. One penurious oddball is left. Like you he's decided that for the time being he'll continue doing what everyone else describes as nothing. He frequently on his hungry evenings comes and scrapes the bottom of the spaghetti bowl. You say, 'Read this.' He says between mouthfuls and brief perusals of your heartfelt scurrilous prose, 'You're crazy.' You pull away the bottle of wine. As he tugs back the manuscript for another look, he says, 'Wait, maybe you're a genius, but get a second opinion.'

The author studies the literary pages of newspapers. And in his incredible innocence mails off his manuscript to the most prominent publisher in sight. Meanwhile he peruses fashion magazines listing town houses and country estates. He looks over the Daimler limozines at the local suppliers. And takes an interest in yachts providing a library and study attached to the owner's suite. But as the silent days lengthen as they accumulate, he goes back to wandering, waiting and contemplating in his favourite cemetery again. And when with a last handful of change he buys a beer in his local pub, he still answers, 'Nothing', to an old pal who asks suspiciously, 'What are you doing now.' But next morning he knows. For at the end of three long weeks a crushingly bulky reply has at last come. From the awe inspiring firm under whose banner these past twenty one days you dreamt you would take your first bounding steps to fame and fortune.

> Dear Sir,
>> Thank you for giving us the opportunity of reading enclosed returned herewith but we do not feel it suitable for our lists.
>>> Yours faithfully,
>>> The Editors.

The first thing you go and do is to sit and write. A furious reply. The first and rudest of which is torn up to write another.

> Dear bunch of Editors,
>> You stupid bastards have just turned down what will be one of the great best sellers of the last half of this decade.
>>> Yours sincerely,
>>> The Author.

And alas, as the glowering wife loudly smoulders and innocent kiddies cower quietly, you realize that the words of both your letter and manuscript are just as effective as throwing the paper on which they are written in a ball as hard as you can against the sky scraping massiveness or genuine Georgian brick in which these titans of the published word reside, daily solving the world's toughest crossword puzzles and trading epigrams with colleagues on their hourly visits to the water cooler.

But the penurious oddball who, along with his deep researching of his own non existent sex life, has been philosophizing elsewhere. He has on the breeze of his eccentricities sailed into the current latitudes of literature and is lapping up a more lavish lasagne and grabbing at the now vintage wine. He says, 'I have a friend who has a crazy manuscript.' And the thin, poem writing many university educated blonde says, 'Hey gee isn't that interesting I have a friend who is a publisher.'

So in a big building sits a guy behind a desk who majored in English and now makes thirty thousand dollars a year, leaning against a wall at various cocktail parties with that look, 'I've read Proust in the original, straight through, one summer in my cottage up on the Cape, and I am sure there is no new Proust budding in the Bronx.' However, uncrossing his legs and pulling up his English woven socks, he condescends to continue the never ending search for new talent and enduring penmanship and says, 'Let us have a look at this crazy manuscript.' And of course this is the novel which would make one's folks, if they read it, drop dead. This publisher reads it. He finds he is glued to every word and shocked into the bargain. He is certain that this is not literature. And if it is it would not make him look good at his next cocktail party. And so carefully disguising the offending tome with the nice blue wrapper borrowed from his copy of *The Shorter Oxford English Dictionary*, he sneaks the manuscript back to the mailing room. And there with it safely parcelled, he writes that under separate cover is returned this volume which the editor finds not only unpleasantly unsuitable but also that season's leading candidate as the most unlikely book for publication.

One more trauma and the author learns a rule, that what is original and vital, and offered, will be rejected. This rule is rarely ever changed, neither by fame, fortune, nor acclaim, and rejection will happen again and again. For in the nature of publishing everyone is searching for what is unhackneyed and alive while handing over a cheque to an agent who has an imitation of last season's best seller. Which the publisher's representatives think they can subscribe in hundreds of copies at the bookstore. So where does this leave the author. It leaves him thoroughly depressed and back again among his neighbourhood tombstones wondering if any soul alive out there will ever hear him, so thoroughly has the loud world quelled his tiny voice.

But the word has at last got round. That the author looks well in bathing costume. And has a criminally dirty mind. Another young woman, a graduate, a doctor of modern English literature, says so. And that there is a socially redeeming aspect to the honest and explicit treatment of sex in his manuscript. And the word sex is soon described as brutish and unbridled. And these words in turn gain those of shockingly explicit. And the whole damn reader's report goes whispered hurriedly from tipster to publisher whose legal advisers counsel that the sodomy is defensible on literary grounds plus a prosecution would immensely help sales. And suddenly the word carnal gets converted to 'Our Standard Contract'. And this latter, as the author sits trembling reading it, is being amended with their most recently fairest option clause for the writer's next six books on the same terms. And meanwhile, 'Have you an agent.' The answer, 'No', and the reply, 'Just sign here.' But through the remainder of that unforgettable afternoon the author's ears are thundering with printing presses, the flash of camera bulbs, and the hundreds of blonde smiling women fresh in from Scarsdale and Sunningdale with their books to sign and themselves free that evening to dine with the author at the Ritz.

But months go by. As the publisher's editor, under the guise of correcting the spelling, attempts to rewrite one's book in standard English. Next the author accidentally gets a peek at a proof of the jacket. And one looks for one's name. And finally finds it. And says to the publisher, 'Make it bigger,' and he says, 'That's the regulation size for all first novels.' Slowly the author gets a changing glimpse of his future. His name insignificantly there on the luridly illustrated cover. And prophetically written on a tombstone astride which is the naked heroine.

Next, the publisher's list is published. And the unadorned print doesn't look half bad. Nor the blurb describing the author as this untamed child of his times whose soul must speak out. And now once again the writer sees himself at long long last standing on high ground, the sailing skiff if not the yacht would be delivered from the boat yard soon. Meanwhile on the three figure advance, the first figure of which is one, his wife has had dental treatment, his children new shoes and he, a new seersucker suit. The wind is gently blowing through his recently tonsured hair. As the distant roar of the printing presses rises. And then subsides. To a soothing spiritual sound. Once heard never forgotten. Of fresh banknotes floating endlessly down from heaven.

Publication day comes. The world does stop. But only for a fractional second as the sun sets just that bit more slowly than yesterday. There are no full page screaming advertisements or even book displays. But you did see an obscure review along with that photograph taken by the wife outside the welfare office. And the words beneath 'shows promise'. And at the end of the review, 'We should await his next book with interest.' But luckily someone else has said, 'This isn't a book for the squeamish or to give your Aunt Christabel for Christmas.' And such words have caught the attention of a few old friends who instead of calling you, call their lawyers. And if you have been honest enough to have written what you've felt and heard, you've also thereby invaded everyone's privacy and held them up to ridicule and contempt, but you avoid being sued for libel because no one dare get up in court and say, 'That's me he's writing about.'

However, following all the dashed hopes, renewed despairs and the unending, 'Well I'm sorry I do read books, but I've never heard of you,' finally, five years later just as you go down for the third time, voices are speaking up. A discerning few are beginning to discover the novel and say, 'Gee you ought to read that.' The book starts to sell. Someone wants to dramatize it, someone wants to reprint it, translate it and film it, and are offering money. The author at long last smiles, shakes his fist close up in his wife's face and, mouth watering, runs to his contract. Alas he reads here, turns over and he reads there, but mostly he turns over again and reads where he finds the words 'the Publisher shall exclusively negotiate all rights, including spinoff, character and merchandising, and receive 85 per cent of all monies accruing therefrom.' After his first feeble moments of white faced anger the author searches in a pitch black soul for words of comfort, fairness and justice to temper his own screams of woe, 'Those dirty rats, they never promoted my book, never advertised it, they let it die and here they are, five years later, jumping with both feet on to my gravy train.'

And yet when the author is writing his first book, it somehow exists, that words written on paper and unpublished are valueless. And they are. Till that day arrives when someone puts down five or more dollars to purchase these scribbles in their published form, when it dawns on the writer that he is in business. Just like anyone else. And the time now has come, if his outrage has left him any remaining sense at all, when the author goes to his local library and borrows his first volumes on contract and copyright. These are two subjects which never occur to him during the years sweating out his creative words. Believing as he blindly must that the world will always somehow discover, admire and reward genius. At least the author discovers, somewhat to his surprise, that copyright is a big pie, full of juicy fruits better known as licences and assignments, all of which can make money. And the author owns all of it. For a while. And for ever in two countries in the world. Portugal and Nicaragua.

Among the countries in which he owns least is the United States of America. Where fellowships, prizes and grants are poured down the throats of writers. Yet an author could not be ensured to receive the rightful earnings of his work, should he outlive the term of copyright protection, or fail to comply with the complicated regulations. Which until recently required you wake up on a certain morning and search your pocket for two dollars and write to Washington for the forms, and fill them out without a mistake, and send them back before twelve o'clock midnight, Sundays not included, on the last day following twenty eight years of publication. The situation resulting from such failure is known as public domain. Into which a living author's work may fall. Which does not mean it benefits the public but does mean that publishers, who preach and breast beat in the name of art and letters, don't have to pay an author a royalty on his work.

And this brings one to one last tool in the writing trade, a lawyer. That few writers can afford. Especially in their first eager innocent steps, which, should he survive these, then for the good author and the best author, litigation will be his lot. For folk, mistaking his heartfelt feelings expressed in his work for softness, and relying on his poverty, automatically try to make him the scapegoat of any dispute. Critics remain always his enemies. Except over the years they hopefully will take more and more print and space to condemn you. Invariably sneakily referring to criticisms of a previous book to see to what extent they dare degrade you with your presently published volume. And the author's weapon at this period becomes silence. In which he remains sacred to that final word he puts on the page. But alas that one tool which the author needed in his first steps, and that he still now needs more than ever, is money.

Through all his traumas and through the too slowly waxing and the too quickly waning of his reputation, hopefully, you finally find the author safely arrived. To that acceptable but declining condition pleasantly known as his prime. Which means you are faintly branded as famous amid the growing hordes of people who have never heard of you. But odd invitations come to give talks at colleges. Interviewers again and again report your daily routine. From dawn nonstop till midnight changing typewriters as they overheat. Yet now you really are a writer. And if there is an occasional glow of joy it mostly comes when walking during your recreation. With a little wine and a little travel. And you may from your country house go up to town. To lie abed that night with a first class woman, in a first class hotel and next morning greet the world with interest. And find the charmingly literate hotel's director has seen to a display of your work in the lobby bookstall. Breakfast is brought. Of buckwheat cakes with creamy melted butter and splashed with pure maple syrup and surrounded by rashers of bacon and golden toasted sausages. Stacked by your hand as you munch, the cities' newspapers both saucy and serious. And you leisurely read while drinking your coffee. Having just listened pleased to sales reports from your most recent publisher on the telephone. And now you make an appointment for tea with an old pal who has long since forgotten he was at length libelled as an unsavoury character in your first novel.

And just as you settle into the lapsang souchong balmy accords of afternoon tea, merely one day like this can nearly answer why be a writer. Forever sweating on a page. Hoping still to find a few voices out there to echo back your own. And make you know another mind, kindred and understanding, has seen your ghosts, felt your love, and had his own worried loneliness broken and driven away awhile with laughter. And meanwhile you've lived the usual story. You can't win. But if you don't fight, you lose. And there is a victory. To remain a writer, reach the age of forty, be solvent and still love your trade.

1977

An Essay in Contemplation
of Writing the Second Volume of
The History of the Ginger Man

Since it involves despair and trepidations in the cities of London, Paris and New York one must be deadly serious about these following words as they are written out in the boglands of Ireland about these glamorous sounding destinations. And which were once and may remain especially alluring to women whose resolves of celibacy in the old days were occasionally weakened when they were by invitation drawn forth, as a magnet might, to what could be thought the illicit milieu of the foreign hotel bedroom. Particularly in Paris where the possibility of romance could be expected, if not always achieved, and where at least hotel proprietors did not blink an eyelash over the clearly lasciviously hell bent couple seeking accommodation.

But for me very little of that sort of dalliance was to be had in that idyllic city on the Seine which was to become for many years of my life a remote unfathomable dark world of jurisprudence complicated by the French language and the wonderful snobberies of its protocol. Now then. Who among you in this age of enlightenment is still antique enough to have ever heard of so called 'dirty books' that once were nearly the sole source of personal erotic entertainment handy to hand and brought back to English speaking shores and eagerly to be found by customs hidden deep in a traveller's personal luggage. And who among you would know what it's like to have a finger of outrage pointed or an accusing hatchetman from a tabloid say you were corrupting the innocent and were purely, if not so simple, a filthy pornographer whose disgusting mind was his only stock in trade. And tomorrow's headline would advise you to flee pronto for the obscurity of some thoroughly foreign and distant land.

Them times now are long gone and best forgot but ah suddenly persecutors all seem to be awake again and in a different guise. The euphemists raging are on the march and have invaded the publishing houses and the world of disseminated information, pointing to the new naughty and forbidden words which are no more allowed to be fictionally said of himself giving herself a well deserved fist in the gob or the root of a boot up the rear. And dare one say it, Paris, as in the past, is again culturally screaming awake and may now be the place of freedom of expression once more. Significant enough when you hear that the scholar's pens are presently busily at work, dissecting a literary period, occurred just after the Second World War, and which has now over the ensuing years hugely come into being. Described in recent books such as *Exiled in Paris* by James Campbell, who, taking us vividly back to those times of personal liberation and exhilaration, re-enacts many a literary drama. John de St Jorre's *The Good Ship Venus* in itself a wonderful study not only of the erotic voyage of The Olympia Press but also of those migrant displaced and alien persons who were the sailors and found Paris a congenial if temporary home.

And then comes that strangest and most curious figure of all, the great sexual liberator and founder of the Paris Olympia Press, and who became my nemesis and sworn enemy, and I his, and who was best known under the name of Maurice Girodias. But then let us dwell a little upon how things were then. The cheapness of living life in one of the most alive cities in the world. With idleness breeding dreams, literary history was to be easily made. There were endless boulevards to stroll, endless side streets to lurk in and numberless cafés in which to sit bemused. Because later your book would be published and fêted across America. Meanwhile the sale of a pair of slightly used shoes or the entitlement to your foreign visitor's petrol coupons could finance two of you in an inexpensive hotel and provide meals for a fortnight. A bag of coffee beans would make you for at least a few hours a mogul attracting the girls. And even though one dined in elbow touching proximity to the French who always seemed to think one was going to steal an escargot or borrow their cutlery, it nevertheless never made the oeufs mayonnaise taste any the less wonderful. Which was why, if you hadn't yet been there, the words, 'Hey pal, you got to go to Paris,' were on every American's lips.

It was then with these now legendary literary figures, and with their books notching up notches on their writing belts, that Paris proved to be where it was all happening. Along with the pseudonymous pornographers there were the writers who were making their names known. Vladimir Nabokov, Allen Ginsberg, William Burroughs, Eugene Ionesco, Samuel Beckett, Richard Wright, James Baldwin and Christopher Logue to mention but a few. Alas, already retreating from the world of words, I of course, but for the single exception of Christopher Logue, whom I got to know later, knew none of them. Yet in the now distant retrospect I can see that I was, because of my own written words, none the less up to my oxsters in this literary demi monde which in France always bordered on the beau monde. But I was not to be seen in deep existentialist discussion over an aperitif in the café but rather with my nose in a tome of torts and with my tail nearly between my legs and slowly but surely becoming surrounded by lawyers, who, all having to sit down and read the book I wrote, were, ironically, becoming my first readers if not fans. With once fourteen of them all collected together in the sixteenth district near Avenue Foch animatedly having cocktails in the grand saloon of my very elegant principal counsel.

At the end of the first volume of *The History of the Ginger Man* I'd achieved publication in Britain and recognition with blasts of both praise and condemnation for this work and a victory over its first appearance in the pseudonymous and pornographic Traveller's Companion series published by The Olympia Press.

But I was not then to know, as several publishers, forty five of whom had previously turned the book down, were now fighting over the rights to publish it, that I was entering a battle which would nearly take up the remainder of my life. But in the vast struggle I was quickly learning things. It became early apparent that in all the opening forays, threats, claims, charges, torts, legal statements, ultimatums, writs, summonses, and where the author was caught in between, no instance ever arose where the scribbler was not immediately cited, to be castigated, inculpated and upon whom not only ridicule for obscenity could be heaped but all blame for legal costs and pecuniary damages could be dumped.

This is not to say that there are not some fair and wonderful people in publishing. But having said that, let me say this. Fairness and humanity sure did seem far removed from the salvoes of writs whistling over one's head. And if a clause appeared able to catch the poor and ostensibly trembling author by the toe, so be it, the poor defenceless scribbler of obscenity deserved it. And yours truly started digging in the law. And where a statute could be shoved down some bully's throat or a clause tightened around his neck, the scribbler only hesitated that moment or two in the interests of historically preserving the concept of courtesy. One's life became seclusion and caution. Friendly correspondence came to a halt. Social occasions became lawyers' meetings. Which surprisingly were not always gloomy and indeed gave me moments during which I took comfort from these astute gentlemen, who were by their professions made wise in the ways of life. And who indeed I found could give their intellectual utmost to the protection of one of their poorer clients.

Ah but many out in the wide, wide world don't know authors. He who by the nature of his profession must get his daily bread from day dreaming thoughts which get turned into words. Like, you no good dirty rat. And the author, as all authors do when pushed, and in dealing with their written remarks, can get just as clever as the cleverest of lawyers, and into whose mouths the author will even suggest those phrases, which only by rude intent prevent their usefulness. And certainly having levered myself up out of innocence, I seemed to be getting increasingly concerned over who got their hands on the money as this seemed to be the most desired prize to be gained by the publishers and their retinue of legal advisers. I was to learn quite early on that the great litigator himself, Maurice Girodias, was heard to say, 'That bastard Donleavy for all his wallowing in self pity is possessed of an astute naïvety.'

The Ginger Man was burgeoning, revenue plonking into coffers. Publications here, publications there, publications everywhere. The pot getting larger and larger for every throw of the dice. With piracy rearing its unpleasant head even new enemies were cropping up and urgently needing to be wiped out. As time and a few further educating trials and hearings went by, trips between Paris, London and New York increased as one retreated deeper and deeper into a not unpleasant seclusion. It no longer seemed strange to come out of one court room, fly to another continent and city and within hours enter another chamber of law. As a little victory here and a little victory there occurred, it became less and less that blame was heaped upon and the scribbler himself made a scapegoat. In fact it was becoming apparent that folk were hesitating to use or even mention my name at all. My implacable obstinacy had somehow grown in the minds of my adversaries to be something to be reckoned with along with a few of my earlier precautionary cables such as:

> Gentlemen
> Only For
> The Moment
> Am I Saying
> Nothing

These words put together homemade I regarded as the quintessence of all letters written by all lawyers. I had learned, too, that when it came time to say something a little more descriptive, such as estimating an assessment of damages, it was a good thing to make the numerals quite odd sounding sums like $300,946.22, and immediately below in the communication, spell out in capitals:

THREE HUNDRED THOUSAND, NINE HUNDRED
AND FORTY SIX DOLLARS AND TWENTY TWO CENTS

Amazingly no one seemed to mind what the Three Hundred Thousand Dollars was for, but my opponents would call in high powered consulting lawyers from distant cities to analyse and find out what the Nine Hundred and Forty Six Dollars and especially the Twenty Two Cents was about.

And finally a new image of the author was to emerge when I unexpectedly found myself on the eighteenth floor of an old sky scraper in a prominent if not fabled New York law office and being subjected to an interrogation on the basis that I happened to be available in New York. Modestly but neatly tailored and in my best innocent manner I proceeded with my own highly respectable and even somewhat stylish legal counsel to such interrogatory as was to be held in my opponents' mahogany panelled chambers. Having now got thoroughly used to the non emotional pincer movements of the legal profession I found myself faced over a desk by a most hostile gentleman who, as a lady stenographer got ready to record proceedings, had just finished shoving a handful of pills into his mouth. I waited for those first few words usually said of a timidly jocular nature and which never succeeded in allaying one's deeply depressing trepidation but were meant to attempt to convey that should you capitulate, you'll find we're all adult reasonable people underneath our vicious attempts to wipe you out. And then just as I put on my most benign air, suddenly this crouched to spring attorney-at-law, glaring from behind his desk, half rose up and, knocking over his vial of pills, blurted out, 'Do you know what you are. You're nothing but an international litigator bringing innocent corporations to their knees.'

I was considerably taken aback and angered in fact that I would be accused of wiping out corporations when only meaning to advise them to behave fairly and honestly. And my own quite charming lawyer interjected that he thought such a remark at the beginning of an interrogatory was quite uncalled for. But there was no apology except that I was about to look behind me to see if some greatly feared mogul sat there puffing on a voluminous cigar who had been guilty of champerty to do with my litigations. But although not quite believing it, I knew something had irrevocably changed. And now that litigation had come to dominate almost all I did, a powerful lawyer's accusation in New York, although untrue, became a comforting thought which was never denied deserved till I feebly do so now.

But further down the line, my nemesis Girodias, too, was implacable. And approaching about twenty years of litigation and having developed a gigantic distaste for legal papers or having it known where my physical presence was, I was even reluctant to admit to my name. But it came to pass that one spring day in New York in front of the Fifth Avenue Presbyterian church a meeting happened that changed the course of all one's litigation and did more unexpected doom to the enemy than my enigmatic messages had. As I innocently stood watching pedestrian life go by from the steps of this church, suddenly this strange little man detoured across the pavement and stopped in front of me. A picture of respectability to whom I apologetically said yes when he asked, was I who I was. I had no idea I was then meeting 'Deep Throat', who, beyond his benignly diminutive size and so neatly attired in his blue suit and brown trilby hat, was to be like an atomic bomb and make me look like a real pussycat in litigation.

'Deep Throat' then said that he'd read my books and that he had written a book for Girodias and that he had been cheated of his royalties, his contract broken and the book disgraced by making it seem blatantly pornographic and that money borrowed by Girodias had been squandered. He asked then would I be interested in what his lawyers had uncovered in spending two years in tracking down and tracing through all the company fronts which Girodias used to obscure his culpability and ownership and that his lawyers had at last followed the trail to the head parent company of all the satellite companies around the world and which at last revealed Girodias as the proprietor. I said I should be very pleased to have the particulars of such discovery.

Litigations with Girodias at the time in Paris were being conducted behind the fronts of companies, his behind that of a Swiss company Eratom and my identity hidden behind an Irish company, The Little Someone Corporation. Eratom's lawyers had long been raging to the judge that The Little Someone Corporation disguised a proprietor who was none other than the notorious J. P. Donleavy. The judge at these repeated hearings would always respond, 'Certainly, gentlemen, just produce the evidence and I shall take the necessary steps to deal with any malfeasance.' As the many months passed of Eratom's lawyers jumping up in protest, one day a parcel arrived to me containing a sheaf of papers. I glanced through and saw that 'Deep Throat' was true to his word. Here it was, Maurice Girodias owner and proprietor of companies which had indeed been traced around the globe with the search ending up in Belgium down a little side street near the old market in Antwerp. Shoved into an envelope off the papers went to Paris.

It was upon the very next occasion of Eratom's lawyers raising a hullaballoo and the judge again asking for evidence that my own lawyers stood up and made their protest of Girodias being behind Eratom and then these quiet gentlemen in grand procession handed their evidence up to the bench which had so painstakingly been collected by 'Deep Throat's' lawyers. And as I sat in the court in sun glassed disguise, to one's immense delight and relief the judge struck out Eratom's action. Ah but the story I yet wish to tell is how 'Deep Throat' continued, even physically, to pursue Girodias across the world which finally ended up with one of the strangest confrontations in publishing history. And indeed it's why, with space being inadequate to tell it here, I now contemplate writing the second volume of *The History of the Ginger Man*.

Suffice to say such are these many strange incidents still left in their silence and still haunting the soul. Which had then, so many years ago, been made to wither on the brink of disaster that you can only hope will not come. Surprised, as you exist further in your bleakness, to awake alive each dawn holding tight to your courage.

> Wondering where
> In the world
> You can search
> To find one smile
> Of love

1995

Shaun Beary –
A Portrait of the Playwright as a Man

I first met Shaun many years ago across a dining room table of gleaming splendour in the elegant east side New York apartment of his aristocratic lady, Ginny Fair Gimbel, legendary as one of the Big Apple's most beautiful and charming women. I was at the beginning of my second marriage, which would come to grief as had the first, plus I had land and farming problems as well. I listened closely as Shaun told that it was a great old country habit in Ireland that if you didn't like someone too much, you threw a strychnine laced chunk of meat across the neighbour's fence to kill his dogs.

Then this man and his stunning companion, an artist of no mean ability, moved to Ireland where one was totally charmed by this couple who took up residence in one of Dublin's most revered old hotels, the Hibernian, while their estate, just bought, was groomed for their occupation. Breeding, raising and racing horses was Shaun's calling as you might say, being that he had grown up in Ireland and, as a fine horseman himself, knew bloodstock ways well. He was, too, descended from the elegant Herberts on his mother's side and from the famed and esteemed jockey, friend of princes and kings, Michael Beary.

Shaun's Elizabethan handsomeness, even seen only in a photograph, often drove women into paroxysms and to desperately pronto make fools of themselves attempting to achieve his rapid acquaintance. He moved imperturbably in the world of the ultra beau monde and the jet set super rich. Singularly stylish in his own eccentric way, his suits subtly cut and his brolly and racing binoculars always so discreet he appeared to be without them, as indeed he mostly was as he readily dealt with a few of life's tribulations and the low life so easily encountered around horses.

Splendidly entrepreneurial, he did with some frequency set about in pursuit of spectacular schemes, trading in paintings, tapestries, electronics and always living in stylish circumstances, especially in New York. When there, I would often take cinnamon toast and afternoon tea with him, marvelling at how, in travelling light, he never forgot to pack his toothbrush, bars of chocolate and a change of shirt and socks, and transported these at his side in his trusty brown paper or polythene bag.

Over the years we would confront by accident in the most unlikely places as once happened in New York when I was busy peering through a crack in an undertaker's door which happened to be next to a stylish café with tables on the street. Customers with champagne dripping from their lips and the unmistakable silhouettes of the supine dead outlined through a translucent glass behind their laughing heads. As I turned from peering into this home for the disposal of the dead and took my attention back towards laughing talkative life, there was Shaun smilingly observing me. For he himself was New York's most compassionate man who could pass no vagrant or beggar without giving him a coin or two.

Also, Shaun had done it all. Produced K2 on Broadway, been a film distributor, become the owner of one of the largest caches of nicely preserved polythene in Europe, traded in sheep, horses, cattle and hay. And possessed of a marvellously practical way of handling money, transporting it in his brown paper bags full of brick hard loaves of cash, he appeared in Chicago one strange year and cornered the wheat market as he bought in the many millions of tons, and calmly waited, as he looked out the windows into the weather from the top of the world's tallest building, for the Russians to bid. It was then that he came closest to what I had predicted for him of becoming the globe's richest man.

I have meanwhile promised to build Shaun a small chapel should I ever hear of his intention to sanctify a relationship. For this is a man whose words, should they ever be shockingly harsh on stage, still harbour in their meaning the gentle touch of a loving hand. Never in the long time that I have known him, has he ever uttered words of downheartedness or defeat. Nor did I know of his long silent struggle in isolation to write plays that, now having seen one, I know will cram the seats and knock the dull hats off the theatre going public in London, Paris and New York. And why not.

> Shaun is blessed
> With enemies
> Who all have
> Such bad luck

1995

PART 2

People and Places

My Own Romantic Bronx

These are words I've quoted over the years to the sceptical and disbelieving. And are words used by the early nineteenth century New York poet James Rodman Drake to describe the Bronx of his day. One uses the words frequently and perversely because it always struck me that no one would ever admit coming from that bereft proletarian mainland piece of New York City. Indeed folk from Dayton, Sandusky or Des Moines are quicker to disclose their origins.

However, once some years ago, in a famous movie star's New York apartment before dinner, a gentleman sat across from me. We were rather prolonging our mildly suspicious pleasantries with one another while our host, better known as Robert Redford, his wife cooking, put their children to bed. I began to envision one of those painful hostile New York evenings with one of those guys who infers by every question he asks, 'Hey do you think you've shot your bolt.' Plus I suppose my accent, vaguely tending to east of mid Atlantic, provided an unsurmountable additional barrier between us. But in the process of withdrawing into my tweedy anglicized shell, the most benign and loving smile appeared on this gentleman's face as I said, 'I was born in Brooklyn and was raised in the Bronx.' It was upon mention of the latter place that suddenly one felt one had been admitted to an exclusive club to which my potential adversary happily already belonged.

Over the years it seems one does tend to romanticize one's origins, especially if the present locale of your life is distantly removed. And one is somehow conscious that Americans who've departed to better climes don't particularly care to go back or dwell upon their previous lives or view their childhoods or old friends as anything other than something beneficially escaped from. Alas, of course, that's an important social climbing principle denied most writers, for their pasts are often more precious than their presents or futures and it is my Bronx past that haunts mine.

My earlier memories are of an area variously called Wakefield and Edenwald. We lived in a two storey brick house in a potholed street on top of a hill not far from the intersection of East 233rd Street and White Plains Road. There was a back garden, a grape arbour, a plant filled vestibule and some Italian neighbours. The vestibule was memorable because I tipped from its pedestal a large Chinese vase which momentously crashed on the tiled floor. Adjoining our modest house was the Crawford estate, with walking paths through grounds under big trees surrounding a large old clapboard mansion with a veranda. Latterly a family, two spinster sisters and a bachelor brother, called Kruger lived there and ran a rest home. At Halloween they held outdoor pumpkin lit dances. It was in the Kruger gardens that I saw my first humming bird hovering over a flower and dug my roads for my tootsie toys and where an older girl cousin, Nancy Martin, taught me to whistle.

In the winter small world on top of that hill, I played indoor war with my younger brother using the living room furniture and sofa cushions as battlements and the rising dust as the smoke from our guns. Summers my father would make grape and elderberry wine. Mr Kruger would come to visit down our cellar where tastings were had from the massive barrels. As the evening approached following their long afternoons of wine sampling, I would watch my father, who was an immensely strong man, lift Mr Kruger in the palm of his hand and place him over the fence to stagger home. It seemed such a rural scene but it was happening a couple of stone throws from the roar of the elevated train at the foot of the hill.

Near us were families with children I was not encouraged to

play with. But occasionally I would disappear to dine in their shadowy cellar kitchen off exotic Italian dishes cooked by their ancient shawled grandmother. They drove cars far more luxurious than my own father's Huppomobile, at least that's the name I remember of that car with its round glass thermometer which stuck up from its radiator. Years later I hopefully imagined that perhaps these seemingly pleasant people were members of that Hollywood publicized underworld who carried submachine guns in their bass viol cases and swore death revenges on those who crossed them. And I learned and can still reel off many of the choicer Italian curse words. But my somewhat lace curtain Irish parents preferred another Italian family, as being more acceptable. They made candles. Indeed they made candles for some of the crowned heads of Europe. My mother and I attended occasionally in their forbiddingly Victorian Baroque dining room for tea. Later it seemed marvellous fun to break these ornately sculpted perfumed cylinders of wax in half when I found boxes of them in the family drawers. I was mystified by my mother's anger at my playing this pleasant game.

On this same hill, one of the highest points of the Bronx, I first heard the radio through earphones. Saw one of my first films, *The Informer*, in a movie house with its marquee fronting on the bleak girders of the elevated train. And went to school. Reluctantly brought there some dusty blocks away in my father's Huppomobile followed on the road by my panting dog Spot. I also got hit in the head with a stone, nearly smothered in a baby carriage and chased by a formerly well to do uncle presently impoverished by the Depression, at whom my brother and I threw lumps of cheese. We modelled ourselves on the Katsandjammer Kids in the Sunday comics and delighted in the uncle's enragement storming out of his bedroom trying to catch us running away down the stairs.

When I was seven years or so of age we moved. Across the Bronx River and to the other side of the New York Central railroad tracks. To an area which seemed altogether more sylvan, a small geographically triangular collection of streets called Woodlawn. Being bordered on the east by the northerly slender ribbon of Bronx River Park and on the west by the thousand or more acres of Van Cortlandt Park and separated to the south from the rest of the Bronx by the garden grandeur of Woodlawn cemetery gave this community characteristics more like those of some small upstate town. With its third of a mile long main street of Katonah Avenue. Along which were an A & P store, post office, couple of beer saloons, bakery, five and dime store, and even a small public library established in the once ground floor living and dining room of an old house.

Here the unsocially registered neighbours were German, English, Scandinavian and some of Irish origins just like myself. With surnames like Duffy, Borst, Luttinger, Dobbin, McKernan, Monroe, Walsh, Silbernagle, Hennessy, Gerosa, Kuntze, Farrel, Meyer, Briggi, Gallagher, and first names like Phonicious, Red, Ger, Bah, Quince, Jab, Neut, Zeke. A sprinkling of more prosperous families occupied the bigger corner houses. One or two of these folk, with a couple of horses and garages full of cars and assets downtown in the city, were even rumoured to be millionaires. But most were of average means stuck somewhere hopefully upward mobile on the social ladder the Bronx so precariously provides.

Under an autumn maple tree on East 236th Street between Napier and Onedia Avenues I heard my first joke. I was told to ask Red, a hick visiting his city cousin, a friend of mine, if he ever smoked. 'Nope ain't never got that hot.' I think I may have only laughed politely but this is how one first became aware of the mystifying tricks and improvisations provided by the English language. It was here amid such comic ability that I learned how to throw a lariat, build model aeroplanes, play hockey on roller skates and really grew up.

Eastwards Bronx River Park lay in its own valley of the Bronx River up which I had always heard battleships could navigate years ago. Latterly I'm told this is untrue but there was a deep part of the river close by the Woodlawn station of the New York Central tracks where there was a swimming hole. Rumoured haunted by twin brothers who had drowned there when they high dived and got stuck in the bottom mud of this polluted water. Into which large sewers flowed and up these dank tunnels my early grade school friends repaired to look up passing ladies' skirts through grates, to smoke cigarettes and philosophize in matters mostly of sex and sin. One small chap broodingly remarking that if he were the result of what his father did to his mother he would never speak to either of them again.

But the place which became one's real stamping ground was to the west, Van Cortlandt Park. Falling running here one day I cut my knee so badly I was carried home shoulder high covered in blood and was stitched together by a doctor somewhere below in the Bronx. But otherwise one roamed in safety in the relative isolation from the rest of New York City. My friends, before young ladies fatally entered their lives, spent their time in ancient pursuits as had the Mohican Indians who once wandered these same lands hunting with their bows and arrows. Instead we used slingshots made from tyre inner tubes with handles fashioned from the dogwood tree. These perfected were lethal weapons of astonishing accuracy. A friend, Alan Kuntze, set out every dawn each autumn to trudge booted through winter snows to plant his traps in the muskrat runs under the icy water of the Tibbet's brook swamp. After skinning and curing in his attic he would sell the pelts to the Hudson Bay Company, making the then massive sums of money of two hundred and fifty dollars in a season.

But all was not death and killing. We kept pet racoons and crows. The former fond of stealing ladies' jewels and the latter, when they finally flew away, always temporarily returning each year. Wandering the woods with Alan Kuntze, although I was more interested in growing up to be rich and famous, I did learn from him to climb to the tops of beech trees and swing to the ground as the Mohican children did. He also taught me Indian lore. How to follow trails and leave or not leave signs of your own. How to set snares for small game and in these woods we often sat around late afternoon camp fires dining off squirrels and talking of the mysteries of hawks, snakes, owls, fox, opossums, racoons, mink, weasels, skunk and the occasional deer which inhabited these lands.

Here, too, one would like to think one took what must have been some of the first steps ever taken by Bronx conservationists. In the part of the woods adjoining Woodlawn and extending to Jerome Avenue with its then cobblestoned roadway and trolley tracks and now Major Deegan Boulevard, there was a swamp which the borough engineer had decided to drain. We blocked the big ditches dug and sabotaged all the efforts made to dry up and fill in this ancient wetland where one hunted and roamed. As preservationists, we wore big paint pails held up on our feet to trudge in the mud, building dams to save this natural oasis of rats, black snakes and big vicious snapping turtles. And one supposed one helped, too, those hikers and mushroom hunters who on Saturdays and Sundays walked along the path on top of the Old Croton aqueduct and detoured into the woods to have their picnics and find their toadstools. These people somehow seemed so foreign, as indeed most of them were, having not that long ago, like my own mother and father, got off the boat from Europe.

My parents by buying new houses and not selling the old one became landlords and when I was twelve or so we moved again. Just a few blocks away to a somewhat more spacious street and to an older house. Having graduated from pranks like projecting unripe grapes in blowguns to smash unpleasantly smearing on car windscreens and folks' front windows, I now, with the athletic boy up the block, started exchanging the wash hanging out on adjoining neighbours' lines, or stuffing their backyard chickens in their bedroom windows, or spending Friday nights transplanting their entire gardens or smashing ripe tomatoes against their screens as they sat on their back porches playing games of bridge.

Utterly appalling behaviour but at the time one thought justified by the constant dirty looks worn on neighbours' faces. Nor did my conduct improve when I began my first self employed job delivering the *Bronx Home News*. My constant late or missed deliveries had folk forever waiting to glare or shake fists at me, which demeanour alas only confirmed my opinion that adults were simply no damn good.

But more profoundly and somehow always hauntingly close, casting a spell on one's life, was the cemetery. Its lavish stone monuments peeking through the trees. And its acres full of tales. Told by the uncle at whom my brother and I threw the cheese and who later became employed there. Of the woman who nighttimes appeared hitchhiking in her flowing robes at the southern end of Webster Avenue. And when given a lift along the cemetery wall adjoining this barren roadway would alight at the northern cemetery gates and disappear. A local mildly deranged tearaway nicknamed the 'Tombstone Cowboy' often invited the reluctant rest of us to climb the formidable fence and spend a midnight maurauding in and among the mausoleums.

It was in this necropolis through the good offices of my father under whose jurisdiction the cemetery came in his work as the fire department building inspector that I got my first and last job. Cutting grass during a school summer vacation. My colleagues were mostly European immigrants, one an ancient Polish gentleman in his eighties who had toiled there for forty years. Another, an Italian, a squat swarthy bachelor, told me about Mussolini and every Saturday payday was the highlight of his life when he went back downtown on the train to his tiny room on the lower east side to play poker and drink wine with his cronies late into the night. And I'd always ask.

'Is that all you do.'

'Sure, that's all I do.'

And of course, unappreciative of these most sensible words, there was also the usual consternation when I'd fill with grass cuttings their sweat drenched caps left drying on tombstones, and as the green shavings poured down their faces, I'd roar with laughter. To then drench them with sprinklers or tap them on the shoulder and disappear or jump out from behind graves as a ghost. Which set me to wondering who all these people were, locked up in their sumptuously vast mausoleums, stacked in there richer dead than I was alive. Some with names out of history books, others tycoons, or robber barons, admirals and explorers but most just plain prosperous citizens. And during my long bouts malingering, one wondered about the mystery of such lives which brought them so respectably here to repose in such comfort and splendour. Only many years later, having returned from Europe, did I learn that my unduteous grass cutting took place just fifty or so yards from Herman Melville's grave.

One had read authors like Jack London and Howard Spring but my first vague literary awareness arose when, on top of another hill on East 238th Street under another maple tree, I heard the name James T. Farrell uttered, a writer who, I was told, wrote about life as it really was. The hot news came from the lips of a young gentleman with the splendidly simple name of Bill Pain, who wore a tweed jacket, grey flannels, white buckskin shoes, Oxford buttondown shirt and black knit tie and called my argumentative ethnic prejudices fascist. He nearly convinced one that words could be as effective as action in life. For previous to that my only serious brush with neighbourhood intellectualism was an attempt to start a local rival newspaper when my implacably patient route manager in his natty convertible Ford coupé finally hysterically exploded and severed my relationship with the *Bronx Home News*.

High school years made my Bronx expand. From the local Catholic grade-school of St Barnabas where we were tutored in the Gregorian chant and played handball and a chasing and tagging game, ringaleevio, in the schoolyard, to places easterly. Where beyond these strange bed spring fenced wastelands, my father once drove by the apprehended Lindbergh kidnapper's house. And now one went kayaking in the sheltered sea of Long Island Sound and swimming at the man made Orchard Beach where my friends became lifeguards. Swarms of people coming up from the city's lower east side on the hot summer days to sunbathe jammed on the imported sands, or to crowd in curiosity round someone dragged out drowned. While offshore barely a mile away was Hart Island in whose potter's field half a million unclaimed bodies lay buried with the quietly eloquent epitaph 'He calleth His children by name.' Yet out here, too, were the spacious golf courses where, as I grew up, another uncle called Jim brought me with him to play golf. And City Island down whose quaint New England clapboarded streets one found fishing piers, yacht building yards and evening beer and clam chowder.

My daily excursion to Fordham Prep took me further south into the Bronx, to an area where the spacious boulevard of the Grand Concourse housed its modestly successful citizens and seemed like a giant spine to which this residential part of the borough clung. A nickel ride on the bus took one half around the cemetery and down to Bainbridge Avenue and across Gun Hill Road. One's day either brightened or crushed by the eye recognitions from girls attending, as my sister did, the Ursuline Academy where I alighted and walked down Bedford Boulevard hill and along the edge of the Botanical Gardens to enter the university's back gate. I knew who Edgar Allan Poe was but couldn't imagine this magnificently maudlin minded man, as his young wife lay dying, ever walking near here in a countryside sprinkled with edible herbs and without the roaring Third Avenue elevated train or the thundering New York Central track.

Three years later I was duly expelled from Fordham Prep as a bad influence on the student body. For among my heinous crimes of attending in a pool hall under the elevated trains and taking lunch of beer and free appetizers in a nearby saloon, I also made efforts to found a fraternity of which I would be instant supreme brother master to whom all dues would be paid. But before I departed I did at least get to take my first encouraged

45

steps in writing, concocting a spiritual visit to Westminster Abbey in which foggy European part of the world I had never been. And my mentor, a young apprentice Jesuit, pleaded on my behalf that a young man of literary gifts was being booted out whose name might be the school's only claim to fame one day. I of course took this fact so much for granted that I never thanked for his efforts this idealistic, charming and dedicated gentleman.

The Bronx now became my stepping stone. To other adult city climes and places. Fordham Prep having brought me to painfully polite Saturday afternoon tea dances and on sentimental school June boat rides up the Hudson, also introduced me to downtown life in the city, when a school chum who admired my suicidal nerve in and out of the boxing ring invited me to show my stuff to Frank Fulham and Arthur Donovan, who presided in an historic room of fisticuffs overlooking the corner of Seventh Avenue and 58th Street. Following our daily boxing ring blood baths, we sometimes affluently in the same building wined and dined, and my friend told me that we were under the rich man's yoke. The first of which I thought I felt one day driving Bronxwards with this young man's father in a big bullet proof limozine in which sat another sombre gentleman in a black stetson hat whose face was saluted by police all along the roads. At a big dine and dance emporium there was a famous band practising and this darkly dressed man put a big diamond ring on a brightly dressed lady singer's finger as she sat on his knee.

It was somehow that the great towering anonymous borough of Manhattan made that of the Bronx equally strange. Early evenings, heading east along Central Park South in its city glamour and glare, I went home by subway, with the crush of polyglot passengers thinning out at each stop north. The swaying train on its gleaming tracks roaring under Spanish Harlem to rise up thundering past the hundreds of stacked up blocks of apartment houses and their thousands of yellow lighted windows. The noisy abyss of the street below. The day time flashing glimpse of green of the baseball diamond down in the Yankee Stadium. The station stop with the Indian name Moshulu. Till in the nearly empty train one felt a curious loneliness descend as the last few folk made their solitary footfalls on the terminus planking to go down the steps glad of each other's proximity to wait flanked by woods and cemetery for the bus to take them further north and home.

Following a six month sojourn at a spruce tree fringed coeducational public high school in Westchester called Roosevelt, where my academic pursuits were totally obliterated by the presence of a particularly attractive lady, I was promptly parentally steered back again to another exclusively boys' school in the Bronx. Now heading in my new daily direction westwards of Woodlawn, poetry had entered my life. Which I recited to a friend I had persuaded to shortcut in the same direction with me to school. She had the marvellous name of Ann Henry. Daily reminding me of the only American history I ever remember, Patrick Henry's impassioned declaration, 'Give me liberty or give me death.' Miss Henry's large blue eyes were full of a smiling amused wonderment at my brash mispronunciations and whopping grammatical errors which even then I began to stubbornly insist was the way English should be written and spoken.

We met these frigid late autumn mornings along the Park at the intersection of 239th Street and Kepler Avenue and crossed through the fallen leaves of the first woods to the windswept uninhabited corner of Jerome Avenue and the cemetery. I reeling off tall stories plus my poems scribbled the night before, and she politely listening as we, sometimes with ice skates slung over a shoulder, strolled a snowy cinder path along this winding road down to Spuyten Duyvil Parkway past a frozen 'Vannie' Lake and the old Van Cortlandt mansion. I went to the pleasantly cosy little school of Manhattan Prep, tucked away serenely in an ivy clad quadrangle just up Riverdale hill while my intrepid friend coldly continued alone on her way to the College of Mount

St Vincent further beyond on the banks of the Hudson River. And in this area of substantial houses and some splendid estates one found that no one ever called it the Bronx.

In my growing up world of New York City the word downtown, if it didn't mean the excitement of horn blaring crowded streets and department stores, it meant an illicit tinged Manhattan and drinking Tom Collinses in the Hotel Astor, or kissing someone goodbye beneath the stone towering vastnesses of Pennsylvania Station. I early envied the people who lived behind their anonymous doors in those swank tall buildings with their nice square low ceilinged rooms. Of how hot water, just like some of their private incomes, came out of their faucets from some hidden source to pour soothingly down in their stall showers and not from one's own oil burner one heard leaping into action under the dining room floor. Or how their food came nicely wrapped, packed and full of preservatives and not as mine did out of our fruit cellar or fresh from my father's gardens. And then upon my return to America after living away seven alienating years, the downtown city seemed a more grit laden shadowy manic place harassed by its endless streams of cars. My acquired materialistic Europeanized outlook had now made me conscious of the simplest of pleasures to be taken free of charge in my part of the Bronx. The privacy of its unused quiet residential pavements, its woods, zoo and the cloistered peace of its cemetery became encouragement to one's legs and lungs and sagging spirits as I daily walked for miles. And I then first began to sing its praises to unbelieving ears.

By this suspicious time in American life, no one if they could help it was putting foot out of their cars, or eyes anywhere but on a television set. And there was the odd occasion when police squad cars were dispatched by mistrusting citizens to investigate that bearded man standing staring on the corner, but I continued to take my undisturbed novel writing reverie on this open land. Pondering as I did so the sombre stories come to pass of one's growing up friends' lives, many having moved to establish in

48

bigger and better houses on bigger and better lawns. Their childhoods left behind to gather dust in this triangular little piece of one's Bronx which I thought had begun to deserve its own small historic legend. Being part of somewhere so unsung, unknown and unclaimed by those who had lived there. Yet gaining its own Gothic aura just as mystic as a fog shrouded Westminster Abbey. With some of its sons now having made themselves at least felt on the vast unfeeling fabric of America. John Duffy, who composes music, Richard Gallagher, who catches criminals, C. Donald Kuntze, an eminent gynaecologist. Plus my own brother T.J., painter, composer and engineer, who still, after everyone has fled, alone holds out in that old white house on the top of that hill in the uttermost northern Bronx.

And now, over so many years and three thousand heaving ocean miles away, looking back. Watching from a high rear bedroom window on East 236th Street, out across the stretches of Williamsbridge, Soundview and Clason Point to the nightly fireworks streaking the Flushing Meadow sky over the 1939 World's Fair. Or on an outdoor stairs, seeing a bolt of lightning strike just above the head of my ducking father. The festive Labor Day parades, a band booming and blaring, bunting waving, floats passing, ice cream frozen in smoking dry ice and hot dog picnics had on these Indian hunting grounds and battlefields. My evening visits with a paper bag of sandwiches for my father at the old 233rd Street fire house as the alarm bells tolled repeating other far away fire alarms in the city. Being given a dime and a compliment of what a good boy I was and departing to see the light over his desk where he worked on his reports or wrote his poetry in a window which looked out over the cemetery. He died only a stone's throw away. In a hospital converted from a building where my young close friend Alan Kuntze, before his own airforce pilot life ended in the last days of the war, went to junior high school and equipped me with my first three words of French.

'Vous êtes stupide.'

49

He also tried to teach me a gentlemanly deportment over pineapple sodas and strawberry milkshakes. And to walk on the outside of girls along the street as I did with his sister Carol on those autumnal high school afternoons when the maple leaves were falling and the poly noses fell.

And one consoles oneself that perhaps one day the neighbours, who growled and swore seeing me come and go from my front porch, would convene to hold some redeeming ceremony, at which this borough's former children who had made some small mark out in the rest of the world, and who were now unashamedly publicly admitting their origins, might now be welcomed back on some podium, while the assembled tax payers, whose gardens one once had desecrated, gave thunderous applause as one was ushered with bands playing to step up on a raised red, white and blue taffeta trimmed dais. To stand beaming in front of this cheering audience. Who no longer shook fists or sneered. But now proudly handed to one a radiant brass plated Bronx Oscar.

But alas, even with long buried sentimental memories awake I cannot see even as patient a man as my erstwhile *Bronx Home News* route manager, Mr Baumgartner, forgetting the stacks of free sample newspapers I daily slammed down the sewers, or my shouts of drop dead to the complaints of the paper's many yeared subscribers. One felt they were the authoritarian oppressor who had to be chastened before one stepped from this modestly favoured little community to go out fighting in the world for fortune and to further enlarge a scandalous name. And when, just a few years back, I last walked on a Woodlawn sidewalk, I came upon a corner over one of my favourite sewers and found conspicuously scribbled in the cement two of my childhood friends' names, written when time, alive only to one's dreams, spent itself so carelessly, silently ticking away in the promise of endless leisure years yet left to live in the Gothic grandeur of my own romantic Bronx.

1983

An Expatriate View of America

Stretched on shady warm Mexican sand, I write this in the tropics by the Pacific ocean's surf under pale green coconuts ripening high up in the sinuously waving arms of the palm trees. And hope to finish it, as I am presently doing, in a far away more northern latitude where a whole gang of strange bugs having a circus are not seething through one's alimentary canal. As they have now recently ceased doing and I contentedly rewrite and watch the apple trees blossom and hear bird song in a midland Irish orchard with the rain gently falling from its grey tumbling source on this roaring green land. And I sit thinking, as I often do, of America. Where on that ancient continent and in that then hundred and fifty year old country, I was born fifty years ago in Brooklyn to be raised in the Bronx. And except for my first twenty years in the King of Cities, New York, I have been an alien nearly everywhere for most of my life.

Although that nation is now two hundred years old, it seems by its din, violence and energy that it only decided to begin yesterday. With its weaving concrete highways aswarm with citizens encapsulated in steel. A society rolling on wheels and daily fanned by a consumer propaganda to buy, buy, buy. And keep the vast coast to coast heap glowing. And the horseless carriages propelled on the infinite highways heading anywhere and everywhere in a million streams that by day snake like long dark threads and at night make twin white eyes moving one way and red tails the other. Only slowed or stopped momentarily by tornadoes, blizzards and earthquakes. And these itinerant occupants steering and tapping a throttle with their toes. Nudging over speed limits, listening to jazz and symphonies, lighting cigarettes and making phone calls in the vehicle they put on like a coat. Wearing it with its brand name. And by the colour, style and size, telling the world who they are.

Each time I go to these United States I start anew trying to figure them out. And after two weeks I decide that like anywhere, greed, lust and envy make them work. But in America it is big greed, big lust, big envy. Laced liberally with larceny. And unlike most of the rest of the world at least everyone gets their chance. And if it's slow in coming, you can always buy a gun. Stop someone on a highway or street, or walk into a bank. And give me the money. Or I'll blow your fucking head off.

But when growing up there, I remember it somehow more peaceful. Playing marbles on the dusty hard ground. Along summer shady streets of the uttermost northern Bronx. Or wandering woods shooting chipmunks with slingshots carved from the forked branches of the dogwood tree. Folk would give you an apple and a quarter if you mowed their lawn. Fights could be mean but were mostly fair. It seemed then a safe place to be. Except someone might pull your trousers down, smack you in the face with a snowball or bust your model aeroplane. And you knew where the bad places were. Where something really awful could happen. And that's where you didn't go. Or if you did you were ready for trouble with your fist curled up. And your legs ready to run.

But mostly, across that wide spacious land, you could get big continuous hi theres and hellos. As I did when summers my Irish immigrant father took us motoring west. Always in a brand new car. Crossing on the Lincoln highway. Out as far as Nebraska. Reading the rhyming signs of Burma Shave along the road. Or shouting when we saw a Hex sign on a Pennsylvania barn. The plenitude of the endless waving tassels of corn under the blazing sunshine across Indiana. The only fear was in Chicago. Where there was an epidemic of infantile paralysis. And I saw ambulances and fire trucks roaring through the streets. With the stories of the whole city once burning down racing through my mind.

But out in each small town you could always find a sweet smelling tourist house with dew on their front lawn in the morning. Big creamy thick milkshakes at the local drugstore at night. And across the darkened plains, the wailing lonely sound of the freight trains. My father would with his big hands folded behind his back go down main street. To find any local philosophers taking an evening sit on the community bench. Or members of the volunteer fire department to tell them fire stories of the sky scraper city back east. For him America was great. Bigger and better than anywhere else in the world. And Ireland where he had come from was where they didn't have a pot to piss in.

And while I was growing America grew and grew. With those dreamland suburbias spreading ever more widely between the cities. And even the right side of the tracks sometimes became the wrong. With enough get up and go go go, you could, provided you didn't try it by writing poetry and symphonies, grow up to be merely a modest millionaire. And one hardly remembered the hungry men begging door to door during the Depression. Who would call at our brick house on the highest hill in the Bronx. And although my father would not give them money, he would invite these gentlemen into our tiled kitchen to sit and eat with us. Great heaping helpfuls of meat, potatoes and vegetables. And glasses and glasses of my father's elderberry wine. Before midnight came, with my father's roaring laughter and telling and listening to stories, the men would be at least well fed and distinctly unsteady on their feet. Departing down the front steps to navigate the steep potholed hill to the bottom. Where an elevated train thundered above the road. And it was the only time I knew there were poor people in America.

Because we had some neighbours too near who drove big bullet proof touring cars and never seemed to work for their money, we moved to another community and a lesser hill two miles across a river and railroad tracks. Here the Bronx streets were cosier. With lots of nice little boys just like myself to play with. Summers we spent in a shingle house back from the road

between potato fields out near golden sand dunes and a pounding
sea. With the haunting names we'd pass getting there, of Jericho,
Babylon, Patchogue and Ouoque. Making me think we were
heading away from civilization. And one autumn, nightly, from
my high bedroom window in back of the house, I could watch
the rockets exploding their rainbow of colours over the distant
World's Fair. Or on clear days see the trihedron they called a
trilon and the big silver ball they called a perisphere. And
everywhere and everything said that America was big strong and
beautiful. Then came the Lindbergh kidnapping. New Jersey
was suddenly somewhere awful. But the culprit was found in
the east Bronx, a waste land of ugly junk lots, vegetable patches
and shacks. Just where someone ought to live who would commit
a grievous crime.

Cans now took the place of the glass jarred preserves that
used to be made and stocked in our cellar each summer. My
father's big wine barrels disappeared. I played street hockey on
roller skates. And America seemed eternally peaceful. Until a
foreign power did something evil on Sunday morning. I got
expelled from a prep school and narrowly graduated from
another. Just in time to go to war. And as a sailor one lonely
Saturday afternoon with a twenty four hour pass, I left my base
at Little Creek, Virginia, where I was being trained as radar man
in a crew. To sail an amphibious landing craft on to the Japanese
occupied islands in the Pacific. Which I did not delight to think
was really my cup of tea. Especially with the suicidal attitude of
the enemy. And as one did then, most sensibly, instead of
disappearing into the sailor swarming, beer swilling and even
prostitute famished town of Norfolk, I would, if I didn't seek
out the peace of the local library, go and visit another naval base.
And I remember, as evening approached and great flood lights
switched on, walking along the harbour quay of this vast naval
installation. Passing under the giant grey prows and anchors of
aircraft carriers, battle ships, cruisers and destroyers, all combat
ready with their planes and tapering steel guns, one next to

another as far as my legs could take me. And I thought good lord, what idiot foreign power ever decided to take on this.

And someone did. And we saw arriving behind big wire fences prisoners of war. To whom we were ordered not to speak. And the hours were countable till the war in Europe was over. Sailors ran out of their Quonset huts and looked up as if something would happen in the sky. Others took fire axes and chopped desks in half that they were supposed to carry somewhere. Moored flocks of amphibious ships in the harbour were hooting and beer began to flow. I had some time previously, after much insistent begging of a welfare officer that I be given a chance to, taken mental exams and physical tests. And one day, instead of sailing out to the Pacific to land assault troops on a Japanese defended beach, I found myself on the leafy gently rolling hills of Maryland. At a strange institute of education called the Naval Academy Preparatory School. Which stood in a splendid stone edifice overlooking the town of Port Deposit on the shores of the Susquehanna River. It was here, while the Japanese war was daily coming closer to an end, that I first heard among these incredible naval collected intelligentsia, the name James Joyce. And listened to an extremely human and erudite literary English instructor talk about good writing.

Between bouts of algebra, and strange insubordinations inspired by the student body writing to their senators and congressmen that the food was lousy or their pillows too hard, there were also calculus and trigonometry. While a fellow sailor gave private recitals playing Sibelius on the school organ. And these clever young chaps, so many of whom through their influential fathers had intimate connections with power in Washington, DC, could have our entire barracks sound proofed overnight or more peaches and cream for dessert or the commanding officer countermanded when he cut leave to discipline 'you bunch of spoiled god damn congressional ass kissing sea duty shy bastards'. While I further heard of Dublin's wide wide O'Connell Street, a big brewery and the drinking word stout.

It was in the peaceful library of this school where I conjured up a magical mystery about Europe's largest municipal park called Phoenix in Dublin. And the stories of a returned sailor friend who told me you could in Ireland drink quietly and secretly with a glass of this black beer and piece of cheese in a little mahogany cubby hole in a pub called a snug. So with my piss poor high school record being instantly rejected by every university I applied to in America, and my mother's information that there was a college called Trinity, I wrote to Ireland to ask could I come. And I ran around for days looking at a letter emblazoned with an escutcheon of a lion, book, harp and castle which said, yes, please do.

Throughout one's American upbringing somehow Europe seemed a strange and more tolerant clime. From which came the music of Mahler, Handel and Fauré. And from where, refreshingly winging the oceans on short wave radio, you might hear a dirty uncensored word. Spoken out of its war torn wise old ways. But it was its pomp and circumstance which seemed to call. Even as one never wanted to leave the sweat socks, gleaming polished loafer shoes and the lazy just hanging around days of billiards and beaches. Or the beer saloons and dates at night with the tanned skinned, bright toothed ladies. But deep in one's background there always lurked the sense of a foreign world in my parents' lives. For I had always been forbidden soda pop. And whenever I saw Coca Cola in another kid's ice box I was filled with awe. There were no candy bars, bicycles or white bread. Instead my mother daily gave one an eyedropper drop of iodine in a glass of water. And pressure steamed five vegetables from the garden. Enviously I would see my friends trip down to the delicatessen to fetch back their combination salads and bologna meals. And sunny afternoons leaving on my way to the beach, my father, tending his dahlias, would smilingly say, 'You have nothing to do but to enjoy yourself.'

And so one October day climbing on an aeroplane, which three times went down the runway of Idlewild airport and didn't take off, till on its fourth attempt three days later, I flew for fourteen hours via Gander to Shannon. Landing in this toy country. With its dazzlingly white swans sailing on glistening ponds nestled in the quiet green pastures. Straight out of a fairy tale. And in a small prefab building by the grassy landing field, for breakfast I had bacon rashers. These, monstrous and mahogany, were curled thick next to two gleaming sunny fried eggs. The big crystal grains of sugar. A strange liquid called tea. The yellow yellow butter. The corrugated crusted brown flecked soda bread. And the simplicity. In this sea fresh moist air. Here all you had to do was to keep warm. And dry. To eat. To sleep. To listen. And drink in the pubs. And before you froze to death you had to start doing all these things in a hurry.

In Europe's slow awakening after the war, Ireland was an isolated outpost. And you found that you came as a glamorous envoy from an invincible and the most powerful and richest nation on earth. Folk greeted you with a ready smile or with a curiosity titillated by lurking envy. You were an American over and above everything else about you. People came as they might to a museum to look in your cupboard. At the array of your fourteen pairs of shoes. Your fifteen suits and neat tall stacks of shirts and underwear. And like Americans did you even gave some of them away. Folk sought your company. And bought you drinks till, when everyone was drunk enough, they'd ask you why the hell did you do what you did to the Iroquois Indians or tell you that America had no culture. And suddenly, patriotism awake, and with the cry of 'off to the beach fighting amphibians we sail at break of day', an evening would erupt in war.

But otherwise, America for nearly seven years was remote way back west beyond the massive big blue green crashing Atlantic ocean. But you found it in other Americans you met. Always delighting and cherishing to be in their openly spoken and crut free company. Where you could say your whole meaning with a smile. As these handful of expatriates demonstrated things like the jitter bug and how the zoot suit was worn. Or played their specially airmailed records that otherwise would take years to reach Ireland. And when they did and were put on some awfully modern citizen's gramophone, their smooth rendition was usually short lived. Terminated by some sincerely drunk poet who would soon pee into the loud speaker or be thrown crashing against the turntable in a fight. Often started over a split infinitive in the song's lyric. And then you knew that the only America you could now know would mostly reach you in the weekly news magazines. To restir your memory and some of your dreams. Of that wonder golden land being buried deeper and deeper by the new life you knew.

But as far away as you may go, or as foreign as your life can ever become, there is something American that always stays stained American in you. Even if it's only the bliss of slathering vanilla ice cream over the deep blue purple of blueberry pie. And as a land, it always, however faintly, glows with promise. And during those new born years after the Second World War when expatriates like me tried their luck and educations in Europe, spending their days in primitive strange discomfort, chilled and damp in Ireland, albeit with a white coated college servant to administer afternoon tea, or their nights bitten by bed bugs in Paris, they always felt that back there waiting for them across the seas westward was that place they knew and understood, called home. To which, when the chips were down, they could flee for comfort and safety. Back to the oodles of soap, showers, chocolate milkshakes and big purring automobiles. Of the pneumatic thighed drum majorettes prancing amid the cheering, banners, bunting, the hot dogs and beer. Of monstrous sleek money rich corporations where, yes, the grey charcoal flannel suited man would say, welcome back, how nicely, Mr D, you are qualified by your five cultured years in Europe, and by the way I like your accent, I really do, and here, with our board's most heartfelt compliments, is your first monthly big bushel of dollars.

And yet when I read now back in my letters written then

when I, like others, with hope confidently tucked up in the crook of one's tweed jacketed arm, returned to that land of opportunity, I see the word escape, and other words to an intending traveller, formerly of Dayton, Ohio, decamped from Dublin, and now holding out at Mount Ararat Road, Surrey, wishing to join me. And to whom I wrote:

The Northern Uttermost Bronx
A Solemn Saturday.

Dear Gainor,

Unfortunately your letter finds me in a beaten state. Coming here is the biggest mistake I have ever made in my life. Someone who has read The Ginger Man manuscript has pointed out that if it were published here it could mean my passport would be revoked by the State Department and I would be forever doomed to stay in this country. If you come be prepared for the utmost in despair. There will be no pie in the sky as expected. This is not the land of the big noble rich, everyone is screwed. There is a fantastic red scare here, the whole country undergoing a rigorous censorship. I want to go back to Europe where I can regain my dignity. Come if you will but there is no good life here. It is sad and bitter. Where no man has the opportunity to feel any love. This is a land of lies. The whole country is strangling with the tentacles of the Church and various American legions of Decency. It's all vulgarity, obscenity and money. A country of sick hearts and bodies. So tragic that I just sit and sit full of pain. The only good thing about it is that they deserve what they are getting. If there is a war they deserve that too and I'll be cheering both sides on to beat the living shit out of one another. All the wonderful things in me are locked up. But I'll beat them yet. Best thing is to bring the books of Franz Kafka and read them here. However, strangely enough your elegant accent will be of help.

Yours regretfully unencouraging

GUTS

And my intrepid friend Gainor did come. Just, as he said, like an emigrant or worse probably. Arriving in the middle of a hot June on the SS *Georgic*, penniless and thirty years old. He got a job with the American Express Company and took up residence across the street from the Flat Iron building on Fifth Avenue New York. Where I remember that he borrowed a cup of sugar from a girl living across the hall. And that little item of domesticity stunned me. But I was reassured when in his first week, having walked miles with the hot pavements burning his feet through the holes in his shoes, he had socked someone into the tracks of the subway for their persistent rudeness, and being the impeccable gentleman that he was and instead of running, as any good New Yorker would, he called for medical aid and for the good chaps in the station change booth to stop the train. Following all of which he was temporarily arrested and chronically sued.

And so started my friend's saga in the New World. As I rather cautiously hid out, first in a cabin in the woods overlooking the Housatonic River near Bridgewater, Connecticut, stubbornly, resolutely, writing *The Ginger Man*. And then deep in a ghetto in Boston. Where strangely amid all the poverty, stinking garbage pails and packed families, and being frequently awakened at late night by a noisy prostitute, I began enjoying America on my budget of eleven dollars a week. Twenty one dollars a month for rent, twenty cents a pound for kidneys and ten cents a pound for green peppers or grapes and all of it fried in olive oil with slabs of egg plant. And there in these narrow Boston streets with the odd visits of some old friends many years previously returned from Europe, I had flickers of hope. But also in my tiny sunless rooms, bed bugs.

As that year wore on with some encouragement from an editor of Scribner's, Publishers, I sat over a typewriter, having sometimes to retreat to a park bench to get desperately needed sleep. And then peck out more words of this novel I began to suspect would never find a publisher in this land. But there were still some simple pleasant things that I found in America. Unearthed by one's daily life. Like a copy of the *New York Times*. And reading it under the leafy trees near the swan boats in Boston's Public Gardens. Or a walk along the Charles River with the quietly inhabited horizon of the old Back Bay red brick houses. The free symphony concerts you listened to lying on the grass. The penny admission to the local swimming pool. Or my big weekly thirty cent excursion to meet A. K. Donoghue waiting in front of the Co Op in Harvard Square. Mildly telling me as I mildly tuned an ear to the latest conclusions being reached about Russia at Harvard's Russian Center. And the news was that it was a big drab land of grey life. And as I listened to Donoghue's voice and to his constantly fermenting mind erupting with the woes and wonders of sex, power, money and women, faded were some of the other small displeasures, as the fat guy in the corner grocery persistently attempted to cheat me of two or three cents on every transaction.

My beard brought suspicious looks and sometimes even the faint growl of a challenge, which was never pursued when I'd stop, look back and wait. I sustained myself with reminders of Europe, the remnants of which were here and there in the West End of Boston. Behind me, in even darker and smaller rooms, lived an elderly Polish Jew. Who mornings would grab me as I stood on my formerly vegetable store front stoop, his two fingers pinching my cheeks to ask, when I said I was Irish, that why didn't I admit I was a Jew, as such a fine better class yid he had never seen. He wanted to know why such an educated man who spoke so cultured lived in such a place. I asked him the same question. He said because of his old age and independence. That his son and daughter in law always wanted him to take a bath and throw out his junk he every dawn collected. And then he would try to peek through the crack in the door behind me. 'Hey what do you do in there.' I said write. And he gave a grin because he thought I meant I was a bookie. And this too was America, and something that was life between these narrow fly infested streets. Where I could watch in admiration, a kid lie down in the middle of the gutter, and stop the horn blowing traffic while he balanced a spinning top on the side of his nose.

But something in one's bowels was saying no to this land. Where my childhood friends were growing up, just as their parents did, to be trapped trembling and terrified in a nightmare. And to temporarily comfort myself with the reassurance that there had survived before me other writers on this massive continent, I paid a visit, on my return to New York, to Herman Melville's grave. It was in a cemetery I had known from childhood. And in which, during a school summer vacation, I had cut grass. For an author often another author's life can feed him some romantic energy to keep tempered the tenacity of his own brooding pessimistic spirit. But at the cemetery, and unlike Shakespeare's Stratford on Avon, it seemed they had never heard of the man, and searched out the location from his file and helpfully marked it on a map. I could see as I reached the tree shaded hill that not many, if any, previous feet had come to read some heartfelt words Melville may have written on the gravestone of a son who predeceased him. And on his own tomb was chiselled a feather pen. That his next of kin felt him worthy of. To tell a stranger that here lay a man in whose life there had been the written word.

And through that struggling parsimonious year, the idea that America wanted great writers and great books to heap rewards upon them relentlessly vanished. I was told by my father. That you couldn't get anywhere unless you got on a big TV programme like *The Ed Sullivan Show*. And this suggestion was as crushing as alas it was true. And centuries away from my own fist shaking determination and resolve. Which was now that I had to escape or die. For even if I were to gladface on that box to the millions of eyes, I knew that my uncensored two or three cents' worth in their ears would have them jumping in their cars and heading to the studio to stomp and strangle me. But then,

I was getting what writers never really want to accept that they thrive on. Obscurity and rejection. And this is what America gives in abundance. However, with my energy spent, and my vengeance sworn with the words I wrote, I now knew that a lyric voice could not be heard unless heralded coast to coast by a throbbing promotional media campaign. And that that country, be it the home of my birth and where I grew up, was not about to give it to me. And if I stayed, they would, without even trying, or knowing, kill me.

I saved my dollars and dimes in dribs and drabs in desperate anxiety to buy a ticket to catch the Europe boat. Even popping nickels and pennies, one by one into a cigar box atop my dresser. My first wife and child Philip had already flown. And in that white old house on a hill in the Bronx I pulled the shades down to the sill so that no one could draw a bead and shoot me before I got out. When I could muster the confidence, I walked in the cemetery of Herman Melville. And met Gainor Stephen Crist there in the wintry snow between the mausoleums. He approved the setting but mildly objected to the inconvenience. But at least he agreed that in there, sitting on the marble steps up to the sepulchres of the rich or of some robber baron's tomb, we were in peace and safety. Albeit a hell of a lot poorer, even though alive, than those entombed so splendidly dead. And now with the myth of America as the place you could return to shattered.

Slowly but even more surely, one's own life began to explode. On a drunken Greenwich Village spree with Gainor Crist I had badly cut my wrist putting my fist through a pane of glass as I missed something I was trying to hit. A kindly taxi driver drove me free of charge to St Vincent's Hospital. And I remembered a previous taxi trip in Europe when, with me in my death throes, the driver demanded to be paid. And my brother T. J., who played his haunting Knobly Wood Concerto simultaneously on two pianos waking me at 3 a.m., had nearly been stabbed to death by a pair of aggrieved hispanics downtown. Who after he had taken them to a party and his hostess had asked them all to leave tried to kill him for the slight. Daily I went on a pilgrimage to Bellvue Hospital, that massive pile of wards, corridors and morgue by a grey cold East River. Where my brother lay hourly hanging on by a thread of life. My voice becoming fainter coming out of my throat. And Gainor Stephen Crist in his own ridiculous desperations, and now under constant siege from many aggrieved citizens of the United States, supplied the only distractions I got. And even he, a far better survivor than I was, was also setting his sights to recross at the first moment possible that deep blue green Atlantic. But I never thought for one second that in the chaos of his life he would ever make it.

I sat holding on to the edges of my desk fighting and fighting to keep afloat in a sea of despair. Knowing bleakly in my bones that my voice was not going to be heard in America. Where some strange ghost seemed to arise and chase us. And point a finger. Because we were traitors to the wonderful happy way of American life. And this spectre was everywhere. On the ceaseless groaning moaning highways. Written on the faces in the subways, buses and bars. And Gainor for a few days hid out with me in the Bronx. Later saying that he remembered it as the most peaceful and pleasant time he had ever spent. Even my father, weaker in his years and perhaps dimmer in his belief of America's greatness and who himself was beginning to die, voiced contentment. Where, over orange juice, pots of coffee and frying sausage meat in the kitchen, my younger brother T. J., convalescing, regaled us on the wintry sunny mornings with stories of his once selling cemetery plots and gravestones. And how in six months he didn't sell one. Which he thought was because of his well brought up gentle demeanour. With both Crist and myself thinking that soon we would be becoming his first customers. But someone got wind of Gainor's whereabouts. In this tiny cut off community of Woodlawn in this most northern uttermost Bronx. And threats suddenly got closer, deciding him to retreat to what he was sure was absolutely secure rural harmony with sympathetic friends in Woodstock, upstate New York.

And some days later a letter arrived written January 25, 1953, which began:

'My dear Mike, My God !! this has been an unbelievable nightmare.'

He related a story which even I, who had always been of the opinion that he was more than mildly lacking in certain discretions and unheeding of clearly impending pitfalls, thought he did not deserve. He had, in sandals in a snow storm, begun by hitchhiking from the George Washington Bridge. And got picked up three successive times by three successive and persistently aggressive homosexuals. To whom he kindly explained that his life was already too complicated for him to do justice to or encourage their advances. And would they please just let him out in the snow storm again. His letter ended with 'May B.O.P. intercede for us all.' These initials stood for the Blessed Oliver Plunkett, Ireland's martyred Bishop of Armagh of Cromwell's time, who now, as a result of such intercessions, has by the power of Crist and Rome, been made a saint. Gainor had, among other unfortunate things, been at the wheel of a borrowed car on an empty road while rescuing a lost lesbian. And, forgetting what country he was in, drove on the left Irish English side. A marvellous custom those two races retain in common. And shortly there came, with the first other car to approach in the middle of a continuing blizzard at 3 a.m., a head on collision.

Without a driving licence Gainor Crist had been arrested, and stood trial at 4 a.m. before a pyjamad Justice of the Peace in that gentleman's cellar. He was humanely only fined but, having no money, the reluctant judge was compelled to imprison him in Kingston jail. His knees as a result of the accident were swollen up like footballs. Late the next day, his hostess with whom he was staying paid his fine. He returned with her where they both decided they needed a good stiff drink. Gainor sat in his sofa chair with the bottle next to him. His hostess crossed the sitting room floor to get some ice. Half way there she disappeared from sight. For the first time in his kindly gentlemanly life, although he did however reserve moments for administering violent instant justice, he did not instantly leap to aid a female surely gone somewhere in distress and certainly out of sight. But instead Gainor uncorked the whiskey bottle and lifted it to his lips. And in one long Dublin gargle swigged nearly the entire contents. And though Protestant he was, he then blessed himself with the sign of the cross and said the Roman Catholic act of contrition.

When hobbling to investigate, as noble chap he always ultimately was, particularly with ladies, he found himself staring down into a black chill abyss. His hostess had fallen through a trap door under a rug on the floor and plunged fifteen feet down into a cellar where she badly sprained one and broke her other ankle. And when Gainor had a reflective moment to express words again. They came to my ears from his very heart.

'Mike, pray God I may escape this bloody place before further disaster overtakes me. I must get out of here before I wind up in an asylum for the insane.'

And so on a cold 3 o'clock afternoon in February some twenty five years ago, hysterically mute and with the western setting sun bleakly blazing a red tint across Hoboken, I stood on the stern of a ship ready to set sail for Europe. The pink lights glinting on the thousands of stacked up sky scraper windows of Manhattan Island. The Hudson grey dark and cold. Fleeing this nation on the back of the good ship *Franconia* and on one of that vessel's very last journeys. Leaving this land that was, in its culturally commercial way, conquering the entire earth. As well as me. They were serving beef tea in the garden lounge topside. The skipper on his bridge. Lines being cast off and tug boats waiting to nudge the vessel midstream. And then I heard Crist. Racing and pounding down the pier. With his paper bag, and a wicker basket covered gallon of chianti. He was shouting as they drew up the gangway and he jumped the last couple of feet. Together we watched the New York skyline disappear in a winter's gathering afternoon mist. My voice gone, I wrote on the ship's stationery for my stalwart companion, Gainor Stephen

Crist, words that have gone through my mind on my every visit to the United States since.

'There it goes, a runaway horse, with no one in control.'

I had spent my most solitary Christmas eve ever, in the front bedroom of my Bronx childhood home, listening to the choir of King's College, Cambridge. Heartily homesick for some gorse and heather covered piece of land I hoped would await my return somewhere in Europe, somewhere in Ireland. With all the latter's sanitary shortcomings. And Gainor Crist had spent his last days sleeping on the subways. Carrying with him his trusty immigrant's brown paper bag. Which contained among other sentimental and practical things, two child's cowboy suits for his daughters in Europe, a sweater, corkscrew, piece of cheese, length of rope, and an Aran Islander's hat. This last a navy blue thick woolly head covering with a tassel which he wore on his interborough rapid transit journeys going nowhere from last stop to last stop. And one wondered, what didn't America have for us. It could have been as simple a thing as that bushel of dollars we always dreamed was there. But even though one could have taken fistfuls of that mullah and celebratorily thrown it up to come down again in a soothing shower from the sky, one somehow felt that with no kindred spirits like our own ready to speak and say, 'This place stinks.' That money alone would never be enough. Even though money is always enough. And yet if there were voices of dissent and if they did dare speak. One could have said, 'This place really stinks.'

Yet, in my first months in New York I had my marvellous long walks. When my work each day on *The Ginger Man* finished sometime after one p.m. and I would go down the steep hill to Katonah Avenue to catch the bus along the cemetery fence to the elevated train. And stare from this roaring vehicle into the stacked up windows of the Bronx until it plunged downward past the Yankee Stadium and let me off walking up into the sunlight of the downtown city where I would wander, wander and wander. Full of reverie born from the streams of faces, buildings and streets. Where each man was carrying as carefully as he could his fragile breakable spirit. And I clutched my few feeble dollars, wondering more than a little where I would get some more.

Late afternoon I'd return to the New York Athletic Club, a tall greystone tower overlooking Central Park, to work out in the gym, followed by the boxing room. Where one talked to the resident philosophers Arthur Donovan and Frank Fullam. And this latter boxing instructor, who did much more for my hopes and contentment than he did for my left and right hooks. And would, when I said I had painted some pictures, greet me next day with introductions to the best galleries on 57th Street. And when I said I was instead now writing a novel, he had ready the next afternoon further introductions to publishers and powers extant in the Book of the Month Club. And as much as anywhere else in America, I remember this room. Peopled as it was then, and in the years before I went to Europe, by admirals, a prep school friend, Thomas Gill, film stars, former mayors, present judges and local city eccentrics. It was an oasis where I could disappear behind my whirring skipping rope and pounding boxing gloves and run, swim and later read. And even trade verbal fisticuffs with the then Commodore Manning and exchange pleasantries with Commodore Baylis. And then early evening sometimes to go visit with a childhood friend, John Duffy, down Thompson Street who was also fighting his own battles, perhaps even harder than my own, as a young American composer and one of the few who did not think me strange or changed. And sometimes even see another, Richard Gallagher, one of the few old friends who had come to visit me on my bearded return from Europe. And to whom America had given little as he grew up. So never expecting much, as perhaps I did, America gave him more than it gives most of us. And he now and long has reigned as a New York philosopher of many profound findings gleaned in his Kojak job as a police lieutenant in command of a thriving section of Manhattan homicide. And these men, I think, must have retained something I had lost in Europe, which enabled them to stay and fight and live. And they were and still are America.

For many years afterwards, wherever he was, Crist wrote me a reminder, lest I ever forget, of that day we both stood watching silently from the stern of the departing SS *Franconia* as New York disappeared into a dull winter's afternoon. Fleeing for ever that land. Which quotes no gross national product of the soul. Which still vibrates, throbs and swarms with machine, media and people. That gives rise to twenty thousand murders a year. Many beneficially committed in the punishment of discourtesy. And where, if they make car bumpers one pound lighter, they can change the whole economy. Reducing fuel consumption by 1 per cent. And make Arab oil sheikhs bite their fingernails. The country where your media mesmerized brain shuts off when the media does. Where the poisons used to preserve and flavour food and the smoke you smoke are preached as patriotic. Where an alleged Mafia member is described as having a tall specially built domestic chimney attached to his residence where he conveniently cremates his rubouts and the other affluent locals are too timid to object to the extremely unpleasant fumes. Where parents, bereaved by a son being stabbed to death on a subway train, have their house and home ransacked and robbed while they're attending his funeral. And you find that both father and mother are blind to boot. Where the elderly move in terror through the streets hoping to get back to their lock enfettered doors alive with their groceries. Where prestigious periodicals carry advertisements for porno films. And where as you fall asleep at night you think you hear, and you do hear, the distant screams of victims and wails of sirens across this quasi criminal nation. Ah but then, but then, it practically is, it is, a free country. Where nobody seems too elegant to lie cheat or commit larceny. Or sue you for negligence committed in an act of mercy. Where someone can be killed in an argument over who discovered America. Or a Prince of a President smashed dead who, if nothing else, made America appear to the rest of the world to rise like a phoenix from the graft, ashes and ethnic hates and shine in a splendour it had not known for long years before and it has not known since. But yet it's still a place, become over these years, and growing slowly out of this spilt blood where now the honest voice is more than mouselike amid the lion loud deceit. And a young man, because he knows you're hungry and broke, will give you a free hamburger from behind his counter even though he also knows he will be fired for it. And men like him grow little gardens of beauty in some still desperate slum.

And unquestionably it remains, but perhaps at certain places and in certain times, a country corrosive of the spirit. For each time you arrive anew in America, you find how small you are and how dismally you impress against the giantness and power of this country where you are so obviously and, with millions like yourself, so totally fatally expendable. And as you wake up to the throbbing airways and roaring cars, you wonder when will it ever be solemn, quiet and calm. Where no one thing matters further than at that peaceful moment. Where everyone who has his constitutional chance to shove his elbow in your ribs, as he constantly does, will step aside and say excuse me. Where your ears can hear a telephone call. Without the garbage trucks grinding in a giant hullaballoo down the street. And that somebody is going to wake up some morning in that wide awake land and say stop, don't tell me things. Let me for christ's sake have my breakfast in peace. And give my wife a sock to darn and a fist in the gob instead of the new dress she wants from I Magnin's. And maybe then when he's told his damn noisy kid to shut up and be thankful he has a skate board, he himself will be a good gentle honest citizen. Even though, as you always know, that it is a country you can't beat. It only beats you. And gets plenty of practice in two hundred years.

1976

Rat Holes and Magic Places

Upon being asked by the French magazine *Actuel* which place had been magical in one's life and what was the worst rat hole you visited, the following are my two answers.

The place which I have always regarded as being magical is the small cemetery of De Passy, the walls of which border the Place du Trocadero in the sixteenth district of Paris. This small oasis behind its anonymous walls on the edge of throbbing boulevards to which one would walk years ago along Avenue Kléber from the Hotel Raphael. Arriving under the stone archway and stepping through the gates, one would always find, in late sunny afternoons, black garbed ladies lurking within its tiny paths polishing and cleaning and replacing flowers on the graves of their departed spouses. In this quiet place reeking of respectability and sadness it made one feel that there was hope for us all as husbands. Its narrow lanes, some lined with shady trees and faded elegant mausoleums, were haunted with their departed lives. The reposing souls of so many distinguished inhabitants made one feel this was the one most marvellous place to fall in love, reminding one as it did of women who must have worshipped their husbands.

The worst rat hole in the world is a place I have never actually visited. But have imagined it to be from the description of a friend, an eccentric English peer, who was always in favour of sampling the bizarre, whom I had sent there, the friend thinking that I had already been, and that it was a place possessed of some astonishing special beauty. I was staying in Copenhagen in Denmark at the time and each morning from my hotel window I could see departing a boat or hydrofoil or hydroplane which said 'Malmö'. For an entire week I attempted to catch one of these boats which left twice a day for this town in Sweden, and each day got more and more desperate as I would invariably rush out of my hotel and down on to the street but always fail to catch the boat before it departed. Back in London when I heard that my friend was visiting Copenhagen, I said you must absolutely must visit Malmö. Somehow my desperation over an entire week of missing getting there made me imagine Malmö to be one of the most amazing and stunningly beautiful places on earth, which I might now be destined never to see. Then a month or so later, upon confronting my friend, again I asked him did he get to Malmö. I could tell by his slightly quizzical frown that something was very wrong. Especially when I asked him what it was like. Then he said my God, you mean you've never been there. I said no. He then, with a great sigh of relief, told me that because he felt he somehow was missing the point of Malmö, which was nothing but a depot and an industrial wasteland, he sat hungry and cold, all day long on the only bench in the place, patiently waiting for the miracle of Malmö to reveal itself until suddenly he thought he had at last discovered the reason I'd sent him there, when a man wearing white long underwear came along riding a tall ancient bicycle.

1983

To London from Mullingar

It's a great century for the Irish. For never in the history of nations has such an abrupt about face come. Literature, art and music sweep this island as never before. Where the creators of such may now dream of their profits tax free. Under legislation which has made much amend for all the great previous wrongs done to its word makers. Who indeed are now in turn this nation's benefactors. As much as Shakespeare has for England, James Joyce now awakens a tourist industry which has every Sean, Finn and Patrick tradesman coast to coast, who may not have read more than three of his four letter words, now eagerly vending artefacts by the dozen in his memory. Reverently marking the spots in Dublin city where he tippled, stopped to think or bent to tie his shoelace. And yours truly, as much a huckster as any man, may as well get in on the act. For James Joyce slept here. Under the same roof under which I write.

Instead of purveyors of banned literature and their plays taken off the stage, authors have now become revered saints for sightseers. No longer pilloried, their mini busts are cast in bronze and even an effigy of one of them reposes in a glass cage stationed in my local hotel lobby. And not without a deservedly justified reason, for James Joyce, while his father was doing a census, came to Mullingar. He now sits sedately life sized in wax, his legs crossed, feet shod in plimsolls and reading a book, not two miles away from where I myself sit and wake up in this mansion arisen out of this glowing emerald land. In his manuscript of Stephen Hero, Joyce described coming up this house's drive, entering its door, walking along its hall and stepping out on its terrace overlooking an orchard where he saw a man sitting in a garden chair.

I have reason to think of James Joyce when I am on my way to London. Following in his footsteps from a stone paved hall supported by a vaulted ceiling below, to go downwards on a flight of cantilevered sandstone stairs to a great stone slab landing and look back up above and then down another flight of chiselled black grey stone steps. Like him, I know I will soon be crossing the great Bog of Allen mentioned in his short story 'The Dead'. I see out over these hills and the shimmering reflected light of the waters of Lough Owel. A pony and trap takes me past the deer park's rolling meadows enclosed by their limestone walls. Enter up the steps of the same grey cut stone built train station where a young Joyce must have also stood in this midland isolation to take the train. The ticket seller who always courteously makes sure he has a cheery tiny conversation for his every customer, making the purchase sound like a friendly sort of bargain. And these little pleasures encountered are needed to buoy the spirits under grey skies in this summer's endless rain. On the station a big clock made in Manchester leisurely ticks away the time. A wire cage built in a corner where chickens straying in transport can be kept to cluck and squabble. With damp seeping down its walls I walk within this engineering miracle under the tracks in the same tunnel where Joyce also lugged his portmanteau. On board the railway car as I look back along the platform, the station master holds open a train door as a late arrived lady and little girl hurry up the steps. A small courtesy you might wait a long time to see elsewhere in the world.

In Joyce's day there would have been steam engines instead of two thundering diesels shaking the ground pulling us out of the station. Past marshalling yards and sheds full of fertilizers and timber, where beyond their roofs twin spires of the cathedral loom over the town. Down below the high embankment of the tracks lie terraces of white walled and grey slate topped suburban houses which would have once been countryside. But soon come

74

the meadows at their purple, yellow and blossoming peak and, with white may waving and poison golden ragwort, the landscape reaches the horizon. Between buttercups sprinkled in the green, small herds of cattle graze, beef to the heel as Joyce said of Mullingar girls. This rainy summer hammering farmers as flat as their crops into the ground. Clumps of hay in the fields rotting dark brown. In the shade of hedgerows tall thistles and sour grass. Symbols of why an Irishman will cut down a tree to catch the seldom sun.

But suddenly there's nothing to block out the sky as we now travel this vastness of bog. Its brown scraggly stems of wild heather. Its landscape lonely, unchanged and bereft. Staring upon its sombre wastes stretches one's mind all the way to the Urals of Russia. Peasant small piles of drying turf stacked above the shiny edged watery ditches out of which they've been cut. To make when they glowingly smoulder the sweetest smoke ever sent into the sky. But from a solitary deserted cottage, ivy overgrown, no smoke comes out as it would have done in Joyce's time. A big handed farmer sits across the aisle staring out the rain streaked window. You know he's noting the good pastures that pass from the bad and that he's got his own cattle to count and watch back in his fields. As we approach this Dublin shambles of a city, a stone hits the train window. A lady sitting opposite assures me we're aseat on the best side to avoid flying glass.

Out of the Irish sky and away from its unkempt capital city, I land in an English summer afternoon and venture into the much and by many loved metropolis of London. I go on the underground transport. Smooth well groomed cool Americans step in the car fresh from the airport. A young man in a yellow tee shirt with a single bundle pack of luggage and just arrived tanned off the plane from California. He can't stop smiling as three kindly young London boys heap upon him their maps and a girl next along the seats tries so desperately hard to be pleasant and gain his undivided attention to tell him what to visit and see. An American mother loaded with guide books recites to her children their itinerary, reeling off the names of places which will be crammed into the next few ensuing days. And the lonely wastes of Ireland vanish in the pleasant sophistication of this city.

As one has done over so many years, I hasten to make my first London act that of going to Fortnum's for tea. Greeted by the waitresses, taking a seat and awaiting the arrival of lapsang souchong with lemon slices and the chocolate yumminess of Sacher Torte. One mildly mourns the passing of this once cosy homey and elegant eatery now become a big shiny and glittering room. But a most minor qualm as an ancient friend turns up. As authors do, we talk of royalties and litigation first and then delve into the wonders of being alive. Especially among these summery golden people strolling these elegant pavements as we set out along Jermyn Street past the men's fashion and shirt shops towards St James's. Instead of walking my fields swinging a gentleman's thistle cutter, counting cattle and petting horses, Ireland's green fields and Joyce are aeons away. And here grazing on the luxury, one can only purringly covet the unaffordable ownership of silks and silver. But all still so alluringly attractive merely to stroll free of spending, variously in and among these perennially soothing byways of Mayfair. The soft brick, the gleaming windows, the domes, arches, posts and lintels preserving their histories. These buildings as familiar as the faces of people and their expressions changing in the late afternoon light and preparing for the glamour of evening. Just as they've done over all these years and for all these passing feet.

Tucked away in the corner of its little park, I enter the secular peace of Farm Street Church. And stay awhile. Before I go to gently click my heels on the white tiled interior peace of Claridge's. Past this hotel's sweeping staircase ascending to its pampering comforts above. Behind a pillar in a corner I sip a pale cold glass of champagne. And think back across the Irish sea. To the Joyce haunted train station of Mullingar. Its granite walls and bow fronted windows facing east. It is night now across the lonely darkness of the Bog of Allen. Where only a train's ribbon of light may pass. Wheels throbbing on the iron rails. Ferns at the foot of the green walls of ash trees wave along the track. Somewhere out there in that sad obscurity. Where another author's mind did dwell.

1986

Come to Cong Where the Glamour is Still Glowing

When God dropped that little bit of green in the north east Atlantic ocean between longitudes wet and latitudes chill, and there was in a trice this pleasantly peasant little island nation resting on the waves, the Almighty had no idea that such bereft place would become an emerald hued mecca for tourists. For in recent years, bestirred out of its moist windswept primitive simplicity, this toy country with its make believe people is now esteemed the world over for the courteous generosity and friendliness of the inhabitants. And although many would say God be with the good old days when we were an oppressed backward ignorant dominion, nevertheless numerous are glad that at last we have not only freedom but plumbing, electricity and also plenty of publicity.

Ah but now let me tell you within the confines of a potato skin, or while you're having your black beer they call Guinness, that despite the avalanche of soft toilet tissue, ice cubes, central heating and other sophisticated hot and cold modern paraphernalia, and even American TV beamed down from orbits high, there's still to be found absolutely a plethora of folksy rusticity here. In a country where pain, frugality and discomfort have long been the norm of the natives and rather than benumbing the spirit, they indeed thrive on it. And perhaps it is not surprising that insanity in this place is less noticeable in the people than it is anywhere else on earth. And alas it suits them, accounting as it does for much of the charm and the curious remarks you'll overhear as you stand elbow to elbow crushed between the natives in a local tavern.

'Ah now this pub is always jammed packed, no wonder no one ever comes in here.'

The first thing to remember about Ireland, where the grass stays fresh and its most famed beer is piquantly sweet and velvety dark, is that there is an abundance of genuine Irish living here who adore having an equally genuine American in their midst. For, though they tolerate, they are not exactly enamoured of the sight of the predictable artful shrewdness of one another. And the more credulous and gullible the foreign visitor the better. And ready to please Americans, who with their matter of fact fairness and half knowing the lingo, and who leave their business acumen at home, are particularly welcome with open arms. Especially by your man in the old shambles of his antique store as he points out to you the genuine Stradivarius violin he's only recently rescued from a monastery. And which, although a bit banged up and needing only a few new strings, is signed inside with the name of its maker. Indeed there it is, to be seen legibly writ through the vent of the sound hole. And you could do worse than to ignore the little legend you spy underneath, 'Made in Germany', and buy it for the rock bottom price of twenty two pounds. You might only get a piece of junk but it's perfect for breaking over the head of an indifferent waiter back home and you'll also have the remainder of your days vociferously blessed by the wishes of good luck from the proprietor.

However, in spite of the friendliness and the bargains to be had everywhere, always keep a wary guard up while you're enjoying a quiet refreshment in your better class of hotel lounge. And keep your violin near, as you might get a fist in the gob meant for someone else, when Paddy from beyond the bog comes roaring drunk into the village and, angry about being alive, rages in every direction knocking over the modern invention of the lampshade and then wears it on his head as he tries to make love to the wall. But as soon as he finds out how solid the latter is, he'll sing you ballads and tap dance a jig.

So with so much vicarious entertainment to choose from in

Ireland, the mind boggles at where to go west to a small personal place in which to take a singular pleasure. Be there so many nestled here and nestled there and tucked in beyond everywhere. And being that every village and hamlet is suitably small and particular and gets personal in an instant. In fact the land coast to coast, if you ignore the miles of bogs and mountains of granite, is veritably dotted with them. Ah but a little caution here. Many tiny metropoli would make your hair stand on end with the barren loneliness and the crumbling and deserted houses. Albeit that more than a few of them are disguised with their rotting remnants of lace curtains left still hanging in the windows, and with maybe a rusting sign still readable on a shopfront to say there were once cigarettes sold there. And to which vicinity or village a hapless American couple might venture, and stop dead in their tracks while the husband wasted no time to gather up his sensible courage to say to his wife.

'Hey, Mabel, what do you say we get the hell out of here.'

Yet there are those places, although not leaping and jumping alive, which at least have their buildings intact and into which and out of which goes living life. And few would be so pleasant, peaceful and purring as a little place of three hundred souls, called Cong. Out on the western granite dotted reaches of Galway between the lowland plains of Ellertrin and the bulging grey mountains of Connemara, this village, made an island by rivers, sits quietly safe from harm on a corridor of land dividing the great long loughs of Mask and Corrib. These two haunting bodies of water lie like seas stretching north and south, and the winds blowing upon them can raise white caps and in the force of a storm can sink boats beneath their waves. And you might, judging by the natural isolation, think you were coming to a place of desolate obscurity. And you'd be wrong. Because once a Hollywood film was made here. To christen it with a lasting fame. And to this day the older inhabitants have never forgotten the stars of *The Quiet Man* who once briefly glamorized their world.

In a cluster of bright painted neat little terraced houses, enclosed by four streets nearly in the shape of a square, and centrally divided east west by a fifth, Cong is compact to say the least. And walking in any direction if you keep turning right or left, you'll never get lost. It is populated by a decent sort of people, both by day and by night. Evidenced by not a single sight of the law, other than a tiny and pretty house situated in the main street. And would that every police station in the world could look so invitingly bijou and quaint. And why wouldn't it all be, with so much benign for miles around and pleasing both to the soul and eye. For once upon a time, too, now long ago, some Anglo Irish were here. Who, before 'our own' took over, built and maintained much more than a little of what is architecturally attractive and still left standing in this land. Before the natives, in their struggle for freedom, burned, pillaged and knocked more than plenty of it down. Especially the 'big house'. In which no grand piano, mirror or marble console table escaped reduction to smithereens. And where special elbow grease was administered to belting to kingdom come any Italian neo classical parcel gilt walnut and fruitwood marquetry commode. Ah but at the same time they did at least leave the walls of the premises looking natural enough in their demise. With mushrooms sprouting out of the ramparts, thistles growing from the windowsills and vines climbing up the stairwells. While cattle were put to graze on what was left of the rugs in the drawing room.

But all that now, be assured, is nearly safely past. Even the house wherein I write has been identified as a protected structure in order to preserve the heritage of the county. But to this day in this Catholic country, if ever you spy ahead on the road rhododendrons and towering old trees, you may bet your life that if no Anglo Irish Protestant still lurks there, one once did, once upon a time. And it is here at Cong where such a family turned three thousand five hundred acres into a garden paradise surrounding this little settlement. Cheek by jowl with the village streets of Cong are walls enclosing these tended wooded policies. That are entered upon through massively imposing entrance gates. And if you motor on the long winding narrow drive, climbing up and descending little hills between the mown lawns of a golf course, you will see suddenly ahead, framed against the lake, the spired and castellated grey sprawling edifice of Ashford Castle. This massive monument, hauntingly elevating from one of the most exotically beautiful settings in the world, owes its existence to the black beer originally brewed by Arthur Guinness which allowed for the amassing of the wealth necessary to create this place. Where with its ancient trees and battlemented gardens extending to the shores of Lough Corrib, it still sits surrounded on its moated island by the roaring rapids of the Cong River through which the salmon and trout darkly and silkily slide.

In these days and times and with more than your usual number of louts now loose across most nations and with peace and tranquillity at a premium, you could do no better than to enjoy the latter inside the sumptuous interior of this hotel. With every antique still intact across its soft carpeted, panelled reception rooms. Indeed the romantically modernized paintings look good in such setting and if you stay awhile and stare south west out of these windows you'll memorably taste of that which is the exotic Ireland. With the sound of the river's rapids and the chattering birds, early morning mists pass over the lake. Even through winter, there remains the feel of a subtropical sombre splendour. And by summer, under an evening pink aflood in the grey sky, swallows flash in the air and the water hens dive in the lough. And if there be a damp wind whining and whistling around the windows on a wild pelting day and the cloud is shrouded down over the mountains and the waves are white tipped in foam out on the waters, open up your heart to the rain. For it will seep in there anyway. But remember it's a downpour which isn't the kind that wets you. All the same, the natives advise, there's no need to rush out into it if you're already dry and warm.

Ah but come back to Cong, only a stone's throw away out the back gate, and you'll be seeing a new and completely different country now. For an architectural start you can ignore the noble ruins of the ancient abbey and turn instead to confront the exquisite cut stone elevations of Cong's public convenience. With its mahogany stained and bright green handled door. With not one of its beige and tan tiles out of place but all aligned gleamingly spotless framing the white vitreous china toilet ware waiting to be used in its skylit interior. And it is why Cong is so charming. For there is hardly a sign of dereliction in sight. Even the ancient ruins are restored and tidily preserved. Its pubs, guest houses and little hotels are all neat, clean and chaste. There's a small but dignified pharmacy. And in every little shop awaits a good natured proprietor willing to pleasantly please. Who if you asked to buy a medium sized elephant would not hesitate to ask you wait a second till he had a look out in his back yard to see if he had any left.

And Mabel and her husband, coming here, would ooh and ahh at the reassuring evidence of modern civilization amid the natural native beauty. All within the sound of the nearby salmon rivers even pouring subterranean underground and flowing every side of the town in which fishermen fish and upon which the glistening white swans go. Their breasts bucking the swift current, their orange beaks dipping deep underwater to chew on the river bed. And what else is this small beguiling capital of Cong good for. And I'll tell you. It's perfect to travel from. To go westwards to the Atlantic ocean of Killary harbour, on one of the most astonishing of roads that traverse this boggy loneliness and the stupendous silences that hang over these landscapes. And not to worry if an occasional road sign with a destination in Irish is unreadable. For these are frequently bare handedly torn in half by the natives as a demonstration to the passing traveller of the strength of the local inhabitants. This is a long established custom widespread throughout Ireland's rural parts. And you'd be right if you thought the might evidenced by such act was formidable, for indeed such signs are of cast iron a quarter inch thick.

But sign or no sign, there's usually nowhere else to go on such roads but to continue west. And on this byway to Leenaun you'll look down upon Lough Corrib with its flat black and silver waters sprawling through the hills. And further along this valley you'll come to Joyce's River and see the flash of the sun in the distance on swan's wings. The gleaming yellow of the coconut scented gorse. Sheep grazing the patches of grass. The stone walls so carefully stacked as if teetering, criss crossing the sparse meadows and some dividing land through the heather and boulders to the very tops of the mountains. And here stop awhile. You won't know where you are till you get there and by God you're not there yet. But in the sweetly moist green air, high on a hill an old lady stands to look from her doorway under its golden thatch. This small rapid river of bog water tumbles by. Baby trout lurk in the brown tinted pools. Lichen's timeless grey patches stain the outcroppings of granite stone. A single shiny beer can is near. And Cong is back there gently nourished by its waters. And where its glamour is still glowing. While the west's awake. And remember, the Irish always believe the lies they're telling. You own a genuine Stradivarius now. And the hush you hear while you play hands you back your own soul.

1986

PART 3

What a Sport

Georgian Cricket
or Whither Goes Those Wickets

And here doth be assembled as pleasant as flowers these Georgian people in their finery, glasses to their lips, bats to hand in this sunshine joy. Upon this parkland meadow with its hay bundled in big round mounds, and cordoned by these ancient trees of beech and oak. These people undaunted who never give up the battle against the relentless philistine vandal. And who daily endeavour to keep safe a moment longer the jewels of life. Someone must preserve the architecture. Someone must cherish the porcelain, paintings and marquetry. And care about the trees, flowers and butterflies. Someone must love enough again in this unloving land. To keep the air sweet, the waters pure and the grasses their natural green.

On this pale golden day I drove out anciently rusting gates that squeak open early morn in these midland hills to head east across the lonely Bog of Allen towards Dublin. Stopping first to play a game of De Alfonce Tennis in the summer perfume of a rose bowered court secluded in the trees. My opponent came by helicopter, rotor blades roaring in over the fields, with the Wicklow hills purple grey in the distant mist. The great motor bird's spinning wing, hovering it down to land on this country house lawn. And Laura stepped out, purple bloused and in white linen slacks, her black hair blowing down from a yellow silk band tied around her head. Pearls at her throat and a Côte d'Azure tan on her splendid slender exquisite feet. The laughter still there on her mouth, just as it was when I last heard it cheering me up when together we went to the Lawn Tennis Championships at Wimbledon.

'Ah, J.P., you poor old recluse. So nice to see you out of your prison loose once more.'

And in my reluctance to go out and confront the world, it was essential in doing so and nice, too, to have along this beautiful and blissfully solvent companion. Who said she'd come with me to a Georgian cricket encounter anytime but only after we'd played a De Alfonce Tennis match. And so losing balls under shrubs and run ragged on court, I succumbed as usual to her shrieks of laughter as she again and again left me lax in my tracks with her top spin whip lashed passing shots. Wrong footing and leaving me, as she had already left so many men, devastated. And now there she was, in the midst of all this green of Ireland, looking resplendently apple gleaming fresh following an ice cold dip in a not altogether sparklingly clean pool.

And tucked away in this grand land are all sorts of surprises. As was this hotel. In its shady situation in the near Dublin countryside. Strangely secret rooms full of couches and settees, plates and bric a brac covering the walls. Laura and I repaired for midmorn tea which included a glass or two of restorative champagne. A graciously attentive gentleman pouring the chilled wine from its moisture coated green bottle. A wood fire smouldering in the grate as is frequently needed in this land even in the midtime of summer. And before departing towards our Georgian cricket, Laura back into the sky, and me proceeding old fashionedly on the road, Laura poured the last of her champagne into mine and leaned to whisper against my ear.

'I'm so glad you've stopped gathering dust, J.P., and are getting out more in the world, even if it is only to play with an antique wicket, ball and bat. You're not really all that bad at conversation you know, and believe it or not you're actually even funny at times. And if you would only allow people to get to know you, they would like you. Loneliness can be, if you let it become, the most dire of all pain.'

Buoyed up this bit from down in the dumps and visions of dying in the gutter somewhere unnice, I thought what the hell, let's thumb a nose at rejection and the shyness bred thereby and even if everyone is out to use you, why not step out into the world. I drove along the Maynooth to Dublin road making an abrupt turning up the wide cobblestoned drive to my host's house, Leixlip Castle. Welcomed by genial Patsy, the butler, and led by an obliging Eileen, the housekeeper, I climbed the scrubbed wooden stairs ascending to this ancient attic to try on my costume. Fitting on one military coat after another but each one too tight across the shoulders and certain to hamper even my American styled half arsed swipe of a cricket bat. But a naval lieutenant's jacket combined with a red waistcoat at last didn't altogether stop me breathing and at least would allow me to appear in the swing of things. And driving a mile or two over the narrow winding country roads, through this county of Kildare, where recent rumour has it that between the ancien riche and the nouveau riche a hotbed of socially sexual intercourse has vividly erupted. Even to the point of someone spotted sporting liturgically purple lingerie. However, keeping a wary eye out, I arrive morally unscathed among the gathering of eminently respectable guests assembling on the pebbles fronting this great edifice Castletown House. And oh my God, the haughty particularity in the splendour of this setting. Vowels echoing, the glory of the clothing and the glamour of the people everywhere to behold.

Sited within its ancient meadow lands and worlds away from the now honky tonk tawdry town of Dublin, this massive Georgian mansion of grey ashlar stone faces its windows like many gleaming black eyes out over aprons of lawns and sentinels of yew trees. Inside behind its walls proceeds a lovingly meticulous restoration which for all these past eighteen years has kept this house still standing. As have remained a few other Anglo Irish edifices which were too damp for the nationalistically inclined native ever to burn down. But now all within this great structure, with its slates pushed back into place, dead leaves removed from roof gutters, cures injected into the dry rot, the crumbling joist ends repaired, new and restored wallpapers and fabrics adorning afresh its fine rooms, all continues preserved. And all faithfully seen to be done by its various diligent guardians, many of whom will wield a cricket bat and cut upon a ball this day.

And miraculous, too, that after sodden weeks and months of smouldering skies and rain drops that by persistence break the back, at long last the seldom sun beams warm. Arrays of bottles from champagne to Armagnac and from gin to bourbon are uncovered in the back boots of cars. The costumed figures raise their drinks sparkling in the sunshine. I overhear further gossip that an English vicar's daughter had run amok among the neighbouring counties, bedding both husbands and wives and proclaiming she was looking for multiple orgasms. And one sadly realized that this once sacred isle of saints and scholars had caught up finally with the concupiscence of the rest of the world. Albeit I took chaste solace from the unblemished folk gathered here from both the Irish North and the Irish South. And was relieved to be reminded that my redeemer still liveth.

Meanwhile one's heart quickens, all loneliness flees. For this was the trooping of the Georgian colour so to speak. As a pipe and drum band stands assembled playing on the wide steps of Castletown. Behind them, framed in the front doorway, in his swallow tailed green footman's coat, his hair waving in the breeze, his blue eyes blazing out over the parklands, his attentions focusing on the contentment of his guests, stands the estimable founder and original host of all this, the very Honourable and the very Hospitable Desmond Guinness. His ears pricking up as he enquired did that recent roar deceive him or did he really hear a helicopter land beyond the trees. And someone said he did and Desmond delightedly smiled and said.

'Oh good.'

I didn't tell him it was Laura, the shyest of all shy people. But who was in the habit of telephoning me at midnight when she wasn't telephoning me at dawn, to merely laugh and say, 'Galvanize yourself into action, J.P., and roll out for some frivolity, you curmudgeonly old grouch!' But now today, tippling before the match, it was tons of frivolity just as it was time for lunch. And never was anything so good. Like lasciviousness, many a culinary delight has at long last reached these shores. Even the cuisine of the Chinese and Japanese has come. And as we trickled into the great ancient tall ceilinged kitchen with tables groaning with victuals, wine flowing, I thought that nothing anywhere doth be as generously delicious as that still served by the Irish Anglo Irish, and the few of them left, God bless and keep always safe from harm. Since dawn that morning, Penny, Desmond's pretty wife, had prepared a magic potion of horse-radish sauce, which upon one's lips I could already feel it curing all ills. And clearly everybody else's, as a piper played and singer sang and all were having a glorious and golden fine old time. When a sentimental tear dropped from my weaker eye, Laura wiped it away and said.

'Ah apropos of nothing at all, J.P., don't you think the space over one's head in one's house is the elegance under which one lives. And that is why some of us prefer to make a roof of the sky.'

And that's where we went. Following behind this little group in all their own many hued colours. Wandering across these meadows waving golden ragwort and the purple flowers of thistles. How then do you have the best time of your life. Ah, all you do is sit, wait and watch and play cricket while sipping a cool wine of Sancerre between the overs. And I wholeheartedly entered into the fun. Never having held a cricket bat before in my life. Or known that in the eighteenth century version of the game two wickets stand and there are four balls in the overs instead of six. Plus the Georgian bat weighs seven and a half pounds and takes some strength to wield. And not surprising someone was overheard to say that the indomitable Desmond, behind a hay bale, was lying down for a bit.

Appropriate in the distance, in this county of Kildare, music, 'Ain't Misbehaving', requested by Laura, who had now in her purple shirt fled from her picture being taken. Just as clapping and flattery came louder from the sideline supporters. The bloodstock breeders, Julian Lloyd and David Grenfell, were at bat. Big hitters both, showing their form. And Julian, also a world ranking De Alfonce player, cut a thirties figure in his golf outfit of silk shirt, checked trousers, cream cap and buckskin shoes. As he and Grenfell raised a storm, elegantly slamming run after run in every direction far afield amid the thistle and ragwort. And as I came hopelessly to bat, to soon be put out by a catch in the deep, Charles Lysaght, the umpire in his judge's wig, was kindly biased enough to shout bravo as I sliced one accidentally aloft over the heads of the slips. And earned a run. And one wished all judges and umpires could, like Lysaght, look so welcomingly benign and be so encouragingly kind to the unskilled amateur.

Ah but don't go away. Listen to me just these seconds longer. All any of us simply and solvently want to do is to go on living in this world. And I'll tell you now about life in this nearly bankrupt Ireland, of which my own long dead father used to say, 'They haven't got a pot to piss in.' Poor it may be but it at least remains an intimate country. Where someone you've recently libelled is suddenly only two feet away trying to grasp hands around your throat to throttle you. But here today, peace and pleasure reigns. Joined under the larks rising singing in the air. These of the Ulster squirearchy, and their southern counterparts, accompanied by their long gowned beautiful ladies under their wide brimmed hats, ensure that posterity will rejoice. For there still are and shall doth be these Georgians who love this old land and the houses they save from decay. And by the way. The South of Ireland won. By a run and a wicket. And not yet gone in her helicopter, I looked for Laura. And found her inside Castletown House. Seated in the gloomy shuttered dark of a big old room. Where a fire smouldered and a few flames licked atop a stack of grey ash. And in the loneliness she warned me of, she was like a votive light in that summer sombre chamber.

1987

Sexual Exercises for Women

I suppose a contrasting setting could be extremely important in reading this volume and as the owner of the world's most
famed dirty book publishing house, The Olympia Press, Paris,
one is already primed not to add to one's aura of possible
prurience. A not unpleasant night chill was settling on the moist
streets of Mayfair, and I had just been into a wine shop to view
exotic bottles and had André Simon's wine list in tow. At two
minutes past seven p.m. following a wash and brush up I entered
the lounge of that hotel of hotels, Claridge's. Quietly ensconcing
myself in the north west corner in a comfortable high backed
chair behind a suitable discreet pillar, gold leafed upon its capitals.
The small string orchestra having played a waltz now launched
into Gounod's Ave Maria. And with a fresh sparkling brew of
champagne graciously placed by a liveried gentleman's gentleman, one opened *Sexual Exercises for Women*.

With London's literary scene rapidly increasing its American-
ization and in turmoil, one immediately thought one's leg was
about to be pulled. Especially with such precursors of jape and
spoof as that now famed literary figure William Donaldson, who
turned and continues to turn English Society upon its ear every
few months under his own and various marvellous pseudonyms,
prime among which is Henry Root, fishmonger. And then lo
and behold, when I saw the present protagonist of this present
volume as having been educated at Trinity College, Dublin,
one's suspicions further aroused. Then the name of the intrepidly
innovative publisher, Quartet Books, behind whom is that man
Naim Attallah of many up market triumphs. And just as I am
beginning to put two and two together and to nearly get four, I

open a page to the author's indeed quite beautifully written words that we might apply to much of life. 'Hasten slowly, do everything gently, and above all, don't rush.'

On my second glass of champagne I then encounter his eminently sensible words on zinc and selenium, and as a scientist of sorts oneself, one's total suspicions are dispelled. Clearly, as a product of Trinity College, Dublin, and, as one would expect, a brilliant scientist, easy of manner, precise of advice, especially on nipple tweaking and buttock clenching. And on zinc, ladies require this in only small amounts. But so blissful is this splendid information, so masterfully and fluently given, that you know down in your bones that it is simply not only going to be damn good for women, but for men as well. The only terrible thought is that Dr Harris reveals what appears to be the long held female American tenet, that happiness is chemical. And therefore should be available to all females in the right amounts and God help the poor bastard who fails in the supply.

Ah but dare a woman be seen with this book. Or might it perhaps even be better read by men. The latter feeding such information to ladies in small doses. The volume in addition has Shari Peacock's colour illustrations of dramatically handsome ladies in the nude, the drawings of whom, where a wash is used, are quite rivetingly spectacular. The work as a whole is elegantly presented as a paperback providing a carnally smooth surface beneath one's fingertips. And as one might expect of someone from Trinity College, Dublin, where it has long been regarded that the most beautiful English in the world was once spoken, the writing of Dr Anthony Harris MSc PhD is easy, friendly, comforting and fluent. Eye catching among the headings is 'tongue waggling', which evidently is stimulating to the vagina. And dear me may I doth gently protest. Are there no more romantic secrets left to discover.

Of course I'm on my third glass of champagne now, and as a serious amateur scientist, interested in what increases immunity

94

and promotes healing, and also educated at the once revered Trinity College, Dublin, my mind is racing in all sexual directions. And I spot a single minor oversight. That these sexual exercising stimuli, pelvic pushing, vulva squeezing and clitoris thighing, are all found in serious foxhunting. But since Dr Harris says they are best enjoyed in private, perhaps a wind and rain swept bog in Ireland with sods from hoofs flying in the sky and hounds braying is inappropriate. Nor least important is the fact that the exercises are yours in this book for about seven pounds instead of seven thousand that a bootmaker, tailor, horse, livery and the better foxhunting circles will cost you.

On my fourth glass of champagne I'm thinking, what a pity a woman hadn't written this book. Who could, puffing on her long thin cigars, blush her way in and out of London literary circles. But perhaps that's impossible, as no female woman, I hope, really wants it to be known what tweaks, squeezes and caresses might emotionally amuse or arouse her, in case they did or indeed in case they didn't. But who cares in a cuddle. The important thing is let us, as Dr Harris intends, keep women wonderful any way we can. And away with all nagging sour bullying bitches. For a man, unless he be already edged over into the steep slope down to death, a woman's juices sipped will always cure him of all malady. And even, his limbs broken, will mend faster.

Could it be now that I shall always pass each Mayfair bus queue and view the women waiting. Knowing each is quivering in a frisson of clitoris or buttock clenching. But why should she not. Release her pleasure giving endorphins. So let us go forward, men. Led by Dr Harris. To engage the new and better sexually exercised women. Flags upon our poles in confidence fluttering. Comforted that not all ladies are conniving selfish self centred bitches of the species. And as one who has had one's life saved by the exquisite nurturing balms of a wondrous woman, may this slender attractive volume give more lubricant power and pelvic strength to such females of such species. Who seem even more marvellous now I'm on my fifth glass of champagne. Indeed ready to demonstrate my own brand of sexual exercises for women.

1985

Whither Goeth Those Racquets and Riches at Wimbledon

They goeth terribly well. Thank you. With gracefully arched top spin lobs dipping tightly across this green leafy suburban valley. Upon this fortnight the end of June, when the God professed to by all good English ladies and gentlemen supposedly disposes to shine the year's most sun. Which beams bathing upon London's ultra elegant hotels, booked up with a waiting list to get on the waiting list.

And if, by profound privilege or smug planning, a bed, bathroom and breakfast abide your arrival so too will these revered inns have at the ready for your accustomed lips fresh asparagus and fraise du bois arrived by magic carpet. And their airing cupboards stacked with peach smooth sheets to pamper your skin where e'er your limbs may languish. In bliss enough to drown even your worst of sorrows.

So freckles sparkling, limbs tan, from near and far to these shores from distant shores they come. To squeeze into the thick of the London season. Each day bonnets bright, top hats gleaming, braving the champagne and the strawberries and cream. Raising voices and binoculars at the racing, parasols at the rowing. And at the tennis, they ooh and ahh, groan and clap. Until, in the silent throes of an exquisite break or set point frisson, those fanatic flanking these lawns of flat green velvet, gasp.

And to this preserve of privilege, one arrives. Meek and mild, if not abjectly humbled. Americanized in one's seersucker, mesmerized once more to watch all these heads swivelling back and forth. These ritualized sun browned limbs poised to serve.

Not a soul mindful that the French Revolution was clandestinely hatched on a tennis court. Nor a care if a commoner like me must explore where one might unchallenged go. Amid the signs which say 'Royalty Only', 'Members Only', 'Players Only'. And one stands forlorn searching hopefully for some entrance somewhere where it might welcomingly say, 'And You Only'.

And little and much have changed from yesteryear. But for me this time it's all different. I'm a member of the Press. There is now in fact a not impolite place where it says I can go. And as I do, I remember back all those years. When first I ever heard of Wimbledon. While cowering in the gloom of my pessimism down a grimy working class London street. No love bites on my soul, which bruises might have made brighter the shadows of the great smoking towers of the power station. And it was here, after enduring a socially ostracized and endlessly damp foggy winter, that I happened upon the hints of what was to become an oasis of hope and inspiration in one's life.

It was an early afternoon the beginning of July. As I walked out of a narrow crooked alley, to stroll to greener, less grim streets. That as I crossed this wider avenue, at least cheered by its pruned clumped topped plane trees, I noticed the strange sudden passing stream of black sleek gleaming chauffeur steered limousines. Flying colours purple and green. With tanned and healthy and mustbe wealthy folk encouched beyond the sparkling windows. And I wondered longingly, to what gala bliss, distantly happening elsewhere, doth they go. At which these select, in their silks and chiffons will beguile, and now hum through this grey dingy thoroughfare on their such pleasantly whirring wheels.

Ah, and I soon discovered. And found I could get there too. By going to my very own station of the underground train. My few half crown coins clutched, the train's doors opening. And from the platform to step out of my social oblivion into a spectacular delicate fume of scent. A din of chattering voices. Of vowels of such haughty particularity to make one quake. As the English know so well how to make you do. And stand awed in what is left of one's social tracks. In the thick of high pitched and hysterically bubbling phrases only spoken at the best cocktail parties. And there me, taking succour amid them stunned. Aglow on the most elegantly exclusive subway ride of my entire if not so ancient life.

For years afterwards come June, I headed there. To its annual green leisurely glamour. The tanned wholesome faces always encouraging renewed aspirations to creep up out of one's withered hopes. The vision that these wielders of racquets, their day's lobbing done, would vanish hither somewhere immaculately to dine in butler attended private bliss. Or at least in the chandelier lit grandeur of some hotel overlooking some park. And be guests of the sort of folk who lived on the interest paid on the interest of their monstrous bank accounts, and who bid them have, with their crêpes Suzette, another anciently pale brandy.

Till one evening, when this afore dreamed image of splendour was suddenly shattered. When I, late departing from my standing room centre court, disembarked at a subway station Earl's Court, which alas nowhere near resembled the elegance of its name. And here they were, a starring centre court foursome of players I had seen just that very afternoon in doubles matches. Now in their open necked shirts and sweaters hung over the shoulder and scurrying across the street. Far from their gleaming limousines, and disappearing into a dingy restaurant. Where I promptly rushed to stand nose to the window, disbelievingly watching them, their elbows splayed over a counter, their sacred racquet hands already twisting up forkfuls of spaghetti and quaffing the dreariest looking, but albeit perhaps the best of vintage, soda pop.

But now, like vespers vanished upon the still air of a university summer afternoon, a generation of years has gone past. The grim working class street where I once lay low in one's pessimism, and from whence one ventured to savour that peaceful emerald velvet splendour upon which those white furry spheres popped

and bounced, has now become a famed, charmed socially acceptable arrondissement. The soot darkened walls painted white.
Front fences bowered in roses. The upper class polished windows
are uncurtained now. Ancestors displayed on walls, to stare
approvingly down on the silver salt cellars sparkling light across
the glass smooth mahogany. These haughty who once disdained
to venture here now strut prim and smug and climb into their
motor cars, their pukka public vowels heralding their afternoon
plans. As they drive off. Guess where. With their prized tickets.
And who would ever suspect these beautiful new inhabitants of
not having perhaps the most beautiful of souls.

But my God. Inner shabbinesses apart. Get ready. 'Tis the
afternoon before Wimbledon. And everything is stirring. Even
the snobberies as usual. I'm comfortably holed up in Belgravia,
taking tea. Near three not unpleasantly casual polite Americans,
two young ladies and a gentleman. All just arrived from Boston's
Beacon Hill, for the tennis. In their sneakers and other nonchalant
raiment. They are already discreetly oohing and ahhing over the
China tea and lemon, and slathering their scones with strawberry
jam and Devon clotted cream. Commenting, 'Boy, this is really
damn yummy.' A moment later I go for a stroll in the nearby
ultra respectable streets. I pass a man in a very Savile Row dark
suit and a lady in a very tight bright pink dress. She's looking
his impeccability up and down, as she says something disparaging
about his wife, and adds resentfully, 'What's the matter, are you
ashamed of me.'

Alas, can one be anywhere else but back in England. Where
everything yet nothing seems changed. Except for me. Who
instead of downtrodden as years ago, in one's little Fulham
outpost, comes now a full fledged bog trotter out of the midlands
of Ireland. And if the latter origin does little for your ego, it
does make you go boggle eyed at the big sophisticated world. I
take the hotel elevator up. As I step out, one of the all time great
tennis stars of yesteryear steps in. As I walk the circular hall to
my room, other ghosts awake. All conjured from that arena

where they say deuce and love and first service and quiet please. And from a whole wall of window on the fifteenth floor I can see all the way to Wimbledon south west out under this still bloomingly blue early evening sky.

As a shield to loneliness, I invite a curvaceously tall, elegant, extremely rich lady friend with a yacht and two helicopters, who on a hiatus between her somewhat poorer husbands agrees she can spare a few hours to taxi to the tennis. She listens sympathetically as I remind her of all my past spectres looming through these streets. Where jellied and live eels are still sold. And the corner shop where once stood Alf the American Stylist whose windows were invariably broken in any impenetrably thick fog, and his latest USA styled suitings removed. Now here I pass sniffing my friend Laura's spectacularly rarefied perfume. As I hear her laughingly lofty vowels say. 'Oh dear, J.P., in your early struggles you were, weren't you, so badly done to.'

It's eleven fifteen a.m., now nearing Wimbledon, and much better done to thank you courtesy the *New York Times*, and in this bright sunshine far away from my former fog bound glooms. On this one of the hottest of London days. Out of the tube station called Southfields summery clad folk are pouring, overflowing the sidewalks. And still a half mile or more from the ground's entrances queues of eager hopefuls stretch back. Traffic at a standstill. The whole of this great ship shaped ground under siege. Best quality barbed wire furled atop the fences. The needfully suspicious eyes of gate keepers. My silk adorned Ascot hatted Laura announces, peering out the taxi window, 'I say, J.P., dear me, one does not wear diamonds this hour of the morning but aren't some people rather mal soignés.'

Ticket touts everywhere. Talking out of the corner of their mouths. Surreptitiously plying their business on this open air stock exchange. Centre court currently quoted at one hundred and sixty pounds to seat one backside. These toughened brokers promptly turning up their noses at any insultingly lesser bid. Reminding victims of the now mile long queues. The alternative being for Laura, in her Italian made high heels, to follow an Irishman a mile around the ground to get in through a back gate. I depressingly dig deeper into my wallet. Laura watching the dismal expression on my face, 'Ah, J.P., your hair may have gone awfully grey and thinned but you remain, just as always, so charmingly cheapskate.'

I get blatantly ready to tear up twenty pound specie under her exquisitely beautiful nose and actually dare to make a tiny rip in a five pound note. When to my relief, Laura admonishes that I should not allow myself to be so bilked. She mercifully volunteers to take over. 'Dear poor J.P., give me that wallet and let me handle these greedy buggers.' And while Laura disappears around a tree, I ask the Irishman why he left Ireland and ten cows and thirty acres in Tipperary. 'Ah you can't go on chasing moonbeams for ever.' Some seconds later Laura smilingly appears having reduced the opposition to fifty pounds. 'You see, J.P., you do immediately jump to the gloomiest conclusions, you must, just as in love, firmly negotiate in these matters.'

And ah at last, the sun rising higher and hotter and just as I part from Laura, other rich, in their limousines with their privileged tickets, are beginning to arrive. I'm met by a quietly soignée diminutively pretty young lady, who courteously conducts me through the main gate. I find I'm number 249 on my primrose non transferable Press Rover Pass. Which straight off lets me waltz freely in and out of where it says 'Press Only'. On this most crowded first day in the All England Club's history. With all these people who have their own pleasant reasons to throng to see these gladiators whose weaponry, woven of stradivariously stretched strings, and wielded on these rectangles of velvet green, can wipe an opponent not only out of his or her ranking and adulation but, far more mournfully and horrendously more painful, also out of a fortune in gold. Not the least of which can accrue from every square advertising centimetre of their tunics.

And the nation is waiting. With bated breath. Not for the first ace to be served. But for the first tantrum to be thrown. And a player to point to a sign under which the umpire is directed to go, which says, 'Morons Only'. And for such insult, who and what referee would be so bold in front of witnessing worldwide hordes, to dare banish from court a Midas man so rich. Whose symbolically obscene and aggrieved signal has been magnified into a nearly international edict. And whose aggravated verbal assault spans this present globe by every phonic and multi-coloured visual means. Raising the curtain on an electrifying drama. Of the four penalty procedure acts. The performance of which can end in a cataclysmic chief referee's finger pointing. To a sign. 'Outcasts Only'.

But maybe imagine. As I'm always doing. That this umpire is a dignified retired Air Marshal of the Royal Air Force, descended from a damn good family. And was once a Battle of Britain fighter pilot, who having shot down eleven Messerschmitts and who normally calmly controlled, and forever imperturbable, now slowly untangles himself from his judging equipment and wires. Descending from his high chair to stage centre of this velvet greenery. His microphone still held firmly in his hand. The knob of which is now raised. And laid suddenly resoundingly down upon the head of this offending player. Whose naughty finger had first gestured in such an unheavenly direction. And whose noggin now has just been bopped with a bang heard around the world.

With a breeze cooling the moist hair on the back of my head, I go up the concrete stairs and shove along a hard green bench. A smiling eminently diplomatic elegantly tailored and spoken gentleman, the Press Officer, has given me at my timorous request a green edged ticket to the Centre Court Press Box. Indecipherable squiggles in a reporter's notebook next to mine. The line referees in their olive green blazers and light pea green trousers file in. A lady player nods her serious nod to the ball boy. New born temperately cooled white fuzzy spheres are bounced in her direction. She slowly gathers her poise to serve. To another tanned intent specimen, whose muscles flex crouching and uncrouching the other side of the net. I watch tennis. As if nothing has happened in one's absence over all these intervening years. And how round now these buttocks how vast now some of these thighs.

It's time to meet Laura. Feeling some terror that she might have been bored to tears. Or ended up sitting accidentally on a tack. But no. She smiles. In her queenly radiance approaching out of the swarm of people as I wait across from the order of play and the so many unfamiliar names on the yellow signs. Having scrutinized my wallet, this present revengeful cheapskate is taking her for champagne. Amid the preordained privileges designed to end pushing and shoving for ever. But knowing already somehow she won't be impressed. And with not a word about tennis, she promptly slams me in the spiritual solar plexus with her thought for today. 'Ah, J.P., it's very painful being a man but it's not all that amount of laughs being a woman. Better on all counts to be a horse.'

But even here. In all the elegance. And amid the snobberies that have kept it thus. The ordinary world makes itself known. We pass a group of gentlemen fiddling with rods over a blocked sewer, all good naturedly smiling with the ironic indignity of it all. Laura sheepishly and shyly acknowledging a gushing greeting from another socially registered face. Whom she not unkindly accuses of looking for an invitation to Monaco where her yacht is presently purring. Then comes howling and squealing. A brand new player heart throb plunges sidestepping through the crowd chased by an hysterical group of schoolgirls clutching and tearing at his clothes. He eludes them through the pedestrian stream but smiles back over his shoulder a bright smile as pleased as sunshine. This is indeed the golden sport. Gleamingly excruciatingly alive. To make the universe seem nowhere else but here.

Popping back the strawberries, sipping our champagne. Nearby, a regrettably pompous Englishman informing a visiting Swedish referee, 'We have here in England our own very nice little language to umpire matches with.' And one is so sorely tempted to tell him in his smugness that animal loving Britain each year is executing two hundred thousand dogs and three hundred thousand cats. The wine corks pop. A lone pretty American girl in a black straw hat who out of her eyes is staring at something else in her life. Balanced on the back legs of their chairs, a group of shirt sleeved rich barrow boys cavort at their table covered with ice buckets full of empty bottles. One knows by their self contented laughter that not one of them has seen a single tennis ball float by. And it's time to remind Laura how nice, without a dull husband cramping her style, the luxury of life must be. 'Ah but, J.P., men may be a necessary nuisance but pursuing pleasure is a rough road to travel as the least deviation from such path becomes such pain.'

And I await. A sadness, as it always does, to strike me. As the sun and feet are turning pedestrian grass to dust. And drawn by the magic magnet of a famed player's name. I go to investigate a strange bunker deep down within the bowels of Wimbledon. Where members of the All England Club will surely safely huddle in any nuclear holocaust. A subterranean sanctum which one imagines might be like one under the Old Bailey. Where a player convicted of winning arrives conducted along a secret tunnel. Jailers on guard to keep back the jury of journalists until he climbs up into the dock. Under the bright lights and cameras. The cross examining questions come. And answers respond. 'Yeah my lobbing was a little off today.' Listeners listening with the same awe and portent accorded heads of state when pronouncing the fate of nations. Till his protective keeper beckons and the prisoner is taken away. Without a soul asking such player has he read any good, or maybe even obscene, books lately.

The sun descends. Shadows lengthen an afternoon to evening. Their notebooks filled, whither goeth these gazetteers. They goeth where it says 'Press Only'. Where wine by the bottle is cheap. Where gambling is strictly banned. They confer in their tennis shorthand. Telling each other what happened at matches where they were not, because they were at the other one. Two Irishmen lash each other with invective. Because one said boo to the other. And the other said boo back. Typewriters drown them in their din. The words of fifty languages go flying to presses around the world. Reporters pause scratching their heads. Tomorrow's fresh paragraphs are already being born.

And so, each day variously, nearly the whole of Wimbledon has flown by. The outside courts slowly lonely abandoned. The action peaking in the midst of the packed terraces held by these great tall ivied walls. Ticket prices on the touts' stock exchange soaring through all previous ceilings. Suddenly alas, without my humbled conscience warning me, I no longer on my low press priority can get to centre court. Or can summon nerve to accost my courteous Press Officer who is anyway somewhere else busily engaged. In newly laundered seersucker, and as all Englishmen at least pretend to do, how does one in this irritating ignominy stay as cool as a cucumber. In the smell of beefburgers at the back gate, I join the bus loads of these centre court rejects who have not slept overnight in a queue.

A telephone call and Laura rescues me. A taxi, taking me in dignified perfection to an elegant house in St John's Wood. Under a mulberry tree China tea is silver served with slices of lemon and Fortnum's Sacher cake. In stately splendour behind white drawn shades on a smooth leather sofa, mine eyes witness these last gladiators smashing acute angled winners in their struggle to triumph in singular glory. A camera zooms in close up on a celebrity spectator. And Laura speaks. 'J.P., please tell me. What is it that is so objectionable about an actor being acclaimed on the crest of his most recent wave.' And of course I don't have a vestige of a clue. But imagine it must have something to do with his overly large smile.

To watch the player princes and princesses play, the exclusiveness of these finals' days becomes positively ominous. As the financially aristocratic squeeze out the disadvantaged commoner.

Silks and perfumes abound along the centre court's corridors. Royal seats kept waiting to be filled with regal bottoms. Me retreated above the tip top towering plane trees of this London square. Safe from the shoves of ladies thronging through a swelteringly hot Knightsbridge, fingering and tugging at bargains. Blinds drawn over the swallows zooming by my window. Once more waiting for the tennis to start. Over a late late breakfast, viewing a previous day's vintage newspaper headlines. 'Palace Denies Prince Was Caned at Meal', 'Five Figure Sum Awaits Old Etonian Tramp', 'Al Capone's Jockey Beats Off Colonel's Baronetcy Claim'. And in the personal column, under a daily reassuring quote from the Bible, five grateful souls thank St Jude for favours received.

And again one watches. A slender arm looking as if it might break, her hand opening like flower petals as she lifts her racquet to serve. Such tableaux upon which memory dwells and awes. While an ace is exquisitely inflicted, a cool fresh orange juice is delivered to my own hand. Making one naggingly wonder how high mounts the hotel bill. Suitably mountainous I'm sure. Dare I be, instead of once downtrodden penurious, now the most costly reporter in the history of Wimbledon. Who is not even there. But here. In front of the multicoloured dancing cathode rays. Listening to the literature of tennis. Takes the ball so early. Cross court reply. Forehand approach made on the run. He dines on a feast of winners at the net. And I lie upon this king sized bed, sheets coloured pink, feet stretched in slippers as a blocked return forehand pass makes a winner down the line. And suddenly, the sweat pouring down at match point. With the ball in a loose volley bouncing where it shouldn't. And this Wimbledon. With hardly a rude disturbance sensation. Is all over. In a blaze of flash bulbs and clapping.

Now the lurking sadness really comes to dwell. As one waits for evening. And the sweltering afternoon to cool. To go stroll in Hyde Park. Hangdog horses wearily heading home from the bridle paths. All of fashionable London now vanished to the country. The city left to burglars and commoners like me. Laura, worst of all. Gone to Monaco. Not to bedazzle or play with the other idle rich. But to entertain a group of orphans she takes on holiday. Leaving me, as she usually did, with a final thought. 'Oh dear, J.P., in the brief struggle we call our lives, money has superseded manners in the worst possible way. And I suppose, should it make one weep, one must thank God for waterproof mascara.'

But the end. The utter end. Is not over yet. There is more. In Rotten Row I pause to rest on a bench. Near the fragrance of roses boomingly blooming. Holding a marvellously reassuring conversation with myself. Answering each question asked without any of my usual evasion. Suddenly a figure looms above my head. A Welsh voice accosts me. An arm points to a statue. 'Its curvatures are as beautiful as the words of Dylan Thomas.' And this vagrant gentleman beseats himself. As if a liveried servant of Claridge's had just brought our glasses of champagne.

His name is Jones. He was born a bastard in Swansea. And was down the coal mines at fourteen. Leaving him with a crippled finger and a long scar on a thin white leg. He served in the Second World War as a desert rat. He now keeps a green sliver of a bar of soap in one pocket and a comb in another. He speaks with the wisdom of those without hope. Still possessed of his rage, he shakes a fist at the world but then suddenly crumbles into tears. As I hear his words, so many snobberies away from the glamour of Wimbledon. 'I don't know who you are, but I'll tell you one thing, you're a charming man.' I reach into my pocket for a one pound coin. And a smile breaks across his weathered face. 'And I'll tell you another thing. I bloody well knew you'd finally give me some money.'

Under the ancient soaring plane trees over the long empty avenues. Darkness descending on the park. And I search for the new moon across the sky. Finding a deck chair to sit in under a great shady tree. Upon the last of all these pleasantly passing London days. In my cleanest coolest seersucker suit. Wondering when tennis players are not playing tennis, upon what do their minds dwell. A breeze blows cool, tinged with a faint smell of scorched grass. Suddenly collar high upon the centre of one's back I feel something splatteringly land. From a great leafy height, a pigeon has copiously deposited upon me. Whither goeth those racquets and riches at Wimbledon. Ah they goeth. Not as I slink away in my latest ignominy. But with the night sweet scent of lime blossoms in the air.

1984

Dublin Horse Show

With its litter strewn streets and the city still tumbling down in neglect and decay and women's rights crushing men all over the place and many a man looking for any means of escape, you'd be wondering, is there anything dignified, unmarred and irreproachable left in Ireland. Well come here till I tell you. There is. And it's the Horse Show. Where the only disharmony might be a mare kicking a passing stallion.

Now during the whole of this glamorous August week with the city en fête, splendour is all to the eye of the beholder, and the buildings are standing up straight and looking their best in their faintly shabby glory. All through the year you'll listen to Dubliners wielding their superlatives, that there's one thing that you mustn't do and that is to miss the Horse Show. Don't we then have pouring in international celebrities by the boat and plane load from everywhere, and the very latest fashion in fashionable people. Sure you could pave a carpet to Timbuktu out of the smoked salmon and sail on the champagne all the way to Hong Kong.

Now exaggeration in all spheres is the name of the game in Ireland. And didn't I find myself suddenly seeing Hollywood stars or their ghosts in sunglasses there sitting in the shadows of the Shelbourne Hotel's Horseshoe Bar. And I must confess I immediately myself went spreading the news that there were your actual personages of a major calibre, if not prancing wild all over the place, then at least discreetly incognito flanked by their usual body guards. But alas although I tried, not once did I work up enough nerve to approach and ask, hey are you really somebody.

But despite the rumours of glamour and notables and that it should not be missed, amazingly I did, systematically year after Dublin year, miss the Horse Show. Suddenly finding that again it was the middle of August and it was well and truly over. And the nearest that I was ever to get to the judges posturing about in their hacking jackets, beige breeches, black boots and bowlers, and other official chaps in their morning suits, was one evening when a gentleman still in his riding kit came striding in the front of the stately red brick edifice of the Shelbourne Hotel. I was not to know that just that day he had won the Puissance with a horse leap that would make you gasp and the lobby audience, to a man and to a woman, broke into cheers and clapping. And still not knowing what all the fuss was about I did what most Dubliners do in the circumstance and stood up tall and shouted out my least timid Bravo.

Now in Dublin plenty of the bashful brave lurk in the pubs waiting for someone just as meekly courageous to come and talk to them. And as a long time professional recluse and more than an occasional public poseur, I often and secretly crave company. Which when it happens, an awfully unselfconsciously democratic upbringing as an American allows easily for. So gathering my wits about me I get myself up in the necessary kit which at least suggests some resemblance to the Irish variety of a country gentleman. Eschewing perhaps calf tight jodhpurs and too horsy a cut to my tweed. And minus the few de rigueur blades of grass to decorate behind the ears or odd stems of clover poking up through one's cap. Then appropriately booked into the Shelbourne Hotel, surely nearly the last of the stately once horsy places still standing, I head out from these midland acres to cross the great Bog of Allen to Dublin. And hoping to see at least one live celebrity.

Of course they would have you believe that Dublin is booked out. Even the worst of scruffy desperate dens crammed. And with every stable, closet and sheltered space packed with humans sleeping upright in their confines. And by God for once they're telling the truth. For isn't the kindly Garda Siochana providing the fatally stranded with a jail cell to sleep in. And now let me tell you, never did you see such a wide spectrum of people sauntering across the social scene. The streets aflood and aflow with visitors and speaking languages you never heard of as they stream past. But ruddy hell, still not yet a celebrity in sight.

Ah but parked in the Royal Irish Automobile Club, I'm now ensconced high up in a junior suite of the Shelbourne Hotel. With two great old windows that look west across the skyline of Dublin. And although spoiled with antennae there still remain Dublin's steeple sharp church spires. And here I am looking out the window at Dublin and I still haven't got to the Horse Show. But racked in my usual low key humility, and to cheer myself up, I'm going. Down into the lobby. Passing through persons none of whom sport those faces bewildered by life which at least do one the honour of readily admitting that we are all mostly drowning our sorrow and fighting back our despair. And more than ever now, to bolster the significance of the day one needs to see someone famous. But for the time being a horse will have to do.

Now let me tell you. There are over one hundred of equine classes showing. And there used to be a time in the hardier days once when the horses pranced through the thickest of crowds and you'd see some great fun as hoofs occasionally went flying with the throngs of pedestrians going down like skittles. And sure without a bother on them they'd arise again brushing the hoof marks off, and remarking on the good omen it was to be kicked by a mare or stallion. For such an injury is a big social plus. But these days things do be different. With the whole nation running at the bending a whisker to their solicitors for what is widely known as the adequate satisfaction and compensation. So safety is everywhere in this sixty acres of pleasing show ground where hoofs pound the green sward and over which the celebrities can throw their weight about.

But here, too, in the very midst of early suburban Dublin, the farriers are demonstrating belting their red hot iron horseshoes to shape. Dog obedience and agility competitions are being held which would dumbfound you by their canine dutiful compliance, with pooches walking blindfold in a straight line to even blowing their own noses on command. Ah but let us get back to the horses. And bowler hats. And the chaps with the jodhpurs and the stern lean judgemental faces. Plus the swarm of girl grooms upon whom it is often maliciously assumed that the country squire jumps. Nae. All the caressing goes upon the horse, whose skin hourly is polished brightly. For this more than anything is a horse fair. And prices skyrocket the higher one jumps or the better a nag is judged in the myriad competitions. Out from the far beyond of the nettles and docks, the farm browned wind blown faces of the owners come. Mixing amid the Texas cowboys, priests in wellington boots and tanned Italians in their Gucci natty outfits. With all nostrils assailed by the strong healthy smell of horse manure. And there is no doubt that certain people as they parade and posture about in skin white breeches and boots do think a hell of a lot of themselves. But this, folks, is the Royal Dublin Society. And there is no harm or law against feeling as good as you look.

And as you might have guessed this revered association, with its long frontage of grey stone elevations, was started by its twelve gents in the Philosophical Society Rooms of Trinity College, Dublin, in the ancient year of 1731 with the splendid motive of improving if not the manners then the agriculture of Ireland. But let there be no prejudice here, who knows, there could have been a Catholic among them. And of course this is what Horse Show week is all about. To banish, in its glow of glory, all woes and cares. But where indeed are the VIPs.

And so one proceeds back yet another day by friendly taxi to the dignified comforts of the Shelbourne Hotel. To arise next midmorn following the grand Horse Show week ball. And then to sense action of what seems to be of a big nature. A siren and police outriders guiding someone somewhere. And by the sound it's got to be at least the President or the Taoiseach of this fashionable little nation. But surprise of surprises. Who should it be. But a highly thought of Englishman. And certainly celebrity enough. Your actual proprietor Rocco Forte of hotel fame and his beautiful Italian wife. On their way to play host and dispense, under a great white tent at the Phoenix Park races, the anciently splendid hospitality of the Shelbourne Hotel. And where, and meek and humble of heart, unexpectedly I suddenly find I am invited. To take with the Laurent Perrier Rosé Champagne, miniature tartelettes of Foie Gras and Quails' Eggs with Caviar. The nags are running. Hoofs sending the emerald sods flying. My pretty lady is losing my money race after race. The champagne is pouring down. And amazing, amazing. To wake up out of one's bog trotting life. Surreptitiously wipe the cow flop off one's heels. And find you are having such a damn good time. And got to the Horse Show at last.

1989

Donleavy is Better Than McEnroe

With wry amusement mixed with some embarrassment I read this headline following the inaugural De Alfonce Tennis match which took place in France in Paris. I had first approached Virginia Wade, whom I have long regarded as being one of the most beautiful and brilliant tennis players ever to set her marvellous legs on the lawns of Wimbledon. But alas she was required to officiate as commentator at the Roland Garland French Open.

My publishers, Editions DeNoel, then persuaded Phillipe Sollers, the distinguished author and superlative lawn tennis player, to substitute. So in the hauntingly appropriate confines of the American Church in Paris on the banks of the Seine, an audience of Paris's beau monde assembled, and with hors d'oeuvres aplenty and liquid refreshment kindly provided by Moët et Chandon, the match commenced.

As voices hushed and highly curious faces turned, Phillipe Sollers, without previous experience in the game, sportingly stepped out on court and then astonishingly began to wipe the parquet with me. With sweat pouring from his brow and as if born to the game, Sollers executed every shot from the De Alfonce repertoire. La Balle Flotteus, Finasserie, Le ricochet and Riposte du tac au tac, wrong footing me again and again and leaving me lax in my tracks. His each winning shot deservedly earning explosive applause from this elegant gathering of pleasantly sophisticated folk, who quaffing their champagne on the overlooking balcony sympathetically cheered as I managed a return.

Finally when one found oneself at match point I did what I imagined McEnroe would never do at such a crucial point. I jumped up and down in rage and slammed my De Alfonce racquet on the floor and in so doing nearly amputated my toe. But it galvanized me into implacable resistance, and bitterly fighting back from two chukkas down I finally triumphed in a close match. And it is now that I take the opportunity to extend my thanks to Mr McEnroe for his inspiration, having witnessed many of this superlative gentleman's own battles back from the jaws of defeat. And in the face of linesmen incapable of telling whether a ball bounced in or out.

And so in fairness to Mr McEnroe and following the appearance of the above headline, I must correct the impression that I am better than McEnroe and make it known that there is little doubt that he could abysmally trash me to a pulp on the De Alfonce court. Ah. But of course remember he is my inspiration. So I would be fighting back tooth and nail using Le ricochet, Riposte du tac au tac and my two hundred mile an hour serve. Indeed now that I think of it he might not stand a chance against me on the De Alfonce court. So now I hereby therefore challenge him to a match.

Of course I take instant comfort that De Alfonce as a game is a great leveller, giving even an inept player a chance. Overt expressions of anger and the uttering of expletives are strictly forbidden and, according to the ninth commandment of De Alfonce Tennis, *Thou shalt not be rude nor scowl at the umpire*. I have never spoken to nor met Mr McEnroe but have been present on many occasions when he has blown his top and expressed that certain situations might have been the 'absolute pits'.

In racking my American brain I cannot recall what the word 'pits' really implies but I gather it does not mean anything harmonious. But of course it is to these outbursts that the Wimbledon Lawn Tennis Championships now owe their record crowds. And at such times I'd often wondered if one of the referees would ever jump down from his judge's stand and engage McEnroe in violent fisticuffs. And who knows, with the audience pouring out of their seats to take sides.

Now happily nothing like a boxing match has ever happened and I suspect mostly because underneath it all, as are most talented people, Mr McEnroe is a perfect gentleman and person of compassion and sensibility and such qualities are never entirely hidden even in the most violent of verbal outbursts. In fact I am highly suspicious of Mr McEnroe not only being possessed of a brilliant intelligence which usually comes with a personality quick to irritation and anger but also of being extremely erudite. And when I do see him fleetingly going by in the flesh, I am always amazed that his arms are not full of books instead of tennis racquets.

Once called specially to witness Mr McEnroe being interviewed I was equally a little surprised that instead of references to Sartre, Rilke, Samuel Beckett or James Joyce, never mind Kafka, he is instead discussing disguised lobs and the wristy flick used in a cross court passing shot. And then when he's out taking umbrage on centre court I'm always expecting him to accuse line judges of being illiterate philistines instead of having bad eyesight.

Now of course, as happens to most of us, the fact that one day Mr McEnroe may think of retiring from lawn tennis, and as the playing of De Alfonce relies so heavily on intellectual ability, one does plan to invite him to be the number one De Alfonce player in the world. In achieving this he would displace the present top five, namely Evans Farley, Ron MacDonald, Michael Bernhard, Jules Almand and my son Philip Donleavy.

Amazingly Mr McEnroe may have already actually seen De Alfonce played as it is upon the court where it was in fact first invented, in the gymnasium of the New York Athletic Club and where Mr McEnroe was thought to be once seen playing basketball. The sight of him made the above mentioned De Alfonce players extremely nervous concerning their rankings and that McEnroe might have chosen this as an opportunity to size up their styles.

Over the years one has recognized certain endearing qualities in Mr McEnroe and the one certain thing that I do know about him from my spies is that he deplores being recognized and accosted while pursuing his privacy. Indeed one hopes that he will not take amiss this present reference to him. But there is no doubt that De Alfonce, the superlative game of eccentric champions, would fit McEnroe like a glove. For, if I'm not mistaken McEnroe as a name is as Irish as they come. And as one knows this ethnic minority does not take shit from anyone, even the big, strong or all powerful. It has been long recognized in New York City where I grew up, that even the Mafia, no slouches at looking after themselves, were known to be frightened of the Irish, and that in an argument the Irish never waste time to go away to plot to kill you, but always did it right there on the spot.

As the Honourable Founder of De Alfonce one hereby extends an invitation to McEnroe to challenge the winner who emerges victorious out of the world's top six. And believe me it will be a momentously competitive match. With its serves at two hundred miles an hour, its swerves and slices, riposte, parry and the unique nurt ball, which when struck descends to remain motionless on your opponent's court, McEnroe is bound to take a while to get into the swing of the game before he manages to hit aces across his opponent's bow. And surely he needs a change of ambience.

One always, each new season, going to Wimbledon, watches from the side lines and wonders as the players' faces get older that my God here they are once more throwing the ball up to serve and perhaps for the billionth time and surely they must, if they think of it, feel just that little bit foolish. And one now urges these great stars to throw down their cumbersome lawn tennis racquets and pick up the feather light one of De Alfonce. And we invite them all to join us soon. Including McEnroe. Tennis owes him a great deal and he would certainly be, as are all De Alfonce players, an eccentric champion.

1989

The Manly Art of Knocking Senseless

If you're wondering if any violence is going on in Dublin during the cease fire, let me tell you, there's been just a bit more than a little. On this July balmy Sunday fists are flying at the venue called The Point, down at the mouth of the Liffey River where it begins to flow out into Dublin Bay. This once gloomiest part of Dublin. Of sad farewell to those on the night mail boat to England. And where the mooing cattle on the hoof went sadly as well.

Along these bereft quays passing the moored ships was often a nightly walk I took from my rooms at a usually deserted Trinity College. But these days back up in the city all is en fête. Dress codes a distant thing of the past. In the refined precincts of the Shelbourne Hotel, once the hang out of the fox hunting élite, there goes across the lobby instead of your human hawthorn a traffic of tourists' tread. In this former claret capital where all the polite formalities were once observed. And in a pair of pink shorts and blue baseball cap it'd be thought the balance of your mind was more than temporarily disturbed and you'd be gently arrested for your own mutual safety as if there were two of you.

Ah but on this Sunday where once the church bells rang out across the streets in the quietude, culture has taken over and nearly every inch of the fence around the green foliage of St Stephen's Green is covered in works of art. Long known as a writers' city, there are now brush wielder artists everywhere. And none of them are half bad. Indeed there are nearly too many to be so damn good that you'd have a long walk to find someone that damn bad. With bargains galore, these practitioners sit waiting calmly for a sale. Anything is available. From pure abstraction to the Florentine academic to brush strokes of naked nudity. And, folks, that latter says it all. Carnality is here and seems sure to stay.

But I am in town down from the country to witness the manly art of pugilistic self defence. Or should this be better called these modern days the art of knocking senseless. But blood sport though the fight game is, there is nothing quite like the social life it engenders. At which this present great newspaper, the *Independent*, came nearly not to be represented. Frank Maloney, the distinguished promoter, not realizing that yours truly was a friendly and not a poison pen attending, my appearance much softened in the company of rock singer composer Rachel Murray, Dublin's Dark Angel, her sombre voice known for her dirges and melodic anthems to doom. And following in the wake of her stately tall dark beauty, one was smilingly welcomed everywhere. Able to close up pick out the flattened noses of the retired pugilists, and to shake hands with the more unidentifiable collection of these appreciative gentlemen ringside who are aficionados of the sport.

At eight p.m., America is waiting across the seas to watch the main bout on television. But first lights flashing and booming out is the music of Shane McGowan, we are to see Kevin McBride versus Steve Garber. McBride, six foot five and seventeen stone, is the new Irish heavyweight and Frank Maloney's prodigy. Unbeaten in his string of sixteen fights, his lungs whistle as he plunges in his punches. And unfolds a non stop battle of punishment absorbing, energy spending sweat flying from start to finish and a more bruising contest you've never seen, his opponent Garber nearly giving as good as he got, the brutal battering ending in the seventh round with an astonishingly intrepid Garber from Bradford finally on the canvas. If McBride or Barber had to prove they were tough enough to both endure long careers in this sport this was their imprimatur.

Now let me put a few observations forward. The first time I was ever substantially impressed by Frank Bruno was in the first professional fight he lost, when one could see this man finally obtaining and remaining as a long unbeatable world champion. But somehow English fighters and Irish ones, too, seem to take pride in being hit. And now as Lewis's opponent enters the ring and I can close up see his tree trunk powerful legs holding up his chunky physique, I'm wondering wow, will he whistle upwards a lucky and fatal left or right on Lewis's jaw. By his serious mien one knows this Australian's tough and that he can see in his own surname the prospect of being the upsetting underdog in this fight. And sure enough out he comes from his corner in fiery attack his head down like a charging bull. The strong man stares at middle area Lewis whistling punches as he attempts to adapt the poise necessary to hit such a smaller opponent.

Ah, but here is demonstrated the best of all boxing lessons called don't let your self get hit, while you wait to hit. And Lewis the calmest of calm expressions on his face manoeuvring out of the way of bull was like a scientist examining a variant in a molecule. Looking up from ring side where the bloody cuts, bruises and lumps from the thump and crush of punches are immediate to the ear and eye, one witnessed between Fortune's flurries Lewis's carefully selected punches. These aimed slicing through the air with the sleek power and purpose of a shark's jaws.

But there was no question that up against a tall tower of skilful strength a fearless Fortune showing little sense of defence is also his own tower of strength. And Lewis's almost leisurely but devastating final punches uppercutting and sending your man across the ring and down, but who, leaping to his feet, was ready instantly to go on. The contest stopped by the referee to the boos of the crowd who wanted to see more of this weight lifting tough Australian fighter and of course they will, courtesy of this referee's timely intervention in favour of safety than to respond to a cry from the crowd. And Frank Maloney, as he should have been, well pleased.

But let us not overlook a sign of the times. I found myself becoming aware that I was seated between two attractive women both of whom seemed to be experts on every nuance of the manly art. To my left Cliona Foley, the distinguished lady reporter whose subtle fight opinions one listens to with awe as her fluent gems and acerbic observations arose from an encyclopaedic knowledge of the fight game. And on my right, Dark Angel's matter of fact summing up, who never at a fight before accurately had already predicted the round ending the first two fights. Between bouts I then retired with the gracefully swan necked sultry star of doom and dirge, who nevertheless is never less than marvellously charming, and a stunning contrast to this night. Then as one stood with her over a beer and popcorn, didn't one of the very nearby natives offer his two cents. Who with an amiable honesty said he was laggards drunk but that she mustn't think of him as just a thick Irishman because he had a PhD. And this news one was glad for at least it could mean this conversation might not end up in a fight, and he had the intelligence to ask.

'Now what is the most beautiful woman I have ever seen doing at a boxing match.'

Holed up high up in the old Shelbourne Hotel, the Dublin mountains to the south appear by dawn misted purple and always reminding Dubliners that they are near enough for their own two legs to carry them there. And here in this comfort one has to be careful not to accuse the towels of not being fluffy enough or the toilet tissue sufficiently soft, as one is reminded of the now Sir Rocco Forte, who is no mean handler of his own fists and a marathon runner to boot who, for an impertinence, might pop you one on the snozzle. But by God, he's got to know about the log jam at the check out front desk of the Shelbourne around noon next day that would crucify you with anxiety if you had to catch a plane or train. But with my car parked nearby in the RIAC to take me home I wasn't troubled in the least.

But it was my last Dublin treat to witness an astute young

man fielding the demands of this mob of customers and a constantly ringing phone. And not, mind you, all the hotel's fault, for the crowd growing as it collected, there was a fluently English speaking German gentleman reciting what he had from the mini bar while he then went on to check every item after item listed on his bill and actually winning adjustments here and there. Folk looking at their watches. The young astute gentleman, a prince of patience and diplomacy, continues to field this intrepid German's ad infinitum enquiries as he chooses items he now wants charged to someone else. Finally the prince of patience thanks me for my own, which of course to me isn't that much of a problem as I am busy scribbling some of these very words on a counter perfectly high for writing comfort. Hoping Frank Maloney will again come back to Dublin and bring the best in world fisticuffs with him. Remember now peace reigns supreme everywhere in Ireland except in the boxing ring.

1995

PART 4

Life, Death and Affairs of the Heart

Whither Goeth That Bullet

One hates to have to say this straight off, but the United States is, as all its citizens are already convinced, the greatest country on earth. The place where the story of mankind is being breathlessly told in its very latest chapter. It is also a place where it's damn easy to be killed.

I have always taken every comfortable precaution to stay alive. As a professional pedestrian who pleasures much in his reverie, and as one who does not trust fate to do me well, I have regarded the possibility of being put in the way of a bullet as being an unnecessarily ludicrous way to go. And I have always believed rudeness to be, as much as anything, the cause of violence. Fortunately, I am, to beggars and tycoons alike, unfailingly polite. A trait for which most people are not yet being shot. But it does sometimes leave you, in New York at least, holding open a door for the whole city to walk through. And ready to shoot the next son of a bitch who goes by without saying thank you.

Living in the Republic of Ireland in recent years, surrounded by fields and walls and monstrous dogs at large, one never gets a true feel of danger. No poisonous snakes, spiders or grizzly bears. Trespassers, if they haven't already been frightened miles away by the thundering concert of massive Irish wolfhounds barking, might, unless one rushed to the scene, already be chewed to death. Other places I have lived in Europe, such as the Isle of Man and London, were traditional in their peacefulness, and harm to the person was relatively rare. But now, a perceptible if slow change is in progress. The odd mugging has at last come to Dublin. In London, passengers have been assaulted on the underground trains. One now finds one has to go further afield, behind the Iron Curtain in fact, to be where one is still relatively safe. With maybe a drunken dissident trying to swallow his words on a street corner as one approaches looking as I do, slightly like Joseph Stalin.

But everywhere the world over is growing faster and faster like America. Even in a Prague or Budapest street, there are at last emerging folk who just might want to rob you, and hurt you to do it. One supposes that easy money and greed are the moving forces, fanned by the propaganda of happiness through the consumption of products and aided and abetted by the theoretical equality of man, recognized in the United States and communicated by film and television to the rest of the world. Class and caste barriers, at least in matters of material possessions, are down in America. Where a busboy, taxi driver or mortician can be a hero behind the wheel of a shiny new car. Yet the majority of millions will never swagger triumphantly across the carpet of a country club.

Perhaps because of its vast array of ethnic origins, American culture demands the standardization of its citizens and the availability of what they want. Freedom from scrubbing, celibacy, boredom and self denial. A steady supply of jeans, pot and coke. The throbbing belief in each American soul that I'm as good as anybody. And that why shouldn't I get mine as well if the man at the corporate and political top has his fingertips in the till. And, dear me, does that lead to trouble. Especially when your neighbour on your leafy street or crowded train lets you know by look, sneer or shove that you're not as good as him. And you want to sock or blow his goddamn head off. This is how I have always remembered this country as having been.

But to come up to date. And see America more recently. As I did in spring 1981, on returning from Budapest. Where there is nothing quite like the Hungarian language to keep you in the dark. At a hilltop window staring out over battlements from Buda to Pest across late winter mists lowering over the Danube, church bells pealing, the soul purring in the strange silence one feels far across the eastern reaches of Europe. And with the accumulated days of no newspapers, television or radio, I wondered, sipping my iced mineral water, what on earth was happening way out there beyond the spires in the distant west. Had the stock exchanges yet exploded with the news of a biogenic organism that happily excreted crude oil. Or had the Russians invaded Poland yet, and as the big, powerful nations said slightly more than boo to one another, would the Iron Curtain suddenly slam shut on the toes of this poor, innocent, bog trotting Irishman.

With a military precision provided by the hotel, I departed with ease next early morning, chauffeured to the airport. Somewhat glad, chewing one's apple, to lift into the sky over the Danube past Vienna, out of the constraints of a society rigidly controlled, and safe for the body and unsafe for the soul. I fell asleep all the way to London. Arriving to walk out into a less than bustling airport. My bag for the first time came out sooner than later on the conveyor belt. Encouraged by this omen, I walked on, nothing to declare. Past the single customs officer, his elbow propped upon his knee, daydreaming. As I stepped out into the expanse of the terminal, there it was. A newspaper headline. Held up in a man's hands. PRESIDENT REAGAN SHOT. As I quickly made my way to buy a paper, I was reminded yet again why I, an American born and reared writer with a haunted love and awe of that land, had ever since my twentieth year been living in Europe.

The America I had left in 1946 still seemed, aside from the mob rub out and family feud, the place of the fair fight. Where only the cowardly and the distinctly from the other side of the tracks would pick up a bottle, a knife or kick or scratch. All my own fights, with rare exception, had been in the ring and on the wrestling mat among interested spectators and referees. Then I went to Trinity College, Dublin. To a land where the natives would agree to either side of an argument so long as it could result in a fight. I was horrified to suddenly find overnight that

I was in one brawl after another. In pubs, at parties and, indeed, even in water closets, churches and latrines. With nowhere safe and all the Queensberry rules abandoned. Boots, maces, pick handles and objets d'art flying. But still no knifing, no shooting.

Then in my brief return of a year to America in 1951, American violence, as such, seemed to make its first impression. It was a time of McCarthyism. Suspicion had spread everywhere in the land. Much of it directed instantly at me, being as I was the only man on the entire continent wearing a beard. With perhaps the single exception of a man who came smilingly around the corner of Fifth and 52nd Street early one afternoon and said as we confronted, 'Ooh la la, vive le barbu.' Or French words to that effect. The hair on my face produced hostile stares and growling at every turn. Met, of course, with stares of my own, as I reluctantly readied fists to defend against the first hand laid upon my person. No one did try to sock me. But one was aware that something had changed in America. In their street gang wars, kids were using zip guns instead of bottles, knuckle dusters and chains. The killings once reserved for family anger and mob vengeance had now come randomly to the streets. I heard that a bandit in the suburban peace of the upper Bronx, where doors had once been left unlocked at night, was shooting people dead on their front lawns after relieving them of their valuables. One now knew that America had truly become dangerous.

However dramatic and overnight, the hostility to my beard miraculously abated. Willie Sutton, the bank robber, had been identified on a subway train by a fellow passenger and arrested. The gentleman recognizing him was found slain a few weeks later. And now, as I would enter a subway carriage, instead of being confronted with hostile stares, all faces and eyes were averted. Arriving at the next station stop I would be sitting utterly alone in the car, every passenger having left to be seen along the platform jumping into other cars on the same train. On the street, sidewalks cleared ahead of me. And people apologized if they brushed my elbow. A case, for one citizen at least, of a bullet producing a kind of privacy and peace. And death in somebody else's body.

Then as the years went by and bigger and better people were being shot in America, I found myself one morning in a hotel in Columbus, Ohio, where a man knocking on the door said he was room service and I said I hadn't ordered any room service and immediately pushed my wife, who was about to open up the door, and myself to the wall, out of the line of fire. There followed his long pauses of silence between his admitting he was a fan of *The Ginger Man*. It was a sad occasion as he recounted the influence the book had on his life and that all he wanted to do was shake my hand and tell me so. But one had learned plenty about America, that there now floated aimless men who for no good reason would even kill what they professed to love and admire.

People simply and sensibly do not like people who are not like them. And all of us harbour some vengeance to equate with the slights and wrongs that daily befall us because of our penury, colour, creed, accent, father's job or even the hayseed in our hair that keeps us out of the country club or social register. We all want to rise above our station and, preferably, keep others permanently in theirs. And violence, alas, is the executive hand of this evolution. Whether it be a savage's spear, the big nuclear guns of nations or the .22 calibre pistol of a thief or jealous woman. It is also an intimate part of the spiritual efficiency of the United States. Where the bullet is the ultimate of democracy at work. Relieving the frustrations of a vast computerized nation. Blowing holes through choking webs of litigation. Giving the small man a chance to hold the behemoth football tackle at bay. Or the starving, desperate man who can go to a bank and demand money to feed his children. And even deterring the grasping hand of the grabber at life's banquet. And one can't help feeling that if America had no guns or knives, insolence would be epidemic and intolerable.

America, too, is embalmed with its mythologies of democracy.

The good life, streets paved with gold, where people no longer bend to pick up a penny. The propaganda of products, preaching life without pain, no toil no sweat no tears. Phoney glad faces blaring on every side, 'I'm happy, I'm cool, I'm contented.' Even self importance is sold between the covers of a book, to be learned in 310 easy lessons. Indeed, it produces results. And also, as a consequence, makes life seem cheap, with every kind of personality hearing and seeing constant mirror images of themselves. So why take unpleasant lip from any one of these cardboard reproductions who, according to the Constitution, is no better than you are. And who wouldn't, then, especially the downtrodden, the poor and the not so bright, finally think that the answer to all such bullshit was a bullet in someone else's head. When in your own true heart you squirm at the mealy mouths making noises of deceit.

In the middle of this, I have flown to America, where at one a.m. I stare out a window high up over the trees of Central Park. A great black cauldron of mist ringed with twinkling windows and blinking blue with lightning as the city rumbles with thunder. A symbol ominous and beautiful. A story in the newspaper amid all the other random homicides. Someone in the theatre district is throwing concrete blocks off a building and killing people in the street. It happens that from childhood I know Lieutenant Richard Gallagher, who is handling the investigation. Even in all his years of confronting the gory and gruesome, one sensed his extra concern to catch this cunningly mad killer. And over grape juice and ginger ale I asked this anciently wise and fair minded man what he thought of violence. And he said that what amazed him most was that it wasn't even worse.

In the morning I turn on the television. One channel is telling ladies how not to be cock teasers, and on another channel they're telling ladies how not to fake their orgasms. And this is nearly as mad as the insane violence most of us fear. That which comes without warning or reason from those harried into silent, brooding dementia. In search of their own celebrity and symbolically breaking the encasement of lifelong lies preached to their ears, which in believing them has left them lonely, desperate souls abandoned in ignominy.

But holy cow, it's you who has been randomly chosen, by this malcontent aiming his gun, to be the victim. And perhaps this is the bullet that can't be avoided. Especially if he's at a distance, watching you with telescopic sights while you are out walking your dog beneath the leafy ambience of East 72nd Street, and you have no close up opportunity to smile and promptly yell, 'Hey, good to see you, gee, you look swell. And please don't shoot.'

And to be shot by someone deranged seems sadder than to be shot by cold blooded contract. The latter at least means you were important enough to be an obstacle to someone. As are so many American witnesses before a trial. Who've earned the dignity of a conspiracy to decide their demise. Perhaps brought about by a young, beautiful wife who wants your lifelong earnings sooner than later. Or you want to get rid of this same monster greedy bitch plus her tanned gorilla chested tennis club lover. How many of us, even in wishful thinking, have found it imperative to call upon this kind of bullet justice. And in how few countries is it able to so luxuriously flourish. For what is often now not even noticed about America is its burgeoning subliminal violence of litigation, which murders more than bullets, is countered by those facing it, who subtly murder back. By car accident, by syringe, by snake, by disease. Yet, again one feels the antidote is courtesy. And civility to those made, by marriage ordeals gone awry, the hated and despised. But then murder is one of the most profound acts of life. The self appointed administration of a justice or injustice. Happening in America because people have no faith in their politically appointed judges. That they sense no truth in the words of the rich and powerful. And that there is no king in the land who does not cheat and lie. Who holds aloft a symbol of public conscience. At which they might bend heads and pray. And obey.

But then just as you think of America at its very worst, it's suddenly, in front of your face, a magic and most humane land. A man gives you a free apple and a smile. Another says have a good day and a swell life. You see the joggers trotting along. Happy in their belief, coast to coast, that they are in better shape than anyone else. Bringing to their bodies some of the pain American bodies so desperately need. To counter the dreams. And to sober the kids growing up in this land. Getting what they want. By whines, threats and screams. Instead of a good boot in the ass. Demanding toys, cars and cocaine. Getting them all, till they need heroin. And mom and dad, while jumping dutifully to their every physical whim, serve them up their moral code, which they daily breach themselves. Till these children grow out into the world and suddenly somebody says, 'No, you can't have that for free.' And they find they still can. If they get a gun.

Yet to me all the best in civilization comes simply with being able to take one's perambulating reverie. Along a sunny street. Playing romantic space shuttle in one's own world of dreams. And especially in a land where a novel erupts in one's vision around every street corner. And the language blooms anew in every mouth. At such times, one does not want to have to think of the inconvenience to the spirit, or to feel, as one takes a pee, that one might also feel a pistol in one's vulnerable back. To lose your valuables, piss all over your shoeshine and lose faith in man's humanity to man. And I once asked the artist brother, T.J., who spends his reclusive life between painting pictures daily roaming the TV stations, examining the Ouija board of America's mass communications, what was the defence against, say, a random mugger or an armed lunatic. He said there's only one. Whimsicality. And that a display of your own personal brand of this will throw a mugger or a madman off balance. But only for 2.3 seconds before he again assesses the common denominator of your vulnerability, and then if you can, even with your fly open and urine splashing, you'd better run.

But as one knows, the civility of a nation can be ruined by just one man's rudeness. And so still again I'm thrown back on my solution of courtesy. And that one has nothing to lose even in displaying it with a criminal who already may have the upper hand and who already is fed up with your mealy mouthed corporate guff. One might then murmur at the barrel of his gun, 'Gee, fella, have a good day.'

But let us take solace concerning whither goeth that bullet. That whatever happens there remains the great human failing.

> Although
> One does not
> Want to be shot
> Oneself
> Yet one would like
> To be able
> To shoot others

1981

Sentimental Journey – My Favourite Hotel

Hotels must achieve a great deal of their charm from the fact that people who go to stay at them are, while on their way, temporarily dispossessed itinerants looking for a safe and hopefully comfortable place to sleep, who, unconsciously working up an anxiety through traffic jams, boats and planes, arrive with much relief. Along with the terrorism that now stalks the world these days one's travelling peace of mind is not getting any better. And is it any wonder that one falls thankfully into the casement enfolding us as a door of one's chosen hotel opens and you see there before you a welcoming cloistered elegance.

Now Paris is a place where at least a small part of everyone's life ought to be lived. And it was just following the Second World War, when I was not long removed to Dublin from the wonderworld of New York City and America, that I first heard spoken of the gloriously wide boulevard of the Champs Elysées and that it was perhaps even wider than Dublin's O'Connell Street. I heard further of the splendour of Paris as one stood at an easel painting the university nights away in my austere rooms in Trinity College and conversing with a young Frenchman and undergraduate like myself. And who, in the chill damp of the Irish winter and disillusioned by Ireland's amatory prospects, would wistfully recall the heated comfort behind the glass enclosed terrace of a café on the Rue de Rivoli and there in the morning aroma of coffee and croissants he would watch the chic ladies of Paris go by. As I would proffer him more Madeira, he would then wax lyrical concerning the treasures and beauties that lay everywhere carelessly in abundance under the light tinted blue sky of this city to which I now knew I would soon have to go.

But I should have guessed that this elegant gentleman's aristocratic ways were not what I should encounter on my first trip to that fabled metropolis. As straight off the train at Gare du Nord one had a tug of war with a porter over my luggage. Nor had a financially careful university pal, a scholar in French, who, already in Paris, obtained for me what I had anticipated to be suitable accommodation at an hotel. This was a double bed in a rather suspiciously ornate chamber one short flight up from the street and from whose window one could nearly lean to tap passers by on the head. In my overnight occupancy, and when I discovered upon waking that I was decorated with the little red bites, I challenged my Trinity scholar friend who sheepishly revealed that the dirt cheap room was also rented out hourly by the hotel proprietor for afternoon assignations.

I did learn a thing or two as matters slowly but surely improved over the years. One already knew of and had practically stayed in every cheap hotel there was to be found in the sixth arrondissement between Boulevard St Germain and the Seine. Then my first novel *The Ginger Man* was published in Paris. And this in turn brought troubles requiring lawyers and more frequent visits to a city I was beginning to know well. Keeping pace, as it were, with the number of lawyers was the number of new hotels I tried. Although they did not increase significantly in their merit of stars, they did improve with toilet amenities and in their absence of bedbugs. However, as the prolonged battle of *The Ginger Man* raged, one's fortunes with other published books improved. And finally one graduated from the no star hotel, up to and through one, two and three stars. And then in a great burst of change, and more for convenience than in deference to my elegant lawyers, one switched from the left bank to the right. And at long last to a four star and finally to the Place Vendôme and the de luxe of the Ritz itself. Where the bedsheets felt like silk and one's beer was served in silver ice buckets and where, upon the blotter on one's writing desk, was written: 'Gentlemen are requested not to throw their cigar stubs in the garden.'

Litigation over *The Ginger Man* having now spread from Paris to London and from London to New York, the city in the middle seemed the best place to pursue one's reclusive life and especially as a modest bit of affluence had now come to pass. And it became more than occasional, as one sat in one's eyrie overlooking Tyburnia and surveying the rooftops of London while dining upon leeks vinaigrette and Coquilles St Jacques followed by raspberries, muffins, whipped cream and Château d'Yquem, to declare a homesickness for France. And then reaching for the telephone one would book a taxi to Victoria station for the next morning in time to catch the Golden Arrow train to Paris.

But alas it was upon such an impromptu occasion that the Ritz Hotel was booked out solid. And what if this was the case all over Paris. I had not now again seen my French friend of university years but often thought of him. Sitting sadly and lonely in my university rooms and once describing to me that when great prolonged times of melancholia came into his life he would always go away by himself, not to Nice or Biarritz, nor his family's various châteaux in the countryside, but to stay alone at a Paris hotel, of which, he said, I always reminded him. And I recall as he told me of this that I would be standing at an easel in the middle of my college sitting room painting a somewhat risqué portrait of some trustful lady to whom I boasted this accomplishment. And he would smile and plaintively say, ah and you here painting like this always reminds me of that hotel for it is named after one of the great Italian painters of the Renaissance.

Being only a brash amateur with brushes, canvas and paints, I was flattered by the reference and, in the train on this visit to Paris, racked my brain for the name of this hotel. The anxiety growing that despite my improved finances I could end up again in some dingy bedbug infested room. As the French countryside sped by I was watching one of those affable but quiet and well behaved American gentlemen seated across the aisle having the set gourmet's de luxe Golden Arrow lunch that came with the ticket. And the drama of this began to take my attention. As if he were intent upon getting his money's worth, the American's soup came which he smilingly and hungrily guzzled down while grabbing in turn the three different wines in their three different glasses to help wash things alimentarywards. Then arrived an hors d'oeuvre which equally went down, and instantly replacing it a tasty savoury was set before him. Followed by Galantine de Volaille. The American was now clearly gorged and sated and in some desperation was racking his brains for the French words to say stop, I've had enough. His face was turning green, he was now writhing in his sofa chair. The waiter taking your man's gesticulations as inspired praise and to please keep the dishes coming. Finally, as yet one more course arrived, this defeated American half stood up and raised a limp hand and arm to block as another laden plate hovered to descend before him. And in the most plaintively heartfelt words I have ever heard spoken, declared.

'Hey, gee, buddy, what do you say we skip this one.'

But it was almost exactly at this time of witnessing the American's dilemma over his interminable lunch and as we passed the town of Gisors that the long faded name of my university friend's hotel entered one's brain. At the train terminus I said the magic word to the taxi driver, and racing along gloomy, bourgeois Boulevard Haussmann and dodging around through the traffic circling the Arc de Triomphe and a little way down Avenue Kléber, he pulled up on an entrance apron in front of this edifice of blond stone. Arriving out of the blue without reservation at the reception desk I timidly mentioned the fairly distinguished name of my old school pal and welcoming smiles appeared on all faces.

Now then. Some few years have passed and fewer and fewer of my days have been spent in Paris. Left to be relived and remembered in the pages of *The Beastly Beatitudes of Balthazar B*. The inspiration for this book coming just as strangely as nearly everything now did concerning that city to whence one would go crossing the cold grey waters of a windswept English Channel to hole up in the confines of one's favourite hotel. It was upon a London autumnal day that I was in a taxi passing eastwards towards Knightsbridge and as I looked out the window, there standing on the pavement in front of the entrance to the Hyde Park Hotel was my old French pal from university years. With my taxi proceeding forward and further away, I tried to get the stubborn window down to give a shout. When I finally succeeded and bellowed as loud as I could, a fire apparatus at the same time came swerving out of Sloane Street into Knightsbridge, its electric motor horn blaring and bells sounding, and drowning out my voice crying his name.

And like death upon a face you will never see again, I was haunted by this incident. Recalling joys and sorrows of our university years. His dazzlingly handsome parents I'd see from my Trinity College sitting room window, coming to visit him. The sight overcoming me with a sadness. As it seeming always to be raining. Their elegance carried by their beautifully shod feet stepping along the cold glistening dank pavement of New Square. And I thought. Imagine, they must love their son. Enough to come all the way to these bereft climes from their grand château and Paris townhouse and call upon him in his gloomy, chill college chambers.

And some many months later, following the incident in Knightsbridge and still unable to forget, I betook myself to a table at a window in an eighteenth floor eyrie overlooking the fading autumnal green of New York City's Central Park. Gazing north towards the horizon of Harlem, I was to spend a resolute three weeks to form merely those first opening words of *The Beastly Beatitudes of Balthazar B.*

> *He was born in Paris in a big white house on a little square off Avenue Foch. Of a mother blonde and beautiful and a father quiet and rich.*

And now one does have left this legacy. To come and stay at my friend's and now my own favourite Paris hotel. And since the days of my impecunious college scholar friend who introduced me to my first French bedbugs, my goings and coming from Paris have been much differently assisted. Especially by an intrepid Anglo Irish gentleman called Peter Dawson, to whom the French refer as their own très bizarre and très correct and très endearing version of James Bond. And he, too, has long been an aficionado of the Raphaël. In his efficient manner and in one of his exotically fast motor cars he comes to meet us at the airport to sweep us into Paris. Doing so with the same deft touch the great Renaissance painters used to administer their brush strokes to their master-pieces, as smoothly by a hair's breadth he navigates between fenders through some of the most unpredictably dangerous traffic on earth, while comfortingly informing one that Parisian motorists no longer try to hit pedestrians, as it has got too expensive.

Très bizarre and très correct, Peter has already informed Alain Astier, the manager of the Raphaël, of this, my sentimental return. And Monsieur Astier has replied that no effort shall be spared to make my stay comfortable. And now to enter once again the discreet grandeur of this hotel's panelled hall. Pass by the sanctum of these welcomingly intimate reception rooms. Where in the sumptuous peace and quiet, judicious gentlemen of great power come to sit and confer undisturbed and unobserved. At the reception counter, under the great Turner painting, one books in. Guided by a gentleman of the hotel, my lovely lady and I ascend in the hushed panelled interior of the lift to one's apartment. To be enfolded gently by its cloistered elegance within. Standing again as one has previously done in this suite, a profound symphony of colour upon which the eye wanders across the rug and the soft crimson carpet to the blue bordered cream panelled mirrored doors and alcoves.

Adjoining the sitting room, the bedroom awaits like a pro-scenium stage behind light blue satin drapes and the brass curvature of the bedstead gleams at each end of the crocheted counterpane, inviting one reassuringly to calmly and deeply sleep. Ah, but one hears a sound of a clanking board down in the street. I go to part the window curtains and to peer down through autumn leaves into this quiet rue off Avenue Kléber. On the corner an ancient lady, befurred against the chill, is now being led by the kindly hands of a young man to her car to be chauffeured away. And we know, we absolutely surely know, she is going somewhere very nice. More clanks of boards occur as I continue to watch. The street is being sealed off. A marvellous activity is erupting as lorries arrive. And as always I am ready to be entertained. The tree pruners have come. Like balletic jungle monkeys these acrobatic gentlemen climb, spidering their sure footed way up through the branches. Suddenly, to the loud whine of chainsaws, the boughs and their leaves fall. And no surgeon anywhere amputates with more gentle care and finesse. To stop the sap bleeding, they apply their balm. Worthy of a man to be invited to join any of the great hospital staffs in the world.

Like a meteor tangential into space, a whole day in Paris has passed. One has walked one's usual eleven miles up and down the rues and boulevards, always mindful to stop here and there in a likely café to watch out for the odd great pinball player. One has dutifully stood over the pavement holes the blue denimed workmen of Paris mysteriously dig. Finally to return pleasantly tired to the Raphaël and there in contented reverie lie on the blue chaise longue. I imagine it as the same chaise longue upon which Balthazar B, forgotten by the world, must have reclined in his loneliness. Perusing as he did the newspaper's long list of motor accidents. The clock upon the wall constantly reads ten minutes past twelve. The tree pruners gone. Darkness descending upon the street outside. With a push of an ebony button tipped with mother of pearl, soft lighting glows to life. One visits the twin basins in the bathroom, which made Balthazar's aloneness even lonelier with only one face to wash. And the great crystal tears hanging from the sitting room chandelier might have symbolized his sorrow. But now they suspend above the ormolu mounted marble topped splendour: great curvingly yellow bananas, black and green grapes, red blushing pears, mauve pink peaches and purple dates. A frosted silver ice bucket with a bottle of Hôtel Raphaël champagne, courtesy of Alain Astier, awaits. Just as does this quietly alert elegant gentleman, who comes but shyly and smilingly discreetly near to smile at you and make sure you are content. And perhaps even very happy.

We are now five in this sedately dignified drawing room. Peter and his lovely Katrina have arrived. James Bond's strong hands are necessary to make the champagne cork go pop. But just as we expect, this pale golden wine delights the palate, and is poured for both our beloved ladies. The distinguished photographer David Gamble is here in his black cape and scarlet shirt, his eyes missing no colour or shape as they dart to focus on every face and every corner of the room. For these few glad moments nothing is wrong with the world. And too soon the time has come to go.

Now, with Peter's tyres only briefly and gently scorching the roadway, we go without delay along Avenue Victor Hugo. To stop where a door opens before us to the splendidly modern restaurant Vivarois. With a garden out the window, we sit to enjoy the cuisine of the handsome Monsieur Claude Peyrot, one of France's greatest chefs. The wines flow and in wondrous succession the splendidly delicious courses come. Claude appears and listens modestly to our delighted appreciation as Peter calls to drink a toast to this eminent master of cuisine. And which makes me remember again that sad American of yesteryear on the train to Paris whose hunger was sated too soon, but who inspired me to recall the name of the Raphaël. To the tranquillity of which place we return to take our coffee and Armagnac. On the way we motor along Zizi Street, perhaps better known as Avenue du Maréchal Fayolle but famed for people who show each other their private parts. Peter slows the great twelve cylinder engine down to a deep throbbing purr. But the police this night seem to be too much in evidence and, although these devotees are in their earnest abundance, most parts remain private with no zizi or pomponette to be seen anywhere.

But one always cherishes to return to the quiet elegance of the Raphaël. And in the mornings to go past the flower tinted glass behind the reception desk. Reassured to feel one's step softly upon the carpets of this long entrance hall. The gleam of the marble black and white tiles between the panelled walls. The engraved round globes of glass gently giving light to the paintings. On a grand table of sea green marble sits a tropically bright red leafed flower in a Japanese vase. A large sofa awaits upholstered in its anaconda skin motif. And upon which sit two sleekly groomed ladies on the threshold of entering their riper years. One hears English words spoken between the stream of French.

'Ah, my dear, but I wanted to hold on to Jean Marc's friendship but then it is Pierre's money which talks.'

And, I suppose, just as money talks, nothing lasts. The quiet grandeur is the same, but since the days of Balthazar other things have changed at the Raphaël. The beau monde have come. The très chic just flown in from Nice and Monaco. Sporting the latest. Wrist watchstraps worn on top of shirtcuffs. In long black leathers and flowing robes, foppish and dandified. They stride by so ultrasmart. Earrings clanging like cathedral bells. These glamorous people so in a hurry who live according to a lifestyle. And are here and are there and are everywhere.

Ah, but wait. Early evening approaches again. The sacred moment in the oak panelled, crimson carpeted bar of the Raphaël. The ice bucket stands appear and the golden necks of champagne bottles peek from their chilled confines. Just as they did in those days of Balthazar. Who came here to mourn a lost love. And whose ghost now walks the Avenue Kléber. Down to the Trocadéro and the Cimetière Passy. Where, behind high ivy clad walls, lie those illustrious and respectable who repose in peace under the gleaming marble and faded stone. No longer worried lonely. As living hearts are. Who walk beneath the branches from which the biggest of Paris's chestnut conkers fall. And bop you alive on the head.

1991

My First Love

To stare so far back in one's memory, one wonders how much could be true. But it is all that I know that I find left in my mind. My first love lived where I lived in what one remembers as one of the strangest suburban communities in America, called by the prosaic name of Woodlawn. Its uniqueness arising from its geographical location on the far northern marches of New York City from which it was isolated on its three triangular sides by large open spaces in the form of a wilderness park and one of America's largest and most sylvanly beautiful cemeteries where, in their vast mausoleums, some of America's fabled tycoons rest in peace, richer dead than they were when alive. And where Herman Melville lies along with them.

One wonders too now if idyllic dreams have taken over what must have been then many a sad forlorn time. But those who lived there and who knew it as I did seem to concur that as a place it had all the qualities of your most pleasantly homespun American small town, and a community whose ties were that close that a reunion was held not that many years ago of those who grew up there. In the vastness of Van Cortlandt Park, deer roamed and possum played, and one rode horses, hunted game and also trapped for fur skins, as did my closest friend Alan, who knew all there was to know about the American Indian, whose lore he emulated and over whose previous stamping grounds we wandered. And almost as if from central casting came Alan's younger sister, whom I took out on her first date and who was my first love.

As it might happen in a small midwestern town, the news of Carol and I as boy and girlfriend did, in one day, reach a good many ears to establish that one was 'going steady'. With her two elder brothers, Alan and Donald, the eldest, they were all three handsome and, aided and abetted by their engagingly friendly manners, were possessed of an astonishing natural elegance and assurance. Beautiful as was her face and stunning her figure, one best remembers more than the loveliness of her looks, of which she seemed totally unaware, her warmth and captivating personable nature. To all of which was exotically added the natural musky perfume of her presence.

Overwhelmed as I was by a romantic love, any physical passion seemed a desperate transgression. In any event her brothers, both lady killers as they were called, said they would kill me were I ever to seduce their sister. And I had some proof of this, as it was in their company that I first got to know Carol when we held boxing matches in their large attic. And where Alan not only landed his south paw punches on my jaw but also stretched and dried his muskrat pelts he trapped each winter to sell to the Hudson Bay Company. The attic, too, was where he sharpened the long blades of his racing ice skates and also Carol's, and it was in the valley of the wilderness woods where Carol and I first held hands as we skated by moonlight on Scotchman's Pond and roasted marshmallows in a blazing fire on its shore.

My having a younger brother, T.J., and elder sister, Rita, and despite our background being first generation Irish and Carol's and Alan's and Donald's going back some generations in America, Carol became as if she were a member of one's own family. Our differences came from their owning bicycles forbidden me and they in turn every Saturday morning were routinely made to clean their bedrooms. Although living in a much larger house, I regarded as glamorous their spacious and fairly grand apartment in which was the most elaborate stall shower with a great glass door. Admiring it greatly I was after our boxing matches invited to douche. The family now knowing me well, it would not have been thought untoward for Carol to have scrubbed my back.

Our romance developed with the traditional Saturday evening

147

visits to the local cinema known as the 'Itch' to see such film epics as *They Died with Their Boots On*. Our first kisses in a side back row, as across the screen thundered horses to suitable orchestral strains as the white man mostly beat hell out of the Indians Alan so much admired. Pineapple sodas were taken in the local candy store and more kisses and holding hands walking home along the parkway. Our separations only came in summer time when each year Carol with her brothers returned tanned and smiles gleaming from their long holidays on Fire Island, a long narrow strip of beach fronting the Atlantic ocean.

Feeling somehow we were already betrothed and part of each other's family, and thinking that I was launching her out into the sophisticated world, Carol was the girl I first invited to a Fordham Preparatory School tea dance. Chaperoned by observant Jesuits there was fox trotting and waltzing but no jitter bugging. Carol was alarmingly an immense hit, all vying to dance with her. As I was known as the knockout specialist in the Prep's intramural boxing contests, I felt sure that no one of my class mates would dream of making an advance and daring to do anything as bold as making an assignation. But then I was unprepared for the explosive impact of Carol's smiling graciousness and her intoxicatingly musky fragrance. And I found myself confronted by the class genius, who with damn nerve, if not in some trepidation, was informing me that he was asking Carol out.

Assuring myself that she would be unimpressed by his super genius rated IQ, and instead of glowering that I would break his bumptious little intellectual ass, I instead affected a patronizing magnanimousness pretending amusement at the idea. But when Carol accepted I was shattered. Then promptly came a much worse threatening bombshell. And more painful in the matter of jealousy. The French Consul's son who sat directly in front of me in class and to whom my only conversation was whispered insults concerning French morals, which invariably provoked a snarl and his response 'Léchez mon cul,' had a lot more nerve.

This French bugger informing me loftily that he was not only having a date but was taking this beauty away from her unsophisticated environs of Woodlawn to a Washington, DC, black tie reception and introducing Carol to the international scene.

Despite her avowals of continued love a certain growing tenuousness developed between Carol and I. For that was not all. Closer to home, other contemporary friends in Woodlawn awakened brightly to Carol's charms. Two of whom, old friends, were not only charming themselves but extraordinarily handsome to the degree of attaining the attention of national magazines. And these two gentlemen, John Duffy, later to become the distinguished composer, and Gerald McKernan, a rich industrialist, both fell for Carol, who indeed was now sought by all. And even too busy to come to the nadir of Fordham Prep social activities, the annual school boat ride up the Hudson River, returning by night, dining and dancing as the skyline of New York twinkled in the distance. No one who ever took this boat ride ever forgot it. And to which instead of Carol I invited her brother Alan.

But then in this discreet family's background life something was changing. Carol's parents were separating and getting divorced. No such modern thing it seemed could be contemplated happening in my own family. Their dapper blond wavy haired father who, as Alan told me, had an eye for the ladies, always made me think of a celebrated vaudeville actor, and I was surprised he would part company with these children's vivacious and always to me charming mother. But they had already now, from this small town enclave where they grew up, moved away further down into the lower reaches of the Bronx.

The Second World War on, I went into the Navy and as another young lady intervened I saw less and less of Carol. But then just at the end of the war we nearly reunited, when tragedy struck an almost unbelievable blow. Alan, a fighter pilot, surviving a mid air collision and combat had on the eve of his intending return home to New York been killed in an automobile accident while out celebrating his discharge. And as I entered this funeral home down in the Bronx and went to kneel at the side of the coffin of my closest friend, both Donald and Carol came to each kneel either side of me. But I never saw her again. Donald went on to become one of America's most distinguished obstetricians. Then years later I heard from John Duffy that he'd met Carol's future husband in the subway, a gentleman from Woodlawn who was trembling with excitement in announcing that he was to marry her.

But all of twenty years later Carol did come back into my life one night in my sleep in Fulham, London, down what was then much a dingy working class street, I dreamt that I had returned to America and, my wife having died aboard the ship, I searched for and again found Carol. I asked her out to have dinner at a posh restaurant, where we arrived and were refused service and ignored by the waiters because of my peach coloured shoes. It was a dream so vivid that in the morning I wrote it down. It became 'Peach Shoes', the final scene in the play *Fairy Tales of New York*. And Carol brought back to life in the role played by the wondrous Susan Hampshire, who of equal beauty and charm said she saw the jewels of tears every night glistening in the audience's eyes. Just as they do in mine recalling my first love.

> Which flourished
> In all its smiles
> Of promise

1995

Pasha of Heartbreak House

Having lived now a quarter of a century in a big country house, I am told that I have an unquenchable obsession about the aristocratic upper classes and praise the Royal Family too much. I have even been accused of tweediness and then in this very highly regarded newspaper the *Telegraph*, it was made known in an obituary of a recently deceased Irish author who, while he lived, was quoted as regarding me as a poseur. But worse, a proper English gent watching me on TV lead out the Westmeath Hunt from this present mansion screamed out in the presence of two of my good friends, 'That man is a raving snob.'

Now then. Much truth may seem to ring forth from all this, as these days the image is the reality. However, as an American not badly born and bred, this reputation really stems from attempting to be mannerly and nice to everybody. And as I came to Europe to be educated and later to live, the only people with time to waste in my company and at the same time willing to be pleasant to me have been persons who have had private incomes from inherited wealth which has often brought, through no fault of theirs, a title with it and condemned them to living in large castles and massive country houses located within their splendidly spacious domains. Thus my landed gentry associations and my own adaptation to this way of life have led to the writing of novels such as *The Beastly Beatitudes of Balthazar B*, *The Destinies of Darcy Dancer, Gentleman* and *The Onion Eaters* which fairly echo and revel in this motif. And even an odd passage in *The Ginger Man* has an impoverished Sebastian Dangerfield swearing revenge by imagining that one day he will be back on his great estate where he belongs and will have his game keepers drive away his erstwhile wife, who having taunted and deserted him in poverty now wants to return to him with her babe in arms.

Now all that said, let me please say this. There is no question whatever attached to the fact that I have, through no grievous fault of social climbing, but strictly acquired for professional privacy, ended up myself rattling around in a big old house. The desperate difference being that I am now doing it alone. And more than occasionally teetering over an abyss of solitude such as dries up the soul, which in its weightless frailty nearly vanishes. As an antidote I have a closet full of plus twos and threes and a whole library of walking sticks and sometimes do affect the posture of the country gent, marching out over the parklands. The walking sticks, I hasten to add, carved by my own hand out of the hedgerows. Because I can more often be seen crossing the fields with pick axe, crange and slash hook. But publicized images last. And it is now far too late to allay such aspersions of snobbery and status seeking, if aspersions they be, by jumping on a motor cycle in black leather jacket and boots. Or burning my cravats and taking to the turtle neck sweater, jean jacket and pointy toed suede shoes.

But there are other matters far more real and far more troublesome than the social aspersions wrought by living in the big house, and sporting about in its dilapidated stately splendour as it sits for its two hundred and fiftieth year enclosed on its modest hill by its three foot thick elevations and surrounded by its parklands. For there, within, is the squire and pasha, often bereft, lonely, and having again and again been left in the lurch by one beautiful woman after another. The major problem now being, how do you, in your utter solitude, sustain your reasonable contentment. Yet it is amazing that it is but a few months ago that I first woke up to the awareness that I did so live, and wondered what the hell I was still doing here. That at the departure of the last beauty, I could have myself long also decamped. And maybe sampled the much cheaper and more comfortable confines of Claridge's or Reid's Hotel in Madeira.

But then how does one easily tear oneself away from what one now knows best.

And, too, you never fully give up the dream. They don't exactly grow on trees or jump out at you from the love lorn columns, but what about another wonderful companion. A big agricultural girl perhaps, as is usually sought by land owners in these parts. Not beautiful or lissome, but nearly as nice as some of the damsels who have left. And there's the rub. I may strain my brain. But do not search and seek. Because it all could be so in vain. What you usually find available is someone else who has at the time no better place else to go. However, as Henry Root would say, nothing wrong with that. But if they come, it's just for a while. For you know in truth that what you are running is a ladies' finishing school. Nor again is there anything wrong with that. Except that you charge no fees. And supply in abundance organic vegetables, pure air and sweet water. And by God if it doesn't make your temporary chatelaine learning the ropes look, with her glowingly healthy skin and exuding euphoria, astonishingly good to other men.

As foxhunting season arrives, she hints that she has grown fond of you and still you dream that she will stay. But now equipped for the chase, the cuckolders come. The big house, with its so many rooms and corridors and miles of walks across its parklands, makes you vulnerable to conspiracy. Chaps have asked your would be chatelaine for another piece of soap. Wham. Bam. Thank you, Ma'am. She's been seduced. They now swagger down to dinner dressed in their smart cavalry twill and suede shoes, to even have the effrontery to ooh and ahh over your minor objets d'art. The seeds of departure of your enamoured are sown. But gentleman always, the pasha, politely as he can, tolerates all. For who knows, something new might keep her.

Ah but let us not cast aspersions. Ladies while they last have all been wonderful. And one does not entirely give up the hope of finding a new mistress, especially one wise and a lady of principle. Tolerance and affection, the major ingredients between us. A lady who as she sweeps in her elegant garments along the corridors and pauses perhaps on the grand staircase landing to place a flower's prominence more aptly. She takes heed of one's wardrobe and also occasionally buys one socks. She chooses menus and the placements for dinner and adores to listen to your piano playing. In short, her ladyship is the pearl to be found present in the grand architectural oyster over which she reigns. And never once does she fill a bucket full of ice cold water to throw upon you in bed.

Now this is not to say as pasha that you're not with a stop watch and slide rule working out how much everything astronomically costs. Restocking Guinness barrels and wine cellars. Turning off radiators that keep vast boilers down in the cellars endlessly roaring. But you know that enjoying her free wheeling and especially spending role, it keeps her ladyship staying. Even as she sees you with magnifying glass at the ready to locate the fingerprints on the doorknob to her chambers, to verify the activities of the last randy guest who ad nauseam throughout dinner extolled her virtues. You pretend of course that you scrutinize for evidence of a pilferer who, as the recently rented footman did, may have penetrated the portals in order to case the joint. But aside from her impatience at these pernicketies, she forgives, and inspires all.

But you always know that finally, in your mature ladyship's mind, practical things have got to come first. She can't help wondering, when, as she ferries up breakfast consisting of the pasha's favourite pancakes, bacon and maple syrup, that he might be found dead having snuffed it in bed. As indeed one morning I was supposedly found as I lay perfectly still, staring at the ceiling. The tray dropped and herself was gone. Therefore it is a grave mistake to ever have yourself seen limping, or heard coughing and creaking about up and down the halls. Or even in order to entertain her ladyship, pretending a limp and geriatric shuffle for a laugh. Better to leave available and open for inspection your running book recording your recently run six minute mile. Of course that latter speed might make her think you'll soon drop dead from over exertion.

And in the way you least expect, it happens, the elegant lady is gone. And the bimbo, a waif like slim blonde beauty, who is going to leave you in a thrice anyway, glides in. Enthusiasm is her forte. She is immediately ready to jump upon and be taken away on anyone's gravy train. Openly she kisses visiting gentlemen and gets their addresses and calling cards. You indulge her because she's a laugh a minute, long blonde tresses flowing as she races the halls on her roller blades. You allow her contact on your mobile phone to her new swain. He of course has gone ape happy over this curvaceous miracle who wears skin tight emerald satin jeans, faxing her massive emoluments to the bank account you opened for her. And leaving you wishing for some numerical mistake that deposits same in your own account. And that day comes again, all too soon. You've just loaded her bags in her Ferrari. A kiss on the cheek. And roaring down the drive she goes. And gone.

Once again the dream vanished. Of warmth, proximity, companionship and even hanky panky. Of words, soft and soothing to anoint you while toasting your slippered tootsies in front of the library fire. Of kisses upon the brow and her fingers wiffling through what's happily left remaining of your hair. She likes you enough to suggest a colour change, from its gone white to a youthful black. She's just bought the most up to date kit from the chemists. But none of that is to be had. The big house echoes with your cold footfalls. Sounds made that you must make yourself. You move for cheer from your down at heel chambers to a more luxurious room in the north wing. You are just a statistic, as you would be tabulated in an actuarial table. Young beautiful women leave old charming men. And all you have ever tried to do is make womenfolk content. And they will either kill or leave you for that.

Now, as abject loneliness for sure descends, stern discipline is called for. You march the halls in a military manner. In the music room you play 'Waltzing Matilda' on the piano. Night fallen, you always build a fire. You sit to a set table. But as you scavenge food from anywhere in the kitchen, don't be afraid of feeling sorry for yourself. But don't feel too sorry for those who have left you. No one is about now to slip arsenic in your stew. Or jump on your back to crumple the life out of you. You have nothing now but yourself to get away from or avoid. Time to become a bloody cunning old codger. Choosing careful any beneficiary in making your will.

But having a military or naval background is a massively great asset in helping keep at bay the silence of loneliness as it deafeningly gathers about you. Leather heels resounding upon the pine in walking the long halls remind as you strike your foot falls that you are alive and disciplined. And are not about to prostrate yourself on the chaise longue racked in self pitying sobs. Instead you stride in a military manner squaring turns at the corner of hallways, clapping your hands and shouting cadence and commands to the platoon you imagine is keeping you company. Left flank march, right flank march, to the rear march. Of course to avoid committal proceedings undertaken by your nearest and dearest make sure no one is bloody well around while you're pulling off this antic.

Ah but even when life is lashed by loss and regret, wait yet awhile longer and listen. To a voice that there was once. Of a lady here who said. Let's be a little family, away from the rest of the world. Entwined together in our own little lives and woes. And be in this mansion where are hidden wonders that make children's voices echo joy while playing their secrets. Till they're grown up and gone away. And we chase them. Calling goodbye after their names. Come back again. Where that countryside sings over your grasses matted by wind and rain falls in sunshine. Where now the sadness lurks so deep. It doth make you still. But where, too, was once spoken. A love to one you loved, and who loved you.

1996

Love Letters Straight to the Heart

The saga which led to my soul searing loneliness publicized at least half way around the world found its first seed in the most innocuous manner of a journalist telephoning from London with a pleasantly enquiring voice and hint of an Irish accent asking me to elaborate on Brendan Behan's diet, a single example of it appearing in my book *J. P. Donleavy's Ireland*. Amid chuckles from my listener, I repeated the recipe of one of the most astonishing combinations of foodstuffs ever put together in one mushy mélange. Behan, after an ice cold swim in the sea off the coast of Wicklow, poured and dumped into a large mixing bowl a portion of every ingredient I had in my cottage and drank it off in a dozen or so uninterrupted gulps.

Now then. Finished telling of the incident of Behan's impromptu lunch, the journalist asked whatever happened to that incredibly beautiful girl Rachel, a picture of whom with your good self we have in our files. I said she had with her little daughter moved off to Dublin where she was pursuing a successful career as a designer and an art dealer and was even helping the old boy out back in Mullingar in selling an occasional watercolour and painting of his own. A day or two later, knocking the Royal Family off the gossip page, appeared the stunning picture of the now famed Rachel along with a headline 'Donleavy Left in the Lurch'. Variations of this report promptly appeared in the gossip columns of the other tabloids. Next there was a bidding war for Rachel's story, who besieged rang me in alarm and voiced her reluctance to speak of her departure from the author's mansion to Dublin, even in the light of their offering to pay money. Of course hearing that word money, and as a long time adherent to the principles of a peasant farmer, I said, my God, take the money and feel free as to what you'd like to say about me.

Well now, old Rachel (very young) coming from a most respected and refined family background finally at my insistence relented but selected the more serious and prominent of lady journalists to write the story. Which indeed was brilliant enough, for after its appearance it had perfect strangers shouting praise to me in Dublin's streets.

'Jaysus, J.P., that's a great story.'

Of course I could take no credit for this marvellously written interview but then unexpectedly my turn came. A lady from one of the more conservative broadsheet papers rang from London. She sounded mightily suspicious that I might not be able to write the story of being left in the lurch and to describe surviving thereafter lonely in my mansion. However, they would give me a chance and would even pay for it, but only a fraction of that paid to the beautiful Rachel Murray, whose picture alone could wipe the Royal Family off the tabloid pages, and followed by her forthright opinions give a further sweep of the broom. And one presumes such family would be more than glad for a moment to be so gone. And I suggested that old hat novelists stood no chance in such competition but I would do my serious best to paint my predicament of the lonely old man shuffling about in his empty mansion and how he coped now he was left in the lurch. And by God, I was surprised that what I'd got down on paper, including barking out military commands to himself marching the long halls, seemed to give a pretty good account of the author's brave if curmudgeonly survival.

Ah but there was more to the story so told. Although Rachel was the most amazing and enchanting of all, she wasn't the first beauty to decamp from the mansion and leave the author in the lurch. And so, going back in the years, I recounted the saga of what in retrospect seemed to amount to a free of charge ladies' finishing school over which I unintentionally reigned. And how, as the seasons passed, the swarms of playful, charming cuckolders in gents' natty suiting and cavalry twill riding kit made their attempts to sweep the ladies in residence off their feet. And some successfully did, as it is a signal truth that ladies quite like that. Especially if the sweeping comes in the form of four wheels like a Ferrari and substantial bank drafts from your better banks to pay for the petrol.

But in matters of enticement you realize that you are not yourself, in this respect, free of blame. Although you take care to keep overheads low, you also pay attention to keeping the lawns mowed, the wine cellar locked but not empty, the pool sparkling clean and the sauna full of rare scents and fluffy towels. Foxhunting season comes. The blood gets up. Their horses frisky, the cuckolders get bolder. You know that at all costs you must keep calm and that as a pugilist not lose your temper. There are other and bigger battles. That you're stuck up to your neck in your mansion with bills and the price of cattle and advances to authors are not what they were. But all you know is that you continue to follow that faithful dictum that the author must always remember. That writing is turning one's own worst moments into money. And by which precept you must, through all tribulations, abide. And it's presto, how the novels *The Onion Eaters*, *The Destinies of Darcy Dancer, Gentleman*, *Leila* and *That Darcy, That Dancer, That Gentleman* flowed from my pen. And things still rough, more are on the way.

Ah but now the last of the ladies had left. I was teetering over my abyss of solitude so deep that it dries up the soul. And so, for the broadsheet, I wrote of how one coped with such long term ordeal. Then following one false start after another, it seemed a long time before the piece was actually published. I thought the editor, as they sometimes do, had second thoughts. Has your poor man crazed by loneliness now gone slightly nuts or at least incommunicably and irretrievably eccentric. But then the article finally appeared, spread over a whole page along with a large photo of the author at the side of his mansion. Another insert photograph also revealed the writer forlorn, standing in his empty dining room, with the most glum and gloomy of expressions on his face and his candelabra on the table drooping. And you'd never believe the variety of people who end up reading newspapers. Or indeed where they encounter them. Under the cat's bowl blotting up the milk. Or pages prepared to be rolled into firelighters. But the article 'Pasha of Heartache House' as it was entitled was also spotted and read. And my God, didn't the letters of reaction come.

Some correspondents were savvy enough to refer to a *Who's Who* to get my address and wrote direct. And now the women could be heard. Drawing attention to things as seemingly mundane as doesn't the poor old sod realize that with the bimbos gone his life's a bargain not having to be paying for anyone else to be enjoying it with him. But what provoked most response was my predicament worn on my face of sadness. And without even the faintest twinkle of an eye. However, one or two discreetly pointed out that they wouldn't mind to join me in my ordeal in the spacious freedom of rural surroundings which seemed enviably attractive. But never in the history of opinions came so many. From all over Britain, from France and even a midnight phone call from a distinguished actor and playwright in the USA, the only man to reply, but who did so marvellously and fervently to say the piece had 'touched him infinitely'. Ah but not one single murmur of any description did there come from this dear old place, Ireland herself. Now there's a matter I'm still examining.

Of the written overtures made to get better acquainted one found oneself reverting to one's own lessons learned about women. Which in any case have long come from watching heifers and cows in the herd. Either to jump up on each other or to give a roar to the bull. And it's why farmers know a thing or two about life. And also perhaps why such wise counsel comes from the Irish matchmaker out in rural climes, who was once asked to explain his success in bringing about so many life long unions and replied that it was because all his clients in their anticipations expected nothing and as a result got more. But if I put myself forward as a candidate, I can hear the matchmaker's voice now. Ah Jaysus stay away from that lonely old bugger, sure in the photograph of the dilapidated mansion hasn't he got a big enough roof over his head that you might find yourself out up on a ladder helping him to replace a slate, or worse having to drag across the fields old bed springs to block up the gaps in the hedges.

But also in the avalanche of mail arriving, there were other opinions. Some alluding to their own loneliness. Others to suggest that I seemed to enjoy being taken for a ride. But there were those, too, who were shocked with wonderment at the destruction of an image. Was this the famed novelist as seen on T V elegantly riding out to hunt the fox or with white chamois gloves driving his gleaming Daimler, and who wrote the romantic saga such as that of the poignant romance of Fitzdare and Balthazar in *The Beastly Beatitudes of Balthazar B* and the splendour of their love in the troth they pledged. And why isn't the author now seen standing alongside one such reincarnated magic chatelaine principled in her life long fidelity. Instead of consorting with fly by night ladies who saw greener and richer pastures in bouncing out of his life. Ah but in aloneness, as you cry out in anguished pain, where do any of us go to find love. When no one wants anyone who wants to be wanted. And so rests the heart in that painful verity.

1996

PART 5

Gone But Not Forgotten

W. B. Yeats Commemoration

As the modern world's aesthetic eye focuses ever more intently on Ireland and as one who lives mid way and only a stone's throw from the road and train tracks to Sligo over which W. B. Yeats must have passed on many an occasion and peeked to see this mansion up on its hill, I hereby contribute my tuppence worth to his commemoration. Having oft listened to the singing of his praises and only having to read a word or two of his work full of all kinds of imaginative mystery, one feels Yeats to have been an early pioneer reawakening the north west of Ireland out of its monkish past and instilling there a spirit that has since made it a mystically erogenous zone. Which, who knows, may have also even grown to inhabit the whole of this once saintly celibate land. And together with the profundity of the epitaph over his remains where he now finally lies, Ireland has W. B. Yeats to thank for introducing heavenly apparition into the most bereft and haunted of this isle's landscapes, making them places of romance and enchantment of the same that lurks indelible with every Irishman departed to the corners of the world and yearning for home. And let me tell you your gombeen man selling this place to the tourist has made the most of it. And why not, as, were W.B. alive today, he would have been tax free with the rest of us in this now only mildly repressed and rapidly becoming enlightened nation where every man, woman and child who can string three words together is getting in on the act.

1989

Christmas Recollections –
for Better or Worse

My first ever published comments about Christmas appeared unexpurgatedly in a painting catalogue written near the sea at Kilcool, Co. Wicklow, the year 1961. I composed it from notes and letters. And the catalogue was for sale for six pence at an exhibition I gave in the Dublin Painters' gallery then existing upstairs in a back room of 7 St Stephen's Green. Although I did not sell many pictures I sold plenty of catalogues promptly translated into rounds of stout in the nearest pub. My opinions have not much changed since then but have been mitigated over the years by the fact that Christmas is not for the disillusioned adult but for children's anticipated dreams of pleasure. My manifesto of those years ago reading,

> We are not dead yet. Where there is life there is success. Two days till Christmas the most vulgar and vicious time of the year. The time of the big kill, adultery and commerce when only the child has any purity or love. I have just come from the pub where they are drunk and fighting. In Ireland friendship is on the lips but not in the heart. But then when hatred turns to love, the will to kill is lost and that's bad in these hard times.

Of course any of you who have ever met him will think these words sound, as I now think they do, like the poet Patrick Kavanagh, who sits presently so calmly quiet in bronze grandeur on the banks of Dublin's Royal Canal and near where you might have met him when he was ambulatory coming across the Baggot Street bridge beneath which went that slowly flowing water. And over which often came Kavanagh ploughing like a battleship.

I ran smack into him one late morning cursing at his personal condition in the world, mumbling, grunting and grumbling as he would, especially at this moment of approaching Yuletide and who said with his first salvo of words.

'You see before you the soul of a man fighting through the raging waves of misfortune.'

Upon Kavanagh's head was his trilby hat worn in the squashed down dirty grey form of the battered crown long worn by Ireland's small farmers. And Kavanagh without a fork over his shoulder to head with to the field to dig up a few spuds for breakfast was instead set on a relentless course to his turf account-ant to place the day's bet. And by way of attempting to instil optimism in the mind of the spiritually pessimistic, I said.

'Cheer up Christmas is coming.'

'Well if it's Christmas that devout time of the year, what have you got to give me before I tell you to fuck off if you have nothing.'

Well known for my American sensitivity and for my violence at the merest suggestion of insult and lest I might take offence, Kavanagh already had put out his farmer's big hand on my shoulder. And with a beatific smile bid me join him in the Waterloo Lounge where I would be permitted the honour and pleasure of buying him two double whiskies, not necessarily in immediate succession as he might want a pint of plain in between. And in return for which I would get a tip for a sure thing at Leopardstown races.

'Now, Donleavy, don't mind what the others say. Trust me when I tell you it's a nag who when let loose upon this peerless day to be, the brakes will be well and truly off.'

American bred and of that bland tradition of behaviour, and a non betting man, I have never been as bluntly rude as the poet. Nor had Christmas yet seemed a vulgar and vicious time of the year. But I knew Kavanagh's gruff brusqueness and indelicacy of language was in his case a defence of his loneliness lest someone in the coming Yuletide be too close and sense the despair of the privacy in which he dwelled. But he was, as we all were, walking the cold wet granite pavements of Dublin under its sodden smoky sky, looking for somewhere with light and warmth. And dare I say it, even cheerful companionship. But little of this latter was to be had in this normally non convivial city without first knocking back several short ones or many foaming pints, and resorting to the Catacombs in the middle of the night. And by God then it was Christmas with a vengeance, with the insults and fists flying, 'Cheer up or I'll break your face, and you'll be needing my good wishes for a happy recuperation in the New Year.' And this somewhat dismal circumstance was as unlike anything could ever be from my own Christmases growing up in America.

The small town atmosphere in which I was reared was an enclave of streets in the uttermost northern reaches of the Bronx where, isolated by large tracts of woods, parklands and cemetery from the rest of New York, you might consider yourself as in fact living in Potosi, Missouri. Friends hunted with bow and arrow, had trapping lines and sold furs to the Hudson Bay Company. There were autumn venison parties and some neighbours galloped by on their horses. And here upon the eve of the birth of Jesus, Yule was a magically nostalgic time of sentiment so overwhelming that it could be painful. And one's anticipation so intense that the aura of Christmas Eve could make one's heart start and stop with its magic. You might have upon your mind faithfulness and trust, going to midnight mass with the other devout and the enjoyment of the incense and chasubles and the hymns sung. Then nearing this hour you might call upon friends in their house, the Christmas tree alight in the window. A wreath of holly hanging on their door. A knock. And the words you'd say. 'How deeply glad I am I see you.'

It was not the shopping, the toys, the gifts nor presents. But it was the moment when you came closest to your closest friends. As if either of you were soon to die. A time waited for with bated breath, and savoured, so to make it pass as slowly as possible.

As if such moments could not happen ever again. And you would cling to them to stop them fading, just as did the jingle bells in the Christmas music on the gramophone that one could still hear as we'd walk away down the street all white and silent with snow. On our way towards the ice cream parlour called Stellings. Or one further distant called Kutches. And there to convivicate with our less closer friends and to suck up pineapple sodas with paper straws. And all such so as to make you say, I love you. Please stay close as we wander this night. And please, please don't die. You kissed her. And shook hands with him. And they did. They were dead before the next Christmas. For they went to war. And the wreaths hung on front doors were in requiem.

Later after that Second World conflict was over, the Main Street soda fountain hangouts were also gone. And I had vanished to Ireland never again to find Christmas so saccharine sweet. The time of year seemed to come as Kavanagh did over Baggot Street bridge, without warning, and was aflow with whiskey, beer and wine. But happily too in my early Dublin days there was much solace for both body and soul. For I lived then in the very centre of this now proclaimed Joycean city in the grey sanctum of 38 Trinity College. Along with an invitation from the Provost I also had one from one of my first Irish girlfriends inviting me to Christmas dinner. And enamoured of this lady I chose the latter. But such was Dublin then and me so naïve to this place that I was unaware until sitting at the dining room table that her brother John Ryan was also my good friend. And anything more unlike America never was.

I dislodged late from a chill bed and discomfortingly dressed to shiver out of my damply cold rooms. A taxi summoned by a porter from the boulevard of Dame Street ferried me to Stillorgan village from whence tall granite walled laneways threaded through green fields and under ancient oaks, ash and elms. Deposited on the gravel apron I was saved from frozen death by climbing the wide steps and entering this large country house called Burton Hall. Centrally heated no less. And great hearth fires roaring in every numerous reception room. In this mansion sumptuosity reigned, that poor poets dream of and students too. Mulled wine warmed the hand. In flowing gowns the Ryan stunning sisters appeared as if by magic. Along with democracy, the rose petals floated innocently in the finger bowls. With the likes of Lead Pipe Daniel the Dangerous more thirsty than innocent drinking down the contents and smacking his lips. And amid ham, turkey and trifle there was much to smack lips over. For most of the foods known to mankind lay displayed festooned with gleaming silverware and your genuine Meissen. And if it wasn't on sideboards there was even more to come via the pantry out of the steamy kitchens. And not to worry either. There was plenty of crystal, too, ready willing and waiting to be filled by the booming burgundies and the long laid down clarets poured.

Ah but we all know Ireland to which we flee back home and from which we flee away again. Anciently old and always generous. And is now more than awake in the world. The last pretty park left on the edge of Europe that may not, alas, too soon, remain to be. Yet for the moment at least, west across the Bog of Allen to Mullingar to Tuam and beyond, it glows with every Christmas sign of festivity. Town streets alight in every gorgeously bright hue. Cars parked bumper to bumper. Each one shinier and newer and better than the next. And less than you'd expect of rudeness and fist shaking at the traffic lights. And more of the animated voices in the pubs and bars. A nation in its present whirlpool of moral dilemmas is nearly a country without a government. And why not. With the elbows close together in the pubs and then temporarily full with plenty of chiefs from plenty of clans, what could be better political management than that. To suit the place gone silly insane. Not only to keep up with the Kellys the Murphys and the O'Briens, but also with the Dutch and the Japanese.

And it was not that long ago, upon an early morn before this Christmas, that I was high up at a window overlooking St Stephen's Green watching a lone seagull fly by. The mist was beginning to clear over the Wicklow mountains. The rising sun turning them as purple as I remembered them from long ago. Descending from my eyrie to take an early morning stroll, I hear the sound of a siren. And see motor cycle Garda racing through the street and they scream by escorting some VIPs in their big black car. And who are they in there. Who leaves your standard, homemade man face agape standing outside on the wet cold pavement watching them go by. I enquire who's gone by. In case it could be an example of that most recent phenomenon that has, about time, materialized in the civilized world, and has been long known to the native Irish. That of being a member in good standing of Celebrities Anonymous. Whose code is, as we know, to earnestly plead, give me obscurity or give me death. And my informer answers.

'Ah it's only him, the British Prime Minister come to find out from us what he should do about Britain. Aren't we already telling the rest of them eegits what to do about Europe.'

Such do I find my sophisticated Christmas in Ireland now. Instead of your empty Grafton Street, the walkway is a throbbing hive of energy alive. Buskers shout, poets declaim and music bursts forth from everywhere. There's even a strange someone to say hello to us. And save us from obscure loneliness and a celebrity anonymous death. I think back and back to them long bygone days when the chancers and cads were rife and the poets and painters were few and far between. When Kavanagh, Behan and cronies and John Ryan walked here where only their ghosts go by now. Christmas then was a church bell silence settled over the city. When you nearly could hear the distant cry in the Catacombs.

'Give the woman in the bed more porter.'

And if you had no bed, no woman, no porter, you walked the grey granite pavements, with the spook of despair hovering over your head. And asking not for new sorrows. Nor to be forgiven all your sins. Hearing the click of your heel driving you onwards towards some cheer towards which you hoped you travelled.

Intending to find there whatever it was you thought your life was missing. And it could be little children. And the comfort you might like to give them for their body and soul. And meanwhile be there no fist in your gob. Nor vulgar nor vicious words for you to hear.

And if Christmas
Not be merry
Have a happy New Year

1992

Remembrance of a Pain Past

Having just rescued a weak lamb's life as night comes, out here in the early springtime midland bogs of Ireland, I contemplate my autobiography and sketch the notes which make up these words. And meanwhile I have forgotten the salt for my tray as I dine alone this evening in my workroom where, scanning the TV with my remote control, I sit in a wicker chair which once adorned my eyrie flat in 'Tax Dodgers' Towers' in London's Tyburnia many a year ago. Then I had merely to reach through a serving hatch to the kitchen to lay my hand on the salt, but now, with helping hands away over a weekend, I must up and travel a chilly one hundred and seventy yards' round trip to and from the kitchen. While meditating on the infernal inconvenience of it all, I encourage myself that walking this distance more than a few times a day at least keeps one fighting fit. And, alas, in a much desired condition as one meditates upon one's present work in desperate progress.

I suppose it is possible that the opportunity for the single most stupendous act of self aggrandizement of one's lifetime as an author comes in the writing of one's autobiography. Which possibly embarrassing act I am in the midst of persisting in, and attempting to decide how to go about it. Does one after all the appallingly mean and treacherous and betraying things that have been perpetrated upon one now take up the cudgel and, pointing an accusing finger, batter back, allowing oneself to stoop to heaping ridicule and contempt upon the guilty which just falls short of being actionable. And letting these turncoats who disparaged have it all back paid with compound interest. Licking one's chops while drawing up the ever lengthening list as

to whom shall be made tremble in their tracks. Alas, the vast un-
charted quicksands of the literary world are such that there are
not that many authors who survive long enough to do any of
this. And, too, as true authors they would be constrained by
the code of the writer which insists that you do no man evil or
harm because he trusts while your ear listens to his tale. But
then, bowing to this invitation to revenge and having disposed of these past begrudgingly resentful folk, does one then
point to oneself as above reproach as having been consistently
kind, loyal, beneficent and humane. In short how does one
manage to tell the truth, show up the dirty bastards and yet
stop from looking and sounding like the saint one can't help
becoming.

Now then. As sad as it may be it helps when a whole lot of
the old meanies who did the dirty are safely dead and only their
nearest and dearest heirs are left to squirm in rage. But then the
humane gentleman does not take too much advantage of the
departed dead's inability to defend and fight back, even as
incumbent upon him as the principle is of truth, dispassion and
dueness and making these sneaky and conniving folk of the past
look as horrible and disloyal as they actually were. And of
course having your lawyers double duly check that they are truly
deceased and not still cunningly lurking alive and planning in
an action for damages to use one's assets as their ancient age
pension.

But now in my own innocent case, my autobiography has no
trouble centring upon the first novel I wrote called *The Ginger
Man* and from which much of my humble recognition stems.
And never was there a book like it to give its poor author
tribulation. Coming heaped from every quarter and erupting
across many a continent. The beginning of the writing of this
work was for me at the crucially terrible age of twenty-four, my
last ditch stand against fast oncoming oblivion. My insignificant
fist clenched shaking against the big wide world of art as I began
writing it in Ireland and continued in New York, Connecticut,

Boston, the Isle of Man and finally hanging on by my fingertips down a drab street in London's Fulham. Where, let me tell you, the then middle and upper class in those days absolutely feared in utter dread to tread. Until overnight, almost magically Fulham became fashionable when an eligible royal bachelor was reported in a newspaper dining al fresco in the back garden nearly adjoining mine. But before this happened years were spent in social banishment down this working class street, counting the sardines we could afford to eat, and estimating the risk of buying a weekly bottle of beer we couldn't afford to drink and having rabbit for Christmas dinner. Until astonishingly, almost at the last moment of my survival, I was rescued and literally clutched from the irretractable jaws of extinction, by the *Guardian* for which I presently write.

My final deliverance came about through a brilliant young and sympathetic editor, John Roselli, who chose to publish some short pieces of mine and who made sure that not a word or comma was trifled with. And whose name now will go to constitute my own little personal hall of fame etched in my autobiography. It was the appearance of a piece called 'I Failed' from the MS of *The Ginger Man*. It not only brought the attention of literary agents but eventually led to publication of the novel, already turned down by dozens of publishers. Meanwhile the MS had been sent to Paris. It was not the piece 'I Failed' so much as the newspaper in which it was published which created immediate interest for Maurice Girodias, founder of The Olympia Press. For his father, Jack Kahane, owner of the Obelisk Press, and the first publisher of Henry Miller, was born in Manchester and had long instilled in his young son a deep reverence for the *Manchester Guardian* as the paper was then called. And the MS took on a literary significance for Girodias it might not have otherwise had. But it was from this unsung origin in Paris that the battle saga of litigation over *The Ginger Man* novel began that crossed nations and lasted till the protagonists were growing old and grey. And as one obituary of Maurice Girodias put it, at the sound of my name he would reach up and tear at what was left of his thinning hair. And if at a restaurant, Girodias, known to be a great gourmet, would jump up from his seat and run out into the street screaming and leaving his meal behind. So this publishing event in Paris of *The Ginger Man*, which should have been one of considerable relief and joy to a young writer, turned into twenty two years of litigious woe. And resulted in the author becoming much misrepresented as a ruthless monster instead of the reasonably decent chap he is.

But one's reputation over the years varies according to what country one is in and what nationality is trying to do the dirty. An American lady journalist who asked why J.P.D. was not included at an exhibition of Irish publishers in New York was promptly told that I was regarded as a black mark against Irish publishing. But in Ireland I must forgive if not forget the Irish doing me down. Their now sympathetic tax laws having made up for all the past mistreatment and opprobrium historically heaped on her writers. But along the boulevards and in the boardrooms of Hollywood are still whispered the unflattering words, 'Don't touch him with a barge pole.' For he's the sort who wants to have approval over films made of his books and demands artistic and creative control. Nobody said I was dishonest or even rude but accused me of the unforgivable act of driving of hard bargains. So now, in view of recalling all these opinions and on second thoughts, why shouldn't I in my memoirs, as well as settling old scores, glorify and promote a little and let myself go ahead and sound a bit like a saint.

Meanwhile I've just discovered instead of the salt from the kitchen I've fetched the pepper and so must perambulate on my distant journey to the cooking room again. Ah but before I go let me tell you that if you ever wonder why authors are so racked with humility and are invariably humane, just remember that their most precious stock in trade is the pain they suffer in their ignominy. And the dispirit they feel from the unkindness their openheartedness earns. But to keep one's words readable, it is necessary to lambast a few deserving bastards. And provided a brave publisher sticks his neck out with mine you'll soon hear of these further and better particulars when I do just that.

1991

The Funeral of Denny Cordell

Under the cold stars of a frosty night, dawn arriving chill across the Irish midlands, as one sets off to the funeral of Denny Cordell, of whom one has never heard said a discouraging word.

I first met him many years ago in one of the smaller sitting rooms of Glin Castle while we were both guests of Madam and the Knight of Glin. But I had heard of him long before as a greyhound owner and mostly described through the complaints of a friend who had rented him his stud farm to house his dogs. Then he later produced the music for a piece I authored and narrated about Ireland 'In All Her Sins and Graces'. And the more I listened to this music the less I became impressed by myself interfering with my spoken words. And so as all news does when it spells the end of one still so relatively young, his death now seems a strange betrayal to the future of all who knew him.

But this is Ireland. Where one comes to hate the truth that distorts the lie. You don't die here either. For the lips of those who remain keep saying your name and telling your tall tales. And Denny Cordell was one of those rare who came from afar to this island and stayed. And uncomplaining as he always seemed to me, he sometimes must have suffered its discontent. However, from all I could see, he enjoyed to play an Irish role still played, pleasantly shooting, racing, hunting and fishing in this western-most parkland of Europe. And knowing too that should you need the spice of discord at anytime to stimulate, you need not go far. The inhabitants will always see both sides of an argument so long as it can result in a fight.

Not able to sleep when contemplating so early a morning departure, and at the same time having to see a bull, his good work done, and whose ton bulk had now to be loaded into a lorry to be taken to the meat factory, I worried over him pawing sods into the sky as he would do if approached nearer than two hundred yards. But now I was gone out of sight and the bull out of mind as I motored south from Mullingar under the glowering grey skies, randomly passing across the Irish country-side and viewing the battle for survival of all these suburban homes so stuck out of place with their 'pitch and putt' and 'bed and breakfast' signs, and more recently posted, those plaques warning of Community Alert Areas and thieves beware. The heart can seize up with loneliness along these lonely winding roads. But you're kept alert trying to read the cast iron road signs torn in half. This an ancient amusement practised by some locals as a testimony to their feats of strength. And this is always better than encountering a sign you can read which points the wrong way. But this always done with the best intention so the visiting tourist will not miss the best sights.

I go round and round the roundabouts. Looking for any sign naming a town I've heard of which marks the way. And taking one wrong one, found myself travelling the countryside in a big circle, which took me back tracking on roads I'd just been on. Ah, but now being able to nicely miss the deeper potholes one didn't miss before. I arrive half way there at Port Laoise, where behind great grey stone walls political prisoners are kept. But who knows now in this land where peace has recently struck out of the blue that such walls might not be needed to be as high any more. Further south finally the hills rise and beyond the valleys dip and the town of Carlow comes. But I can't seem to find my destination of Bagenalstown for it is named Muine Bheag on my map. Stopping to get directions at last I find my way through mile after mile of winding narrow lanes and suddenly the gates of Corries House are there.

But back in Bagenalstown I'd already passed the small neat

funeral home where Denny reposed wearing in his coffin his country and western outfit, and holding a vinyl of Duke Ellington, one of his favourite singers as a boy. He's wearing, too, his cowboy boots, footwear when I noticed such first I thought strangely out of character.

I was warned by two locals that I'd have no trouble finding the rest of the way to Corries House. As the vehicles would be parked for miles around over the countryside. And finally there it is, the modest mansion Corries House sitting in its small paradise tucked sweetly in these hills. As one enters the gates and down the drive around the stud railed field, spears of daffodil leaves are pressing up from the ground. And true it is, his attending friends are legion. From every corner of Ireland and the globe, crowded in the hall and standing about in the sitting rooms. His dear, slenderly beautiful lady, Marina Guinness, her face pale but eyes still sparkling blue. Rock stars in their leather rock gear. Music managers and executives in gents' natty suiting. The racing fraternity in their tweeds and cavalry twill. The grooms and jockeys. The Anglo Irish, handsomely represented in the elegance of his dark clothes by David Thomas Pascoe Grenfell as he holds a glass of red wine, in the front hall.

And I stare at an open door into the nearby room. Candles burn on the chimney piece and there on the dining table is placed the long polished gleaming length with its golden handles of Denny Cordell's coffin. On top lies neatly folded his racing colours, his silks of green and orange. Beneath the table a splendid array of pretty flowers, richly fresh and full of the colour of life. Beyond through another door the kitchen, the table brimming with sandwiches, soup and cakes. And from all the other kitchen surfaces many glasses are lifted into which many beverages flow. The generosity that is Ireland. And amid the animated chatter it's hard to feel sorrow nor does one hear a sad word.

Denny's handsome young sons and friends carry the coffin out of Corries House and up the rising drive to the front gates where an exquisite horse drawn hearse waits. The flower covered coffin placed within and outlined by cut glass windows. I stand watching in the drizzling rain with one of his oldest friends whose crinkly ginger hair is slowly getting wet as his gentle voice talks touchingly of this man they go now to bury, and behind whom one is to walk to the church and cemetery. And about this and the distance, there is the lie told that distorts the truth as the word goes whispered about that it is only a mile and a half. Off we go. As suspicions grow as the first two miles and then three go by.

To pass time I count the little rainbow circles of moisture on the road. And I find I am walking next to a woman in black of a beauteous face who is from New Jersey and now lives in Ireland. Then next to her comes a man in Connemara tweed, his head of long hair is truly soaked in the rain. He shows not a sign of tiredness nor discomfort, but chuckles as I turn to look back and report that there are following now more cars and a distinctly diminished number of pedestrians. We shake hands as he introduces himself as John Hurt. And we walk yet another mile past a field where Denny galloped and trained his horses. Relief now as the church steeple rears finally still another mile away. But one knew the ginger haired old friend of Denny's close behind would walk thus ten miles further behind Denny's coffin. The knowledge gives one a strange hope of light to have in all one's own dark dooms where courage must live if life is not to die.

All around the church, the lanes are packed with parked cars. Inside along with his coffin are Denny's saddle and bridle. I do not recite the prayers or sing. For John Hurt is in the pew next to me and the splendid resonance of this actor's voice would be sad to miss when declaimed so near. 'Crimond' and 'O Danny Boy' are sung. And the service ends with the rousing hymn 'When the Saints Go Marching In'.

As the last sounds of song die away, I am reminded of being back in Corries House when asking one of Denny's old friends, Julian Lloyd, how did all this so suddenly happen. And he said that one night severe pain came upon Denny and he asked Julian to take him to the hospital. Where he lay waiting on his back to be attended, and Julian placing a blanket upon him to keep him warm, saw his cowboy boots sticking up and out. And Julian asked him wouldn't he be more comfortable with his boots off. And Denny, still so far from death as anyone knew, smiled and said.

'No. I'd like to die with my boots on.'

1995

The Funeral of the General

A day ago I was looking out across the green rolling hills of Tipperary and remembering my very first ever seeing the terra firma of Ireland. I was waiting to fly on to Dublin in a smaller aircraft and I walked out of the reception buildings which were but a few neat wooden structures at Shannon. I stepped out into the clear sweet air and walked down a winding country lane to come upon two utterly white swans stately proceeding on a shimmering black pool of water. And having arrived out of the sky from the mayhem of a great but potentially violent city like New York this was a stunning and unforgettable scene of tranquillity. And confirmed as I was soon to learn that the worst crime you could commit in Ireland was to have someone slip on a butter ball you dropped on the floor that you were trying to put on a spice bun served up in a Bewley's Oriental Café.

And there was another attraction I more slowly learned of. I did not think it then but think it now, that although there are, in their pain of life, a few people who welcome death, most of us don't want to die but if such time should come, there are few other places of the modern world on earth which can be found where it is a better place to breathe your last than Ireland. Where the dignity of death is preserved and even venerated and will bring mourners from every corner of the local land and even from far afield as time and distance allow. And one does not need to be of any notoriety, and where indeed to be even obscure and unknown, you can be sure as a corpse that more than someone will shed a tear and thought for your untimely departure.

On this just past August Sunday I arrive up in Dublin. Sorrows descend upon one's small world as the mist of sadness of other times and of other visits to past funerals settles about one. But life and business are everywhere in the city as a laden tourist bus pulls up in front of the Shelbourne. Germans are at the reception desk in this hotel which one has attended for what must be at least the hundredth time. But I just sign as another anonymous name. And although one senses an estrangement as they now say in hotels 'no problem' as one asks for what one wants, Ireland is still Ireland.

I am here to perceive the obsequies of this conspicuous man called 'The General' and I suddenly realize that I am not capable of intruding upon another's sorrow no matter how conspicuous they might have been. And for the same reason did not attend the funeral of Brendan Behan, a friend who was my own guide to the doings of the Dublin's underworld and the dangers of the Animal Gang and Gardiner Street. But in those cart horse days crime seemed only to amount to a stolen landlord's toilet bowl tied with a ribbon like a baby and wheeled in a pram to the pawn. But there were pick axe handles and your fists. However, now we have bigger and more valuable items to steal and faster ways to die.

And suddenly now again I think of my old pal Gainor Stephen Crist, that Ginger Man whose ghost or actually himself I saw walking alive through Dublin not that long ago and who, when he first came to Ireland in the days when your biggest ignominy was not having the price of a pint, had once stood in a field somewhere in the north of Ireland where loyalists were practising their marching and beating their lambeg drums and he said of this fury passing by in front of him, 'Mike these people mean it.' And we knew, too, among other friends released from prison for their political crimes and their more menacing work that they had no uncertainty in their convictions either and that they meant it, too.

And as one goes south to Rathmines Road across the Grand Canal one passes on a side street 'The Bretzel', the Jewish baker. And then further on is the Rathmines YMCA built in 1911, a sounding place to which Brendan Behan in making an edict would direct begrudgers in banishment. Grey clouds edged with a faint brightness and move across the heavens from the south east. Fronted by great stone pillars, this imposing church's massive dome is surmounted by a golden cross, announcing to all its architectural significance with its golden letters proclaiming its name. A lightning conductor from the statue on its roof pointing at whatever God we hope is, in his goodness, up and out there looking down mercifully from his galaxy. Parked in the church forecourt a shiny black hearse awaits, its roof covered in flowers. A thickening line of inquisitive onlookers gather to watch from across the street. Limousines waiting nearby. A group of Press and Garda conferring on the pavement. While an endless stream of traffic moves along the road.

The first realization of who this man is comes from the Garda cars of various blue hues stationed everywhere and the white helmets on police stationed everywhere else. In all directions far beyond the church go reporters with their mobile phones and photographers with their cameras. And as the attention intensifies it is hard to distinguish the converging from the diverging. The activity in the street and the crowd seems to reach crescendo as the coffin comes out of the church and is placed in the hearse. The bowler hatted funeral director, an accomplished master in the disposal of the dead, steps out into the road, raises his hand and shows the way. The cortège leaves carrying sombre faces. And shortly the pavements are deserted, with not a soul left at the church.

The action now is at the entrance under old pine trees at the Mount Jerome cemetery gates. And just as at a Hollywood première the crowds are amassed once more. The hearse and limousines slowly enter. Again one feels not to further intrude but inspects and finds in the streets surrounding this ancient graveyard angry motorists wondering what's happened to find themselves caught up in a traffic jam. And also with an astonishing efficiency out here too the Guards are cruising the adjacent surrounding thoroughfares checking all that could be suspicious.

On this very day they shout truce hopes across the land. But watching the Garda do their duty it makes one wonder how any criminal they want to catch could ever hope to get away. Perhaps some are permitted to in order to keep the force on its most efficient tiptoes, and deliberately they do not catch them all. And then I am amazed how easy it is to pick out from the respectable general public these members of the underworld. This strange brotherhood who just as strangely could be a charming friend when you needed a charming friend. And who may even have perhaps come to admire the splendour of this funeral and the small fortune in flowers.

And now another ghost and perhaps a Dublin legend will hover over the rooftops and streets. Or will be felt lurking in the darker shadows of the pubs where one once thought there never could exist an arch criminal in such an intimate place as Dublin. But now as I leave this city and stopping down a respectable tree lined street as I go westward a group of young kids not more than three foot high are peeking into front gardens as they run along the road, looking and regarding doors and windows for criminal opportunities. And it's my last scene of the metropolis before passing out to speed through the green fields of the midlands. And I realize that an arch criminal could exist. And can nearly feel the chastening effect of murder when such a threat is silenced forever lying under the flowers.

1994

PART 6

Castles and Mansions, Conduct and Etiquette

An Open Letter to Those of the Nobility Befuddled by Clutter

Your respectful Lordship,

We sincerely hope you will excuse the diabolical liberty as we take this pleasure in addressing you by personal letter. As high class old established rag and bone merchants, we have instigated this practice for special clients whom we know (By Informed Sources) are members of standing in the peerage and are in great need to hurry in their clearance of rubbish. (In clearing out fast some of our assistants avail themselves of roller skates should a client so require.) If your problem is, above all others, CASH, this is our strict speciality in the utmost confidence.

We have found in our long experience that a client desperate for ready currency often has in his possession, unknown to him, soiled and begrimed oil paintings which to the unpractised eye seem like the work of an old master. We would wish that this was so. But in our experience there are few old masters about these days hidden in attics and recesses and it is such paintings, very old and encased in ancient varnish of the early Dutch school, that we would like to take off our clients' hands at *NO COST TO THE CLIENT*.

Our employees are experts who recognize junk in a flash, and are specially trained and experienced in wading through the bric à brac, the endless tunnels of mansions and down the deepest recesses of the wine of castle cellars to remove the dusty stacks of old Sauternes, claret and spirits past their prime. They are also experienced in blowing open dingy musty safes or making quiet entrance into cupboards where the bulky, out of date surgical or scientific instruments including space consuming heirlooms most frequently are to be found. And even though the latter are often fake, as is more and more the custom these days, we will rid you of this embarrassment without absolutely any charge to you.

We know you will not be surprised to hear that we have come upon your situation by a picture of your commodious premises up for sale in the press and our supervisor is of the opinion that you will be in great need to have discreetly taken off your hands (without the wide publicity shed on your plight by public auction) unwanted tapestries, old coins and medals, disused basins, bath tubs, ancient Chinese pottery (be the latter Woolworth, Sung, Ming or the recent Hornchurch), copper of all descriptions, jelly moulds and the like. We further know that historical curios and silverware can be a burden to their owners due to the widespread burglaries taking place and these we clear out with absolutely the best competitive price paid IN CASH on the spot.

Unfortunately from the picture of your once lovely premises, we see there is very little garden statuary remaining but the spout in your garden fountain must be of a durable metal, brass perhaps, and since these are out of fashion now, we would be glad to remove this and any lead piping to which it may be attached under the lawn. We are sure that you are possessed of many boxrooms packed with the bygones of yesterday which when removed will psychologically give you the impetus to bring your life up to the modern style. We note also you have a farm. We would be pleased to remove any old cows or horses not wanted. Or other livestock thought to be eating more than their keep.

Rag Bone & Metals Ltd
Visits by Appointment Only

PS We all are informed that you have a grand piano. We wish to point out that although this may have been of the highest quality when purchased the heavy treatment given instruments by today's virtuosos will have knocked the best out of it but we are still prepared to cart this space taker away for very small remuneration indeed. On smaller musical instruments we pay the highest prices.

PPS A special rate (this week only) is being paid for any saucy old photographs or reels of film.

1978

Ghosts and Dolls in Donegal

Before you throw up your hands in horror at the rain, chill and gloomy brooding skies let me tell you of a few tiny joys here. The biggest being that of curiosity finally satisfied. As it was once for me over a niggling mystery which grew slowly over the years. Living as I do a little less than half way across Ireland, and resulting in people on their way to the west frequently stopping off with their friends at my house. When I would, as a matter of courtesy, enquire of folk as to where they were headed and I would invariably hear the answer.

'To Henry's.'

'Who on earth is Henry.'

Up till this moment all I knew about Henry's was that it seemed a destination to which only the very grandest of grand people were invited and to which no one declined to go. And upon the occasion of finally asking, after many years of listening, as to the identity of this name mentioned frequently, the first socially registered gentleman to whom my momentous question was addressed rocked back on his heels, wide eyed in awe, throwing up his hands in the air and laughing incredulously.

'My God. O my God. You mean to tell me you don't know Henry. Good heavens, we must fix that. Absolutely must.'

And this is why these words about Honora, Araminta and Amabel must start with Henry. Indeed it was not that many weeks later, when my socially registered friend did fix it for this present socially unworthy midland bog trotter, and I did, as I do now, set out upon these westward dark wet deserted roads that go curving and winding across this land bounded by hedge and wall. Up and down through the brown scraggly wastes and between the small farmers' fields of Cavan towards a distant Donegal. The lonely cottages and haysheds and nothing but isolation across the tiny hills to the horizon. Except suddenly in the middle of nowhere an arrow points down a muddy rutted track with a sign saying BOUTIQUE. Someone's defiant effort in these forlorn climes to keep alive a rose tinted dream.

Across rural Ireland everything is an adventure. If the quarter inch thick cast iron road signs are not torn in half by the stronger natives, or are not pointing in the wrong direction, then they read, as you get closer to where you're going, that you are in fact slightly farther away. A tourist innovation in road travel which is designed to give the visitor a pleasant feel of relief when he finally gets there. And let me tell you. On this particular chill Sunday that I travel, with the roads icy black, I was sure glad to get there. As already upside down in the ditches were the previous Saturday night's crop of cars. And in the morning's sunshine, suddenly passing was a cemetery on a hillside, where the male mourners were each with a shovel and sleeves rolled up, heaping the sods with gleeful expertise down upon their dear departed. Who no doubt had recently come round a sharp bend and, with the Irishman's disregard for what lies ahead in this temporal world, promptly motored into a tree.

But if in Ireland you manage to miss a roadside hazard, you rarely avoid political strife. And I soon cross at a customs check point, bumping over a security hump into the North. At a stop sign, a disembodied hand sticks itself out of a slit in a fortified gun emplacement to beckon me onwards. Through Tyrone and the Sperrin mountains and along the Mourne River. The chimney smoke hovering over the frequently bombed town of Strabane, and a lone soldier, rifle at the ready, patrols through a side street. And in spite of the British soldiers being smilingly polite, one is anxious to recross the border again back into the somehow softer and friendlier countryside of Eire. But ushered on without question, one is also mildly miffed. As it speaks little for one's dangerous appearance. It may have been I smelled much too fragrant. For with the sudden bumps over the security humps, the top had come off a large plastic bottle of hand cream and flooded my ancient attaché case and filled the car with sickly sweet fumes.

You won't believe it and of course it's not true, but Ireland has become fashionable to visit these days. And this lie said enough might eventually defy the truth, and some of you obsessed with curiosity may find yourselves dumped dumbfounded on these shores. And if you are, you will discover there are still some very charming people lurking out in these bereft forlorn windswept climes. For I was now soon to discover that I was on my way to visit not two, but three of Henry's dearest and oldest friends, of whom the ladies Honora Myles and Araminta Swiney were among the last of that redoubtable breed, the Anglo Irish, who once held their squirearchical sway across this emerald isle.

Going west in Ireland, it is as if you are heading towards the edge of the earth. A haunting precipitous place from where you might fall into eternity. And as I approached Letterkenny, wisps of Atlantic cloud were in the sky, and the grey blue tints of night were descending, and I could already feel this apparition in my bones of lemmings heading for oblivion. Stopping at the first traffic light a cow nearby was staring at me, its head out through the fence. As if to point me towards a long narrow busily thriving street down the middle of the town. Boasting not only a chiropodist but a 'Literary Institute', the latter proclaimed on a grey dignified Victorian edifice in large ceramic relief. But as the rain plummeted down along this dark and cold avenue, there was not a single poet or novelist to be seen. But this is the nearest metropolis to which Henry, Honora, Araminta or Amabel might come for a quiet cup of coffee and change of scene.

Invited to a light lunch, I drive along Lough Swilly from the town of Letterkenny, passing on its outskirts these bijou stucco and stone decorated bungalow masterpieces which in Ireland always sit glaringly on close view to the passing envious neighbours. And one has come to know, wherever one sees an unspoilt stretch of countryside and a plantation of mature trees still standing, that there is sure to be an Anglo Irish Protestant near at hand. So as a lengthy frontage of foliage and a forest loomed along the road, something told me that I was already driving past Aughnagaddy House. And turning around in the pretty village of Ramelton, I headed back to find its shrubbery shrouded entrance. Proceeding into a long potholed drive twisting through ancient trees towering over an entangled undergrowth of rhododendrons whose boughs contorted in the shadows like great monster snakes. Arriving finally in front of this sprawling rectory with its windows too close together, as are some people's eyes, and Honora Myles coming out across the ice coated ground to greet me.

Speaking some of the most exquisitely spoken English in the world, as the Anglo Irish do, Honora welcomed me into the front hall with its ship's panelling. My cap and gloves placed on a travelling trunk under the massive head of the water buffalo benignly looming from the wall. Ushered up the concrete stairs which replaced previous wooden ones burned in a fire. Concrete because in those days past, estate workers knew how to mix cement but carpentry was an unperfected art. Turning left on the landing and up further stairs to a much lived in kitchen. Everything in sight of an eye and handy to reach. From baking powder to barley water. And now further mysteries began to unfold.

A Mr Derek Hill arrives. Cherubically pleasant, freckled faced, jovial and marvellously tweeded, Derek's was another name I'd oft heard mentioned out in these environs. And his was as fabled as Henry's. For both were famed not only as world travelled connoisseurs, Derek as a distinguished painter and Henry as a collector, but also for the splendour of the comfort in which they lived and which they dispensed with their legendary hospitality. Indeed the few words of annoyance these two ever exchanged was over the largest of all sins to be committed out in these rural wastes, that of hiring away another's staff. Henry's abode being bigger and his coffers seemingly inexhaustible, Henry was occasionally to be accused. But if much of what is stunningly beautiful in Donegal still remains, it is greatly due to the example set by both these men, holding out on their respective estates, against wind, rain, mist and philistine.

Sherry is poured as we all sit in a small sitting room reached along a hall, and through a bedroom where Honora Myles has a magic world awakening. Her dolls, many known to her from childhood, are each aseat on their antique chairs in their wonderful frocks. Others are gathered together as a tiny audience or as for a children's party in their ruffles, flounces, frills and furbelows. Fiddle de dees on dressing tables and in every nook and cranny. Georgian dolls' houses in their miniature fairy tale grandeur, and with their teeniest of weeniest furnishings, sit up on tallboys. One wants to diminish so one can join at a minuscule table for an eyedrop of tea and take a microscopic bite of a biscuit.

Nothing anywhere throughout these rooms seems as if it has been moved for many years. The furniture taking its time to find its well worn spot where it shall always henceforth comfortably remain. Even to the bumps and lumps in sofas left undisturbed. Yet all is neat and pleasantly in its chosen place ready to please the eye. Including twenty year old Mousings, the cat, sitting regally curled on a window sill. And this is a house like most Irish mansions, where if you are not huddled over a fire or stove, it is colder within than it is without. Even a fine brocaded napkin feels heavy in the hand. And one's pee fumes up upon the nostrils as it descends into the toilet bowl.

But such chill came only latterly to these big Anglo Irish houses, when far off sources of wealth dried up and the local servants and workers dwindled and butlers drowned their sorrows and standards in their master's wine cellars. It took little then, as the odd roof slate fell and the dry rot creeped along the joists, to shrink the lands of these great estates and to make their large mansions crumble. The riding boots always the last to go as the blue and green moulds sprouted on top hats and dancing slippers. While sustenance was maintained by fishing rod and shotgun and the pheasant and quail hung seasoning behind the satin curtains.

But although many of the Anglo Irish fled back to the civilization of England, their parklands and silverware sold, more than a few of the hardier stayed, defying all discomfort and impoverishment. And keeping their eccentric charm, generosity and equanimity intact. But here in Aughnagaddy House something is different. A strange beauty lingering in these faded colours and peeling paint, as all ages and decays with grace. Even where the plaster has bulged or crumbled on the walls. Or near the doorways where ferns threaten to walk in and spread their pale green fronds waving across the floors.

Sydney, Araminta's husband, politely greets me as I do a tour of the house. He sits in a drawing room chair in his gloves, overcoat and cap, an old pair of galoshes done up with string on his feet. With a magnifying glass he reads a letter recently arrived in the post. Due to a slight rheumatism he apologizes for not getting up. In this room where in front of the blazing fire one's breath goes steaming out on the air. Yet all is a hive of industry. Sydney gardens, paints and fixes the roof. Araminta saddle soaps the riding tack. And Honora knits one of her splendid wool spreads and gives Derek a present. A mussel shell for cuff links, exquisitely covered in glove leather. And Henry's name is mentioned. Of how he would manage in some people's houses to undiplomatically comment on the furnishings.

'That lamp, although it does have the virtue of being not unamusing, is, I'm afraid, an eyesore. However, you mustn't get rid of it, it goes so well with everything else.'

And then upon this visit appears another ghost as the beautiful Amabel steps in with lunch. Of country fish pie she's just cooked made of salmon, cod and mussels with mashed potato on top.

Mousings the cat nearly gets mine but a quicker Honora gets there first. Everyone has a second delicious helping. For Amabel keeps an elegant little restaurant in a Georgian house in the nearby town of Ramelton. For pudding there is orange and chocolate mousse with cream. And then I remember the strange familiarity of Amabel's face. Last seen and watched throughout an evening across dining tables some months previous in Claridge's Hotel, in London, where she sat speaking Russian with members of the visiting Bolshoi Ballet.

But there remains the spectre still haunting me, of Henry. Who now looks down upon us all from that great gallery in the sky. Derek arranges for me to visit again this now empty castle. One says goodbye to Honora's dolls, still all sitting prettily in their straw hats, bonnets and berets, their tiny bow shaped mouths and their blue glass eyes alive with smiles. And I go again as I did on that day when my socially registered friend first announced that we were at Henry's. We were approaching some very modest gates with stags' heads mounted on the stone piers. Out all around us mountainous moorlands towards every horizon. A few distant deer grazed amid granite boulders. But not a single sign of habitation or life anywhere on the rocky heathery hillsides. Just some of the most bereft and wild landscape God ever invented.

And I recall that day driving onwards over a well kept but narrow winding stony track. Mile after mile across these moors. Then the road sloping downwards as gradually the growth of rhododendrons thickened at the sides of the lane. Till descending in a steeper and steeper twisting incline, there was an abrupt turning in the road. Ahead lay the stunning blue black waters of Lough Veagh spreading between two mountains. With trimmed hedges flanking a luxurious tarmacadam drive along the edge of the lough, another world began to unfold. Of strange plants and expansive flower beds. Then through more and grander gateways. Suddenly massive granite walls and the turrets of a castle loomed out of the trees, and was greyly silhouetted against the sky. Here at long last, close at hand, was Henry's. And one had arrived on his little spread of thirty thousand acres by the back gate.

Butlers and footmen rushed to take luggage from the car. Leading one past the turf fires glowing, and up a grand staircase under towering crystal chandeliers and along intertwining corridors to one's room. Our host to be met at drinks before dinner. I spent long minutes staring out the windows and down vistas cutting their way through the one hundred and fifty acres of exotic gardens of plants, trees and shrubberies collected from across the world. In all these lonely windswept Donegal wastes, there stood only this castle, filled with fresh flowers every day, whose colours vied with some of the world's fabled paintings. Washing in the bathroom before tea and drying my hands with a magically soft fluffy fabric, I forgot my watch and returned to find the used towels already replaced with fresh ones on the hot towel rail by a secret hand. A selection of mineral waters and all the books one ever wanted to read were by one's bedside. And one thing at least had dawned on me, I may at last be here at Henry's but there was no doubt whatever that I had also come to Shangri-La.

Visitors for dinner had gathered in the great drawing room with its collection of Landseers, and scenes of wolves tearing the throats out of stags. Shyly I entered waiting to be introduced in this glamorous gathering of guests, some as fabled as the paintings. A figure turned, detached from a group, and crossed the drawing room towards me. A face I knew well from Dublin and university undergraduate days. And who had many a time attended parties in one's own Trinity College rooms. He was a man whose civilized company one would seek for reassurance in the more notorious Dublin dungeons frequented such as Charnel Chambers and the Catacombs. And here he was, beaming a smile with his greeting words.

'My God, J.P., it really is you.'

'My God, Henry. Henry is you.'

'But of course. And where on earth have you been all these years.'

'Well as a matter of fact, meeting people. All of whom were on their way to Henry's.'

1987

Upon Conduct Becoming and
Unbecoming a Philanderer

As just your ordinary average looking kind of guy, you need, in this activity, to show women no mercy. For the appalling truth, frequently denied by nearly all ladies, is that they adore handsome men. Especially of the cigarette ad variety. It also matters not that he has the top of a fence post between his ears, which mostly he hasn't as alas even here, too, good looking fellows excel in intelligence. It's nature's way of keeping a tiny nucleus of the race from getting entirely stupid and objectionable. Which is why philandering by tall godlike well featured chaps is so eugenically important. Of course not being able to attract one of these good looking guys, women, being extremely practical, immediately set about ruthlessly to entrap the next best thing. And this is where you flirtatiously step in.

No decent philanderer worthy of the name bothers pursuing ladies who are handing it out to all comers. Otherwise this is essentially a game called 'How to Get Up Her Without a Wedding'. Although a wedding may indeed play a most important part in this activity especially after she's married someone else. Successful philandering calls for a degree of delight with yourself and some assurance that the word lady killer is not misplaced when applied to you. To be skilled and to remain for any length of time engaged at this vocation, single, married minded ladies are to be avoided. As the picket fence around their future house with you office bound somewhere steadily being promoted and providing a larger and larger salary for their future support comes first in their priorities. No. Your saucy opportunities abound among the riper aged already married ladies pampering their beauty on their large estates and in the boudoirs of substantial suburban houses. Plus of course the fairly numerous ones you may encounter dinner partying at the downtown grander tables in the more fashionable larger cities.

Visit your venereal doctor often and willingly provide the necessary specimens, as he may, at almost any time, have important information to disclose to you. Muster about yourself all the civilities that are normally accepted as indicating 'What a nice boy' and which now you hope will be said about you by all these other men's wives that you are now after. And who are to be found most easily accessible in the leisure climes and in purlieus where the folk are reekingly rich. Along with the water and snow skiing these kind of folk sport the pretence of being sophisticatedly liberal in male female relationships. Like.

'Hey, Bob, you don't mind if I take Carol for two hours out to the deserted island to look over the indigenous metazoa.'

Of course, Bob transports by helicopter and doesn't really have the peace of time to mind. He is loudly and skywards clearly seen leaving the area to return to more tiptoeing on the brink of his daily decision making or sweating out his bland faced lack of it and just hoping to hell he doesn't get removed by the board or fired with his mortgage, the cost of three kids at prep school and wife's bills from I Magnin crashing around his bowed head, while you, of course, with merely a pot to piss in, have one whale of a time grappling with his wife's freely wagging limbs.

Albeit you are fooling around in top drawer society nevertheless remember that you are in and about a sneaky occupation. Often requiring a nimbleness of mind and movement. Not to mention speed in donning your clothes and assuming a fast respectable air about you. Particularly if you don't know Bob's helicopter movements. Therefore it is always wise to check out in detail the floor plan of any residence where you intend to let this or any Bob or Charlie's wife have it. To scale if possible. The residence that is. And do this well before need.

There is nothing worse than to hear the majestic purr of a

husband's motor car or roof top roar of his gyrating aircraft unexpectedly arriving and gently and luxuriously squashing the pebbles together on the front apron of the mansion and then not only have to collect together your strewn socks, pointy two tone shoes, highly coloured shorts, and other of your racy haberdasheries but to then have to tear open your badly folded architect's plan of the house and take up valuable time studying this, not only in order to calculate how many seconds it takes to spring the length of the upper floor corridor to the disused servants' staircase, but also to find somewhere to tuck both you and your shoelaces back into some discreet crevice while outside Bob's car or helicopter door is slamming and servants are being alerted to uphand potables and smokables they are enjoying down their employers' wine cellar.

Besides eroding your iron nerve, such last minute alerts will put an unforgettable strain on your heart, severely shortening your philandering career, youthful though you are, and long distance jogger that you continue to be. But on the other hand if you must contend with Bob's silent approach on a hard topped front drive then do at least stack the milk bottles at the front door which crash at his entrance. Otherwise you're in for an even more adrenalin producing situation than just sailing bollocks naked out into the hall with your map half open in your left hand and hubby chomping up the main marble staircase with some kind of weapon in his right fist.

For Bob might have just come back from a duck or snipe shooting expedition. Which lucky for you he hasn't and with relief, on a quick second glance, you see it's only Bob's custom made monogrammed leather document case. He of course has the name of Carol still joyfully on his lips to whom he has just called. He sees you. Wow can Bob's ashen faced jaw drop. And he recalls the two hour trip you took with his long legged softly blonde haired wife to see the indigenous metazoa. Holy metaphysical cow. This really is a time when you should have already availed yourself of departure to secret big enough for one ventilated compartments. Only trouble being that most suspicious husbands know where these places are and make straight for them sometimes even using your own architect's plan you've dropped rushing in your panic. Plus once there it's deucedly difficult to get out of the way of Bob's fist and impossible to avoid his bullets. No. This is a time when you must talk.

'Hey, gee, Bob, the craziest goddamn thing has happened, you wouldn't believe it.'

'Maybe I won't.'

Don't let Bob's sour mistrusting words dispossess you of your enthusiasm, keep talking.

'Well, remember those goddamn metazoa, they weren't indigenous, Christ they were pandemic I'm telling you, you won't believe it.'

'No I won't.'

'Stop saying that, Bob. This is scientifically serious. Do you know what those goddamn metazoa did. They made clothing itch us. It could be chronic. Came right over when Carol called me. We both had to strip. Son of a bitch things, here, Christ don't come near me, you could get it.'

It is better to have had some acting training to deliver these lines. But if your sincerity can overcome your terror and can at all permeate just a few of those words, especially the last few, as you shoutingly repeat them, 'Don't come near me', you will be astonished at how credulity can creep back into the situation until now both you and Bob can walk back calmly to that adulterous room and indeed both peruse the hopefully still naked Carol and the alleged itch. But be on the safe side, let Bob walk first. And do keep your wits about you to slam and lock Bob and wife behind the bedroom door when you run, in case Carol says her skin feels fine.

Of course Carol by nature is a betrayer as indeed most ladies are if they're going to have any fun in life. But you are a real lousy dirty rat and historically the role you are now playing is that of a cad. Most comments about you will frequently be disagreeable. On that score alone it is wise to keep your picture out of social columns and gossip magazines to which people can point or later refer for your resemblance. Your big moment will come along with plenty of large photographs and big headlines when one of your 'talk my way out of this' efforts falls on deaf unsympathetic ears and Bob was carrying his loaded custom made monogrammed shot gun case and swings or shoots at you and although he misses, his lawyer's action for alienation of affection with attendant reliefs and damages doesn't. And you hear his belligerent advocate, with the customary accusatorial pointing arm and finger saying of you before a judge and jury.

'There he is, philanderer, one of those, I saw, I conquered, I came, guys.'

Although you are now and again beset by these little legal discouragements that folk like Bob relentlessly harass you with, you need but remind yourself that in merely looking to have fun up ladies' skirts, most honestly inclined married ladies admit that they are thereby kept thrilled and happier. But alas, you will also be thought a fortune hunter. And although husbands may not mind you taking your frolicsome lucky dip into their wives, boy do they get their dander up when you start munching around in them investment portfolios. Even the unemotional husband who refers to you as a rotter or skunk will seethe as he imagines you having access to minor assets such as silk cravats or scented mahogany trays of socks, not to mention wines, especially the fine ports, brandy and cigars. The slightly more infuriated will call you an unconscionable cunt and after he's had you checked out by investigators will not hesitate to have a man trap set by his game keepers and entice you by his four day absence to sample his best London made shotguns for a day's shooting.

Therefore to live longer plus avoid stymieing your opportunities by looking like a fortune hunter, keep rings off your fingers, jewellery off your wrists and do not under any circumstances wear suede shoes. Such appurtenances as well as any exaggerated matters of tailoring are always a distinct giveaway and particularly bespeak chaps harbouring a financial as well as sexual appetite. To say the least this does give one a rather ignoble demeanour. And although the absence of these trinkets may not automatically put you among the booted and horsed, it helps avoid a husband's early detection. As you can, with your tie small knotted and precise, and ornament clean of wrist and finger, sidle your way through these knuckle cracking squash and polo players to discreetly present yourself to some tasty morsel. Also, in the clement sunny outdoors, avoid form fitting Adonis type bathing costume and other pudenda flattering coverings. Blazers worn indoors or out are out, as are bright buttons of any sort unless worn foxhunting. Which latter could really break your ass before Bob does.

The rule is that no natural ugliness will hold you back or need ever permanently deny you from being a real whiz whoremongering philanderer especially with the plainer and neglected sorts of ladies, but blatant indiscretions in dress or the wrong sartorial inflection or toilet water will. But be cautious. Appearances and smells are not everything. And although these womenfolk may be bean brained, beetle witted and nonnie noddled, nevertheless they will still possess sufficient smarts to sense through your attentive charms your greedy lunch hooks curling in the direction of hers or hubby's wherewithal despite her eagerness to taste and be sated by your own swinging grapefruity balled or avocado bollocked assets. And if you are after their money as, let's face it, big money is just as exciting as ass to get, anyday. Then choose yourself an occupation to indulge both opportunities when you're not performing your modest but not insignificant duties fussing about way low down in the massive bowels of some corporation or waiting on table. And as that question is asked that people are always goddamn well asking every bloody place you go these damn days.

'And what do you do.'

Blast them with it. Snow them. Just smash these bastards and bitches to bits. Have it on your finger tips. Practise it just as you

206

also practise running with your trousers down to be able to get up an Olympic speed over a hasty coverage of short distances which might save a situation some day. A really long title. Get the word international into it. Funds is another nice one. As is industries, securities, banks and bonds. Till you're ready with it.

'I am an international philanderer, con artist and embezzler of securities and bonds and computer defrauder of banks and money houses. And I'm awfully sorry that I can't answer further personal questions concerning what I do, as the matter, which concerns several elderly ladies whose assets I am accused of swindling, is currently subjudice in courts of several different countries of which this particular country happens to be one but I can disclose that in general my nefarious schemes are based on the greed and fear factors of the human spirit. With my ill gotten gains I hope to influence the price rises and falls on the world's stock exchanges.'

To any nervous laughter accompanying your disclosure laugh along with them till their laughter ceases and then continue chuckling till their laughter resumes. Thus they will think you an investment adviser, which means that with your pocket computer you are gauging the minutiae of market movements in order to get the real mood of market indications, and that under your glacially calm exterior you really are a hot shot money and portfolio manager who has long been a whiz inventor of financial formulae and systems. Now you will be able not only to hang around shooting the shit with hubby on promissory notes, shares, hot market tips, special situations, but also while hubby is instructing brokers to buy on your advice, to discreetly visit Virginia's most sacred vestibule.

Quite soon and quickly rumours about you will circulate at dinner parties. Since all folk like to hear of astro profit investment opportunities. And on the terrace as Bob looks to see that his azaleas are not being scorched by the heat of the barbecue, you might approach and come right out with it as if you really were in stocks and bonds just as you are presently incognito. And you will of course, so that you may with impunity enjoy the company of your married lady with some frequency, want to make friends with the husband. Find out what you and he have in common. If this is no more than having the same number of balls, and all gents, by no means, do, discover then his hobbies and make sure one of them isn't rubbing folk out. If you can get him on the subject of the prominent industry he's connected to then ask the tycoon how things are going. Whether or not the last sales conference he momentarily popped in on had unleashed any new fresh thunderbolts on distribution methods to revolutionize the selling of his product. Should he be a large sleeping share-holder, come right out with it.

'Gee Bob, in the uncertainty of the present business climate how's the old arbitrage doing.'

It ought to be doing swell since the whole point of arbitrage, if you're doing it at all, is to purchase in one market and instantly sell in another at a higher price. Therefore reach right out and clap Bob hard a couple of times on the back. You may think that this is overdoing it. And it is. But in making Bob sputter, readjust dentures or, even better, spit them out coughing, you are, although the point might not be apparent to most people, underlining your sincerity. And you will find as you say.

'Gee Bob, that's just swell.'

That although Bob, who employs a temporarily deeply trusted investment counsellor, may not know what the hell arbitrage is, he is going to like your interest. Sidle up close in as nearly a conspiratorial manner as you can without Bob suspecting any homo motives. This will make him feel your glow of sympathy for his wife's thunderous clothing bills he gets monthly. These goddamn charges really knock hell out of even the big money chaps. When that woman who was already dressed warm enough when he first met her now needs teams of carpenters to extend the closets of her apartments to house the new dresses that appear each day from the reigning haute couturiers. With this in mind beware how you admire her latest gown that she doesn't gurgle to hubby that you adore the designer's work and therefore she's commissioning him to do her yet another whole new wardrobe for the pre spring season. Nothing makes a husband clap suspicious eyes upon you faster than inciting his wife to spend even more of his money. But once having got his business confidence, his wife's most innermost portfolio is yours to tamper with next.

Into a special category come wives of chaps who have inherited money and large estates. Better known as the gentry. Here's where your philandering can really flower. And the perfumes of nature and musky heady scents of your amorata can transport you into the memorable vistas and delights of romance. Plus you stand a much better chance of easily putting it up the wife if not behind an attic chimney or upon the musty mattress of your disused servant's bedroom, then at least in an overgrown summerhouse down by the trout lake or north gate lodge. Although do please be careful, since some of these types being extremely spoiled want no one else to enjoy their rococo statuary, fabled architecture, or to sigh at their sunsets splashingly pink upon their parklands or even to take advantage of their big fluffy towels stacked high in their bathing pavilions. Not to mention a dip between the pure elegant soft sweetness of their ladyships' thighs.

So always be ready for the alert cuckold. The persistently sour look on his face is the tip off. Especially as he watches you quaff his Roederer Crystal Brut champagne in his marble floored ballroom where your eyes are glued to the ample gilt surrounding his semi fake art masterpieces which are always those ones fully authenticated as not being forgeries but which are, of course, forgeries. As the real ones are in his Zurich bank vaults. And this gent, educated by private tutors and who was frequently reminded of humanity's frailties, may sidle up to you when you least expect and let you rather have it straight in the haggis.

'I say, sir, if you are contemplating jumping upon my wife

and rogering her in verso and recto, I suggest you also prepare
to pay for her hay and stabling.'

'I beg your pudding, are you speaking to me.'

'Regretfully, sir, yes. And to remind you that you may shell
out as well for her silk and furry evening tack she is most fond
of seasonally acquiring in some quantity when she is not riding.
Not to mention, my dear chap, my better wine and viands she
freely hands out to sundry eager lap dogs such as you who slaver
after her every low and high heeled footstep. But of course if
you have already sundry times covered her I suggest you be gone
the hell out of here, otherwise I may sooner than soon shift her
out for you to watch over for a longer period than I now care to
do. You may then witness at leisure while she gets old, tit
drooped, fat assed and distinctly au blet. Sorry to put it to you
so coarsely. But you are a turd, are you not. You flash Harry
you.'

Now of course this is a rather long speech from your anciently
pedigreed man and should have given you a considerable opportunity to conjure up appropriate words to deal with this crusty
snooty bugger. But you are best advised to simply say nothing
which is bound to make your superior chap add to his little
diatribe.

'Did you hear me, sir. I said you flash Harry you.'

At this stage however you might venture a reply.

'As a matter of fact I did hear you but was weighing in my
mind whether you, when you were last covering your wife, were
in your socks or not.'

'What, sir, have my socks got to do with it.'

'Well, on they would make you appear in a hurry. And off
they would make you appear barefoot. But either way your
toenails, of which your wife complains bitterly, need cutting.'

This riposte of yours, although only gently inciting your
man's intention to visit his chiropodist, should produce bluster
and fluster and redden your greying chap at the temples. But
beware that while during its delivery this erudite gentleman,

Henry, fluttering his tailcoat, hasn't from his classical Greek and Latin background unearthed something in modern English to slash you about your own possibly too tight evening garments with an epoch making dressing down. Calling the instant attention of the other ball guests who now will be by the potted palms whispering about the bang bang really thank you ma'am liaison they think you are having with his wife.

'You pithering ill born upstart impostor. How dare you attempt to pop it so heinously into my Hilda who tells me that your flaccidness has bored her back to fox-hunting which sadly occasions me to employ more grooms, whom, sir, I would not insult by inviting you to assist them in mucking out the stables.'

Of course the stage of your romance just suggested by her husband may have already been reached when Hilda is encouraging the attentions of other instant pricked, satin coated and velvet trousered bed bouncers of bottoms. These chaps could, if you are bright white, even be of the dusky complexioned variety who, if they own far Middle East jungle estates, seem always able to bifurcately excite ladies with their elephant mounted tiger killing exploits. Or as desert chieftains can produce in womankind a yearning faintness with attendant procreative teardrops when these Raja Sahibs climb a minaret and yodel down to her upraised adoring eyes. And you now may indeed, as you stand there in your not too badly selected toilet water, be compared to these other Asian and African operators, and as his Lordship suggests, be merely a flash alabaster Harry. This branding could, if you take it to heart, smash your philandering career with a depressing variety of hysterical impotence.

However, let's say you've avoided such mournful pitfalls. Your hormones are hopping and it's a Tuesday winter crisp evening. And by sheer blatant pushiness you have successfully penetrated another socially whirling charity ball. Crammed with the polo slender booted and horsed. And there suddenly by the caviar bowl is a lady as dazzling as her spouse is rich. Who has an easy going understanding with her husband, as she stands, as she does every autumn in her life, in a snow storm of engraved invitations. Prominently she features at hunt meetings and cotillions and is given to wearing body clinging silk pale peach dresses and matching shoes. Her recently coiffed hair teased by a terrace breeze gently freshening in the Edwardian window. Or in places requiring it, by the powerful air conditioning set in a ventilator grate of rare flush topped walnut construction. And you rehearse your opening words.

'Would madam care to discuss her splendid elbows upon which she might take ease while chewing and sipping in the future some underdone beeves and booming burgundy I should delight to golf down with her.'

She will of course be instantly spotted by other like minded chaps such as yourself who will also do everything in the language they can to captivate this penis engorging creature. And it is best therefore, straight off, to treat this fellow philanderer with a fusillade of sartorially undermining remarks.

'Where did you get those shoes.'

The word 'where' is the key to this enquiry and should be accented. As your man, pleased with your question, is about to loftily tell you of a revered St James's boot maker and purringly looks down, let him have the next one.

'Don't please bother to look, everyone else already has.'

Naturally if you are he who is him being told off concerning your footwear, you need only whisper the following.

'Where vas you Charlie ven dey crucified my lord.'

Of course for those in the know the slightly foreigner sounding reply is.

'I vas baking beans suh, I vas baking beans.'

Now having discouraged if not eliminated at least one of these cheeky impertinent competitors, pay attention to your last and usual obstacle, her well heeled but commoner husband Basil. Consider first his strengths as it is most ill advised to depend upon what you might think are this gentleman's weaknesses. Especially find out if he collects hand guns and frequently has blind uncontrollable rages. Upon this enquiry being negative, check out his routine. Which will mostly consist of absences at tailors for fittings, athletic clubs for work outs and bloodstock sales for brood mares. This latter hobby of course sharpens the eye not only for the best in horsy attributes but no doubt has helped her husband choose what you covet in his wife, Briget. Notably her uncommon head, well turned legs, good front on her breathing box and her lack of sloping in the quarters.

Although this will have invariably been for money, find out if there are any minor reasons why this splendid filly married Basil. These will gigantically have to do with the rated horsepower of Basil's yacht engines if not his gross Lloyd's registered tonnage, which made Briget choose him over all the other equally panting, tongue out, feverish guys wanting maritally up and in her who own vessels of similar length or displacement. And of course here is how you prevent an awful repetition of being caught as you were by Bob or mortified as you were by that aristocratic twit, Henry.

GET YOUR SEAGOING MASTER'S PAPERS

And don't be discouraged by the years it takes to obtain such briny qualification. You will be rewarded by more cuckolding philandering once you've installed yourself as captain on one of these luxury yachts, both at sea and in foreign ports, than you could shake an internationally major symphonic conductor's baton at. Especially when Basil is ashore and Briget is on board. But even when that bastard's luxuriating over his pink linen napkined breakfast in his owner's suite you will still, as a matter of courtesy, be reporting your daily position and weather in person to her in Briget's own quarters. Remove your cap as you step over the bulkhead and secure the hatch behind you and keep your fingers well stiffened in your salute.

'Good morning, madam.'

'Hi, Captain.'

'Madam, it's good to see you looking so splendid.'

'Captain, you say the nicest things so early in the morning.'

'I do regret though, madam, that at o eight thirty hours the meteorological office has issued a gale warning to all shipping which may lash and toss us all over the ruddy wave tops.'

'Oh dear, Basil will be so awfully seasick.'

'We are presently steaming pronto out of its direction but it could be blowing, madam.'

'Then I must immediately order you, as Basil will be so absolutely indisposed with yawking, to personally hove to and stand by me below decks while abiding further blowing. Of the weather of course.'

'Aye aye, madam.'

Madam's blatant invitation may surprise you but stand at ease and remember there is simply nothing which attracts ladies more than glistening white ducks in the tropics, or elegant navy blue serge in the ice belts or the chart in your chamois gloved hand to which details of the gale warning is affixed. Not to mention that gold braid, not only on your sleeve and shoulders but also scrambled all over your hat visor. This latter salty radiance alone would open your ladyship's dimpled welcoming limbs to you.

'Briget, darling.'

'O captain my captain, thank God my fearful spouse is sick.'

But do for heaven's sake make sure you've got a second mate who knows his shoals and can plot ice bergs accurately and navigate ocean currents. It is simply the most awful feeling to find a vessel foundering under your command while the owner's wife is under you gaspingly enthralled. Not only will Basil, once you've grounded his valuable steamer while rogering Briget, most certainly lose his sense of sportsmanship but he will, just to be ornery, sue the shit, lanyards and binnacles out of you. And, if he's a ruthless hot blooded tycoon, will also demand of the liquidator in your bankruptcy proceedings to assess and sequester your gold dental fillings.

However, for those not acquiring master's papers or lacking in other attributes which gain entrance to a lady's ultimate confidentiality, do not then as a last resort ever waste your good philandering time pretending to a lady that you are rich. Standing there erection minded shooting your shirtcuffs anchored together with big boorish gems, she will, if she's worth the philandering, know with the utmost accuracy that you are not. Instead there are other persuasive and inexpensive ploys. Try going arty and sensitive. Good music. Good books. Good films. And yes, even, believe it or not, minor poetry.

'Do you like Herrick, the English poet in whose soul was reborn the spirit of the ancient classical lyric.'

'Who the hell's he.'

Don't be discouraged by the reply. Hardly anyone knows who Herrick is. But an entirely new kettle of jumping slippery fish will be the reinvented you as you interest your lady with your mouthing of beautiful thoughts. But be wary. Stay out of others' ear shot. Because on the end of any yacht stern or as you slaver in dancing attendance upon her in the midships ballroom, these utterances will make you look like the most impecunious pathetic ass hole to the other well heeled guests. Especially when you're overheard whispering in her ear hole.

> No fire that
> Lucifer lights
> Could be, madam,
> Like your burning
> In me ignites

Although this verges on major minor verse you might under a too intense blaze of scornful looks be best advised to then desist and instead profess a deep abiding compassion for the whole of mankind. Have at your fingertips the most recent facts regarding starving millions, plagues, floods, abandoned babies, erupting volcanoes. In mentioning these catastrophes frequently use the words.

'God, it's all so appalling.'

You will of course still attract sneaky eye flicks from these social superiors but only the most bizarre outspoken Texans of them will dare to say.

'Fuck humanity, screw your sympathy and pass the wretched canapés.'

During such south westerly remarks it is especially a time when you want to avoid looking like your more common kind of philanderer. And if you've avoided other salient telltale indications, make sure you can't be spotted for your metal shoe adornments. Which foot flashiness means you have no claim whatever to the deep silent variety of male dignity which any woman worthy of her elegance prefers to the bronco filly busting swivel hipped ladies' man. Unless, of course, madam is in season and unduly randy. So remember that your every subtlety helps against the everywhere roving competition since the kind of females who will take an interest in you will also make eyes at and openly invite the further attention of servants and waiters. Even to the point of remarking to these menials as they approach with their trays.

'That is the most adorable mushroom miracle you are proffering. I shall, with much relish, eat it you know.'

Of course the flattered footman's mind will leap with eye blurring agility to the conclusion that the word he doesn't understand in that sentence suggests something really beckoning from the lady. He may even be possessed of the crass audacity to wet your fly buttons by tippling over a load of drinks on you. And should your private aperture operate by zipper it distinctly deserves to be rusted.

'Beg your pardon, sir.'

'Why you feeble flunkey you.'

But let's say that your competitors are mostly breathing your dust, watching your smoke and merely catching a whiff of your lady's musk in which you have been headily mesmerizing your senses. Then so as not to stifle your growing list of victims, you must avoid the really outstanding regally devastating beauty who is often quite devilishly hard to get up.

'May I mount you, madam.'

'Not, I fear, poor boy, were I one hundred years dead, and you the world's most revered necrophiliac.'

This is the kind of detumescence you get from these supremely exquisite broads. Being as they have long been aware of their total attraction for all gents. Allowing them to select from among the cream of the great thinkers, statesmen and tycoons. And they can easily collar the man they fancy as they bring various empires and corporations to their knees, and change the destiny of nations with a mere gorgeous ajarment of their sacral gluteals.

'I'm all yours, Mr President. For the next twenty minutes at least. As I'm not having tea with his royal highness till four fifteen.'

For this doll to give you a sniff your only hope might be to imitate the highly titled philanderer which may of course require you to attend finishing school, forge Debrett and take accent correction. Plus learning how to rein ladies by the ears. As pukka peers do. But once having brushed yourself up in these previous categories, the addition of a monocle will nicely augment your demeanour and authenticate your appearance if it doesn't complicate finding your way across the drawing room floor during pre dinner drinks. Then when your eye alights upon the sublime delightful beauty of this lady you may wish your optical instrument feast upon the mastermind curvatures of her bosom. And of course agriculture being as it has always been among the pursuits of an aristocrat, you may remark.

'Ah, madam, permit me to moo, while I view your pastures so much greener the other side of your bra.'

And this divine Diana may just find you long enough tempting to her taste in peers of the realm and princes of the blood for you to really make hay even when your phoney accent slips before your trousers do.

'Is that your vowel dissonantly accosting me, young man.'

'No, ma'am, it's my pedigreed appendage.'

But even socially improved philanderers like you, with your

rapier quick prick, light superficial thrustings and flimsy morals, are not likely to interest the majesty of these great tall usually green eyed goddesses for very long. And you will therefore be mostly confined to ladies of the second rank. Who nonetheless will gently fondle the locks of hair grown long past your ears. These ladies, too, play croquet well. Expertly pour tea. And although they may speak three or more languages they will take much longer to discover what an absolutely regrettable fuckpig you are. Plus their bottoms for some unaccountable reason are often more attractive than their busts. Not that this isn't even better, as indeed it is. Plus they usually are quite supple and joint reflexive due to foxhunting. And it is appropriate upon spotting them to ejaculate.

'Tally ho.'

These girls will usually have married gentlemen for their aristocratic or corporation title or much money or both but not usually for one, without the other. They are quick to lose interest in their spouse and to be mounted elsewhere when they discover that neither of his prior two staggering attractions amounts to much now that she has them firmly in her hooks. No need for monocles here. Tweak lightly such ladies right straight on the arse. They will step away and take a hopeless and smilingly raised eyebrow swipe at your hand. But they will get the message. You must fast, however, manage to impress that you might have more money than her present husband. Best done by giving her a laughing crass flash of bank notes accompanied by an invitation to go gambling.

'Madam, may I interest you to go shake the black eyed bones of chance, prior perhaps to later shaking your own entwining flesh covered ones of love.'

While in the gambling palace keep great massive stacks of chips cascading out of your pockets. You may think that no one would fall for such a superficial ruse to indicate worldly wealth and if she doesn't I'm afraid you are then doomed to an even more expensive procedure. Of giving all your chips to her. And do manage to smile as this morals minus bitch loses every cent. And God forbid, as is nearly always the case, that you as a philanderer are nothing more than a middle income married man with hungry little mouths to feed and questing brains to expensively educate.

In such latter case, however, be warned. Your phone bills will get enormous as your wife starts to harass your more serious seductions. She will telephone at early dawn hours to berate and threaten your friend and her blood and even non blood relatives. She will hire detectives or herself follow you from assignation to assignation. Sitting as she will through the wee hours waiting for a light to go on and for you to get dressed and then come sneakily into the uptight view of her binoculars as you attempt to back your inconspicuous way out the door or down the front steps. She will then, no matter how tall the buildings, shatter windows screaming your lady doll's name, Jessica somebody, coupled with the most unflattering adjectives. Don't run for it. Desperately try to keep your dignity. Although being caught like this can really spiritually stymie you and your philandering aerodynamics can be bent out of flying shape for all time.

'You flea bitten whorer up there in apartment six B of number nine Owl Street, with your sluttish ugliness trying to deprive six children of their father and a wife of her infantile husband.'

But worse still is the crack shot Finger hired by Jessica's husband drawing a telescopic bead on you from a nearby rooftop eyrie ready to splinter your mid spine with a deer rifle as you show up on a doorstep entrance with an armful of aphrodisiac delicatessen goodies. Therefore some precautions are in order. It is always a legal, financial and life risking mistake to leave any record of your attentions. Never send your calling card with flowers or write demonstrative letters. Or indeed allow the lady to send such to you. It is astonishing at how these heartfelt documents tend to be discovered at the least desirable of times. And are wagged vehemently in one's face. Covert looks, smiles and eye ogling is the way you go. But do avoid looking dumb, childish and ridiculous doing this. Always whisper places of assignation. Which on no account should be of the one orgasm midday middle price range hotels or motels.

'I have a reservation. Name's Mr & Mrs Smith.'

'Oh yes, Mr Smith, you called five minutes ago. Room thirty six. Have a good lunch time.'

This is the kind of wretched sordidness that can turn your stomach with guilt. Therefore it is de rigueur to spend plenty on dignity and elegance. Also it goes a long way in impressing a jury when later legal contretemps arise. While you get intellectually acquainted, sporting events in which Jessica's husband takes no interest are ideal. Especially the rodeo. And if hunting fox together, my goodness you can rein up your horses in some isolated copse, dismount and with the blood up. Wow. But make sure the fox doesn't come circling back. Followed by the entire hunting field. Otherwise arrange your meeting in only the most dignified of hostelries. And upon these occasions dress in double breasted grey pin stripe worsted and carry a briefcase containing papers which, at some early stage in the lobby or in the dining room, are produced. O God, what a master stroke this is. Especially if the Finger contracted to rub you out is trying to familiarize your face, estimate his target area and establish your non routine movements.

In your most serious mien, hand across these documents to your partner. She in turn takes a pair of eyeglasses out of her purse and studies the papers briefly and then with the pen you proffer, she initials each page and signs the last. Often the Finger, who is despite his dispassionate approach usually possessed of some human curiosity, or the nosy detective gent who has a lot, will carelessly abandon their surveillance to telephone an intermediary or boss of the astonishing event. Wait till he returns before you put the papers back in your briefcase and as you do, your chic living doll Jessica should wipe her hands quite thoroughly and blatantly.

This latter, especially at that seemingly legal point during this assignation time, really stumps the hell out of your begrudgers. And hardly any detective, hired to track down the pair of you lovers right to the dirty deed, at first won't believe it. Loosening his tie he'll rush back to spend yelling telephone minutes attempting to convince his employers that maybe he's not following the right chick. Until the thunderous scene being described to the betrayed hubby finally dawns on him like the end of the world. That his own lovely looking wife has uncovered all his own joyful philanderings taken place in hotel suites from Knoxville to London.

'Holy shit, she's on to me.'

Sending him damn pronto scurrying from bank vault to bank vault checking to see if the transferable bonds and securities are still in his safety deposit boxes. As most gentlemen of big assets know that money can in its sufficiency far outweigh even the most exciting of dalliances with even the most charming flash Harry. And his wife may just be doing a preliminary financial disembowelling before she starts really slashing in the coming legal struggle. Not a surprising conclusion of course when, Jesus Christ, you hear your wife is signing goddamn papers. That might intimately concern the very pure green jade pot you not only piss into but also from which slightly moist humidor you take your best cigars. As you time and time again jump to your feet and put your hand back through the sparse hair over the bald patch, wondering if you're not yourself to be rubbed out by a wife naïve enough to sign a contract for same. And if you're a real whiz as a philanderer she will be. But presto you, Jessica's philanderer, are now disguised in lawyer's demeanour and cloth- ing. But remember, things can go wrong, and bang wham and splat is the sound and fatality of that bullet.

A word about fitness. Although you may not yet have a flaccid paunch, remember a new rippling flat bellied panting generation of philanderers is hungrily hot on your heels. And since this occupation prepares you for no other, and also erodes your money making moral strength, you will ultimately, as the hormones simmer down and back muscles ominously creak, have to depend upon your seduced women for financial support. So give your early middle age some thought as this worrying time creeps upon you. Realize that if you are not to end up evilly depressed in some second rate watering place slurping tea and rotting the remaining enamel off your teeth with Sacher Torte munched in the company of overly ripened ladies, then you had better borrow your non returnable nest egg from your present victim early in the relationship. And boy, this is tough. As such ladies who have accumulated what they've got by previous practised gold digging, usually, aged though they are, go through men like a dose of lethal salts. And she may, even as undignified as it seems to such a practised philanderer as you, be eyeing some quick dipping lip licking and totally unbooted and unhorsed gigolo. While you try to refurbish your jet set externals.

'It's all right, Henrietta, is it, if I outfit with some new socks and set of jaguar wheels.'

'Let me think a bit about it, George.'

At this harrowing time, don't borrow her hemp, cocaine or cigarettes. This may be the only cheap odd way you can demonstrate to Henrietta that you have not fatally grown dependent upon her money. As you did early trying to get her used to seeing you fill out her previously signatured negotiable instruments for your own trifling amounts of alkaloids, haberdashery and the more modest brands of sports cars, while at the same time desperately rogering her with a frequency that shielded her attention from your poverty. And now as you conscientiously thump away, hoping to finally take her for all she's worth, she hornily in a hot flush has decided to discard you for what you're worth. And since this is now not fucking much, you will over your lonely evening dry dry martini occasionally burst into tears. This is only natural. As you are at the end of your philandering career.

1976

Nothing Looks Better Than a
Harris Tweed Jacket and Faded
Blue Jeans on a Sunday

But before I talk of the stuff that religions are made of, or before I say anything at all about wool, please let me rhetorically ask. How lower middle class can you be. Or even lower, as an upper mobile of the blue collar working caste. Let me tell you, you can, in either category and vertical direction be plenty apologetically lower in both. But it does, when you are down far enough in your social designation, allow for having the most appalling taste in the world. And gives one, now that I am about to spout in the crucial field of men's fashions, a chance at least to be totally unbiased.

In my day of root beer was the drape shape, was the zoot suit and was my transformation from short pants and gartered long stockings to knickerbockers to long trousers and short socks. All took place in that strange isolated middle western community called Woodlawn, incongruously located in the Bronx where I had young friends who were astonishingly precocious fashion plates. One of whom, a young handsome gentleman called Alan Kuntze in the period around 1940 chose of his own brash innovation to wear Norwegian bedroom slippers as his daily shoes. Upon his inventing this I was among the few who then followed in such footsteps. And in the years succeeding I have remained astonished to find this fashion continuing to take the world by the foot as a loafer.

There were of course the dress coinages of others my young friend chose to follow, such as tying his tie in a Windsor knot. Daily he would assess every nuance of his attire down to its fabric weave at a local bus stop on our way to prep school, he to Trinity in Manhattan, and me to Fordham in the Bronx. I somehow can't place his elegantly attractive mother, whose laugh was so wonderfully musical, as ever being his laundress but do vaguely remember a black jolly lady who must have been in his and his older brother Donald's attendance, for his handkerchiefs, shirts and socks were all of the cleanest cleanliness and every crease mattered where it should. Till on one Sabbath he did appear and as I regarded his irreligious weekend raiment he struck a pose of deserved superiority and, brushing a finite speck from his lapel, announced, 'Nothing looks better than a Harris tweed jacket and faded blue jeans on a Sunday.'

As much as he must have set an example to follow I don't think I ever quite got the knack. For I fear that in my earliest imitative attempt to step out as a fashion plate I only invited dismay and shock. One school morning sporting the most bizarre plaid, indubitably non Harris, tweed jacket which jumped wildly alive in a blatant rainbow of colours, especially purple, orange and magenta. Worst of all was its tailoring, as it belonged to my older sister. In this memorable garment and in my conspicuous ignorance did I make my appearance within the ivied confines of the Fordham Preparatory School, which sported aplenty its own store of Jesuitical snobberies. One step inside the nearly ancient front hall I was confronted by the prefect of discipline. This black frocked ashplant thin custodian of young men's behaviour delighted in being abruptly precise. Swaying back like a cobra he made a pursed kissing sound with his lips and, with the minimal raising of an arm, pointed with an indignant finger. 'That. Do not wear it again. To this school.'

I did then forever after slump back down into my apologetic world of appalling taste. And have since always dressed only in pursuit of comfort and convenience and in the constant hope of avoiding raised eyebrows or accusing fingers, limiting myself to having upon one's back the clothes that allow for shelter from inclemencies including the sun and can gain me discreet access anywhere in a usual day's perambulations. And nothing worsted, herring bone or thornproof has ever succeeded in covering nearly all the multitude of my sins better than tweed in all its Harris variations. And as such latter weft and warp is from sheared sheep, where then shall we go to find them safely grazing. We shall on the face of this earth go to a windswept moonscape latitude high up on a chill moist longitude. West of Sutherland, west of Skye and across the Minch and upon western Scottish isles called the Hebrides.

But let us go leisurely there. For on the way arise matters which matter to this fabled fabric. In the early morning flood of cars weave by taxi to Kennedy airport. Fly up and out of New York as fast as these ample bodied motor birds will take us. Proceed over Ireland and, as the day darkens quickly, land in London. While meanwhile in my young life I marry a rich wool merchant's beautiful daughter. And take Sunday sherry brunch at the Troutbeck Hotel in Ilkley in a cleft of that moor in Yorkshire, a long way from my own romantic Bronx. And where an inkling of Harris tweed is to be got from these mill owners' sons who have already served their years of six a.m. apprentice-ship sorting wool deep down in the dark bowels of their factories and did, while yarns wove their families great fortunes, quaff pints of mild and bitter ale, play rugby and clap each other upon their broad and tweedy backs. And because of them, and their wool, you might not ever have had today's marvellous Scottish tweed by the name of Harris. For the Hebridean crofters' looms clacking in their huts and houses dotted all over their islands are made in Yorkshire.

But just before I left New York I was suddenly struck in terror of my task. And phoned a previous godsend elegantly rich helpmate in London who still so treasures her privacy, wishes me not to factualize her name. I ask her would she hold my hand on a visit to the Hebrides. 'Good God, J.P., whatever for.' I answer: 'To find me a mill owner while I write on men's fashions in tweed.' I listened patiently while at least fifteen dollars of mirth mounted on my phone bill. Till finally she stopped laughing and in an octave higher, said: 'Heaven's grief, who was mad enough to ask you to do that.' She revealed further she was solidly booked up. But then in the next nearly five dollar silence, she sensed my crushed bitter disappointment. And then just as I was taking the receiver from my ear, I heard her welcome words. 'My God, you poor sod, J.P., with your atrocious taste I had better go with you, hadn't I, for I do when wearing ratcatcher foxhunting still go out in an indestructible Harris tweed jacket I inherited from my father.'

And now awaking in London, catching a breath over breakfast in the comfort of a Park Lane hotel, I make haste for a fistful of money from a bank in Harrods. Hopping into a taxi out its department store doors and on one's way to St John's Wood for Laura. When I said I was headed for the outer Hebrides, my driver's first words were Harris tweed. And immediately we landed in the subject as we sped on this cherry blossoming warmish spring Thursday through Regent's Park. Kind fate having put me in the company of a tailor whose father taught him the trade in the east end of London. In his day anything less than a twenty two ounce cloth for a tweed suit was, it was reckoned, an invitation to freeze to death. And now today in the northern hemisphere's centrally heated climes the weight is more near to thirteen and fourteen ounces so that you do not gently stifle to your grave.

Laura still laughing, telling me that in the encyclopaedia, tweed could be a one time New York City political boss. Or indeed further afield on a map, you might put your finger on the Tweed river of Scotland. And alas neither serves as an origin for the cloth we know today. For the first word for it was 'twills' which has nothing to do with the River Tweed. And as Laura continued to chuckle I asked what was amusing her now. 'Ah, J.P., like the cloth you travel so far to see, I suddenly find I am, in your wild goose chase, enjoying the deeper shades of ecstasy.'

In the fields carved within their ancient boundary lines, green crops budding up around Glasgow. As we arise by air again in a propeller plane with sea blue cowlings over its twin engines, the sere mountains of Scotland below. Snow high up in the crevices of their crests. Laura says they predict the colours of the wools that lie in wait. And in another fit of laughter in this homey aircraft she says she suspects that the solicitous steward so animatedly smiling and making tea in a pot, and so willing to please, must really be president and owner of the airline and would any second pop into the cockpit to help land the plane. Which now angles down over the blue water of the Minch. Dotted below on the faint green of a small island, one's first sheep safely graze. The sheer dark brown edges of bogs which have been left carved empty in the ground, imagines for me one more colour of tweed. On this bereft Stornoway spot. Where we are bumpily deposited as near to Iceland as it is to London.

An orange windsock blowing over the airport grasses. Surrounding all these glacial blue lochs and inlets from the sea is a glorious barrenness. I panic as tomorrow at noon the mills are closing for a long weekend. At our Stornoway hotel Laura gets on the phone. Already arranging I meet the Member of Parliament for the Hebrides back in London. Then her brilliant vowels and charming words have in an instant caught a mill owner Kenneth Harris on the phone. Chairman and managing director of Harris McKenzie. Who says it's mid season and he has to get up at five a.m. the next morning to enjoy a weekend off. And I arrange to speak to him by phone at nine p.m. I learn he has been working night and day non stop. And ask him for how many weeks. And he says, 'Weeks? Good heavens no. For six or seven years it's been non stop hectic.' And even over the wires one can nearly hear the sweat still falling from Mr Harris's brow. I ask does he have a favourite Scotch whisky. He says there's no need to, as like Harris tweed they're all perfection. And seeking such infallible impeccability, agents come to confer on behalf of all tweed loving Americans. To select this cloth first brought to the United States at the turn of the century by Brooks

Brothers. And which is now again being readied since December. Such preparations presenting a new style for every season. Their innovative vogues coming from their sense of the market place. Their representatives visit in the year to see their foreign customers and attend the fashion shows. Then the theme comes. Upon which they perform their variations. Such instrumentalization being an in house effort. Their designers pedalling their own clacking looms. And six to seven thousand patterns are created.

Bright and early next morning Laura appears smiling in a splendid suit of the cloth of which we speak. On this mild sunny day she's mapped out non stop appointments. At the mill of Clansman we meet the marketing director Murdo Morrison in the lobby. Suddenly I'm discovered as an author. Of novels. Out on this literary limb, I assure all that at least some of my soap opera characters more than occasionally wear a tweed which is Harris. Bruce Burns, managing director of Clansman Holdings, steps in. I'm relieved and pleased to be asked on behalf of a young daughter for an autograph. We follow behind his fleet footsteps. Into a skylit warehouse full of bales of 100 per cent Scottish wool. Their fibres cleaned and dyed lime, ochre, moss green, purple, crimson and crotal. The latter brewed from the lichen growing on Hebridean rock. The strands await ready to be teased and blended to make wondrous hues of yarn. His eyes alight, Mr Burns's own expert fingers demonstrate the process beneath our eyes. He matches miraculously the very thread of one colour in my tweed cap. And I realize this man whose practised hand is able to operate any of his machines, is indeed composing notes of colour as one would strum a muted melody on a harp. And when he says they are ahead of fashion and create fashion and don't follow it, you realize from whence his confidence comes.

Nearby a man is walking back and forth on a platform, weaving a great web of wondrously grey yarn like a spider, and in the process tying six hundred and seventy two knots. Preparing it softly folded to be dispatched out to the crofters where it is dropped off and the woven tweed is picked up. And nothing anywhere betrays this cloth that hath covered or shall ever clothe any back, that it comes into being by the most meticulous of man made means. We continue to waltz behind Bruce Burns through the myriad of rollers, shears, knives, cutters and trimmers. Our host taking a wool snippet in his hand. He rushes to wash it in a vat of 'soap', taking it three times out again to the light until finally this man there amid his acres of factory is holding in his hand to his own utter delight this tiny symbol of magic creation, a wee rainbow of delicate bright magically shimmering colours. His twinkling fervent eyes alive as he talks of his 'cook's recipe', from which ten different colours of wool might be blended to get just one shade of yarn. He now takes to the sunlight his handful of fibre, his fingers playing in adoration across the delicate rainbow of colours held in his hand. 'Just look at that, is there anything anywhere as delicately beautiful.'

We are brought to an annexe where ladies drape the cloth up to the daylight. Spying out the least of tiny imperfections to mend. And back in the large finishing room is another lady from the Harris Tweed Association stamping with her iron, authenticating the cloth as it passes beneath her watchful eye. Every three metres imprimatured by heat transfer with the trademark orb of Harris Tweed. And who brought this cloth to notice out of the Hebrides. Ah as you might know as a man, it was a woman. Unmentioned in any encyclopaedia. But nevertheless the Countess of Dunmore to be precise. Who in the eighteen forties in order to help crofters on her Hebridean estate, carried the tweed to London to sell among her aristocratic friends. And now on this day it goes out to much of the world. Still woven by foot power which both mill owners and weavers in 1979 refused to change to electric and larger looms. These isles remaining a political delight without industrial strife. The people still living in their villages. And every crofter master of his own time.

In tow with two dedicated handsomely tweed jacketed

members of the Harris Tweed Association we head past front neat gardens where sheep securely graze around stacks of lobster pots. We reach a crofter, Murdo Angus Macleod. Who with pretty wife and daughters dwells quietly by a cemetery. His brand new shiny house nearly built by himself with seven bedrooms. And in these changing times, has a bathroom with a bidet. Out in his loom shed, even in the coldest of weathers Mr Macleod sweats. He once counted his pedals by foot which took ninety six thousand times to produce his piece of cloth eighty five yards long. Twice the distance of a marathon.

Laura gliding in her elegance, puffing her cigar. Admiring these sunny sunny folk, who with their old wisdom tolerate life so well in such a grey windswept place. Yet where colours lurk wondrous as they do in its most burnished brown of tweeds. And as muted as the bowl of Scotch Broth Laura has for her lunch at an hotel bar for thirty pence. A man in a black leather jacket who's read my books and whose occupation is oil invites us to a crowded smoky room and a last night of whisky and folk songs. And all too soon one wakes up back in London. With Laura gone as she does in spring to her yacht in Monaco.

I sit now waiting in the shadowy plush confines of the Savoy Hotel. Shaking firm hands with Donald Stewart, Member of Parliament for the Hebrides. And although looking sombre like the islands, he is, like so many of the people he represents, a commercially wise and smilingly contented pipe smoking man. I learn from Mr Stewart that Hebridean libraries issue more books per head than anywhere else in the United Kingdom. And the islands also send more of their children to university. He tells of the once herring fishing industry exporting to Russia before it declined. And one knows, too, that out from these isles death is always await on the waves. Lurking within the Gaelic songs they sing and the cloth they make.

And what about men's fashions. My God. Can I with my taste say anything at all. Except that grey herring bone is the all time classic. And there is every season an ivy league check.

Unlike the more conservative Europeans, the typical American collection goes the gamut from the gaudy to the sophisticatedly subtle. Bantam weight is now 70 per cent of the Harris tweed total turnover and forms 90 per cent of the American market. But to recite facts and figures is only to demean this cloth. Wait instead with your magnifying glass to take a close peek when next you see it on someone's back. It's worthy of such scrutiny. And enjoy your awe. And listen, too. To a voice whispering. Will ye nae come back again. To this passion here. On its lonely bereft moonscape. To the pub, the darts, the songs, the whisky, the warp and weft and beer. The perfume of burning heather. Remember a young friend, standing on a New York street. Displaying his jacket which came from this clime. Out of the spin of a bobbin. Out of the clack of a loom. And upon his back lavishes its draping properties. In all their deeper shades of ecstasy.

1986

PART 7

Dear Old Dublin

Trinity Quatercentenary

It's a long time now since the ecclesiastical powers of this Irish nation, once immune from public sin, descended to chase *The Ginger Man* off the Dublin stage for being an insult to religion and an outrage to normal feelings of decency. And a lot of moral water has flowed under the bridge since. While the lonely pilgrimages continue to England for abortions and venereal afflictions multiply, condoms are discouraged. But never forget that this is a singular country where all is opposite to logic. And still the domain of a beautiful funeral that you nearly might wish could be your own. A postal strike rages to stop all the good news you're expecting in the international mail, but allows the enormous native telephone bill to get through.

This is now a land where women's liberation has given birth to voices raised in rude suggestion to men as to what they can do with their Friday night after the pub appetites when wives were once driven out quaking in the chill of back gardens or locking themselves for safety's sake in their water closets. It's women now who have made their own fists to give himself a round house jolt in his own gob. But also, along with the recent emancipations, other rectifying influences have come. There exists the ultimate contradiction of the Catholic Protestant. A beneficial phenomenon whose number increases. And whose virtuous uncorrupt tweedy behaviour is nearly beginning to set the tone. When suddenly out of the celestial blue, the moral fabric of the Republic is rent in tatters by the storm force gales of scandals, ecclesiastical, industrial and agricultural. The ship of state yawning and groaning as it heaves beneath the massive moral swells, its political and religious hierarchy impugned in the eyes of the people. And as all the banned writers over the years are chuckling behind their computers, and those of them as have already sadly departed and are turning over in their graves to try get a look at the latest headline, it would make you wonder where on this isle could you go in a hurry to find a bit of ethical certitude.

Everywhere you look you find that gombeenism is on the rampage again. Just when you thought that enlightenment had come and the bijou bungalow would be soon stopped from defacing the landscape and architecture at last had a chance. Could it be that there's no more to be squeezed out of the once reviled James Joyce and they're fed up with the expense of unprofitable renovation and preservation of your genuine architectural culture and that the nation is roaring for the bulldozer again. With as a first priority a tourist charabanc highway to gain access to those ash grey hills of Ireland's sacred monument the Burren. Where from the start of time the winds have hummed across its stones to make music of its loneliness. And where the hushed veils of rain anoint and cleanse all with silence. And can anyone stop them as they go paint a moustache on Ireland's Mona Lisa.

Ah but by God, with so many things changing for the worse, you'd desperately need to go find some solace from all this urgent dilemma. And I choose to go to Trinity College's Quatercentenary Ball. Heading out over the pebbles of my drive on a blue skied day motoring by antique Daimler on the straight road to Dublin. And some graciousness is still found as I park myself in the luxury of the Shelbourne Hotel and my car in the cool shadows of the Royal Irish Automobile Club which latter sports one of the last remaining cognomens acknowledging that England once had more than a little to do with this city. As it did with this famed university. On whose ancient grasses, flat green and velvet marquees are set and cricket this day is played in the sunshiny breeze. College gentlemen go by wearing their elegances. Gold watch chains swinging across their crimson waistcoats, straw boaters atop their heads. Their ladies asmile in their long dresses and wide brimmed hats. Music blazes away. I pass among them like the eccentric ghosts of yore who once went here. As I go now in their memory, the loneliest man in the world.

But now night comes. A round moon rises out of the Wicklow mountains and beams down on Dublin. Like the ten thousand others in black tie, I and my lady friend in a cerulean blue gown whose beauty heightened hearts of the undergraduates of my time, stroll through the mild clear night down Dawson Street towards that sparkling jewel in the city's very centre. Where after nearly four hundred years of the English and the Anglo Irish, the Irish Irish now hold sway in the same ancient splendour polished and glowing as never before. Ah but as one arrives amply on time, the champagne at the champagne reception has already run out. I feel a sentimental twinge of disappointment as Jean-Marc Heidsieck, the brewer of this famed wine being served, was a college companion with whom on many a chill Dublin evening I dined in this hall where we had once actually discussed the growing of grapes in Ireland. And I can't remember now if Jean-Marc said it could or couldn't be done. But never mind, on this festive night, I've been given a bottle of reconstituted orange to drink.

One waits to see if out of the migratory massive horde who traipse back and forth across the ancient cobbled front square any of my own old die hard graduates show up. If not from lands across the seas then at least out of the local woodwork. But somehow one feels the past of Trinity is more than just dead and gone, it is abysmally forgotten, overwhelmed by the swarms of these new Irish minds and faces. Out of which not one do I see even vaguely familiar. And it was about this time of night those years ago when the BBC's anthem blared God save the King and God Save the Queen from open Trinity windows to fade out across Dublin. To incite patriots such as Brendan Behan to come as he did beating fists on the college front gates. And as the college porters held their own, Behan shouting 'Ireland for the Irish' predicted what was to be. But tonight instead, to lower the tone, in over the fences and through the barriers, Trinity Ball interlopers and trespassers come. And hard they are to pick out from the invited.

But don't you dismay. And let not this nation be held up to ridicule. All's not gone and lost. Gombeens and their like are not certain to win. There are still champions who fight. And as the fireworks and flame throwers erupt in front square I look out the window of the college common room. Another pair of elbows come to lean next to mine on the sill. It's a young voice extolling and mourning the greatness and passing of Trinity traditions. He is a Trinity graduate and a young beefy ecclesiastic of the Church of Ireland who has taken holy orders and is a tenor no less in the choir. He's proud to remain and be what he is. He would like to take up a sinecure where good Protestants still remain in their isolated spots in Ireland. His strangely delicate fingers play with the stem of his glass. It is as if I am for a moment listening to Beefy out of the pages of *The Beastly Beatitudes of Balthazar B* whose lonely sad story was set in this very place. And for whom it took so much steady emolument for him to traverse his daily life unhindered. And one is reminded now that although the Trinity ghosts are dying, they may not yet be completely dead. Thriving as they are in this romantic young man's mind. Who dreams this night at the Trinity Ball.

1992

The Dublin Ghosts Remembered
on Bloomsday

Look down from the sky and divided by the Liffey and
caught in a great loop by the Royal Canal you've never seen a
better web of neatly woven little streets below. And an item not
yet known to be recorded in any record book is that there are
more favoured spots in Dublin than anywhere else upon earth
upon which one can stand scratching one's head and from which
one can walk in any direction and not have to proceed more than
thirty paces to the privacy of a public house, thereby proving
the existence of greatest convenience to your thirsty pedestrian
the world has ever known. This greatest of all urban assets,
where you'd find a stool out of the rain upon which to place
your ass and reach your lips to swallow a brew to slake your
thirst and between tipples and among cronies coin phrases that
would fill as many volumes of *The Oxford Dictionary of English
Proverbs* that you could shake a black thorn at, is also not alluded
to in any record book.

Now then. Is it any wonder that this island has produced
writers and raconteurs galore or that you would have someone
like Joyce and his Bloom the tourist envy of nations everywhere.
In every Dubliner's mind, as he steps forth in this city of intimacy,
there is also in his mind always awaiting a Dubliner to whom
his feet urge to take him. Where he knows may lurk other cronies
who'd pretend not to be waiting for his arrival and would utter
sotto voce ridicule and would look up as if they weren't glad to
see you. But never mind the rebuff and undisguised rejection,
for even the briefest of acquaintanceships in a Dublin pub breeds
begrudgement. And a pint or a ball of malt might be the cost of

contented companionship and to let them know you'd learned your silently taught lesson in ignominy. Ah but then as Joyce said it's all in the provocation of intelligence.

Now all this gossipy turmoil of insult and spiritual injury was before the neon light came to Dublin and when the principle of chauvinism was exalted and thriving. And the world of Bloom had hardly faded then in the first year of peace just after the Second World War. The pub life in those days was a sea battle of withering witticisms, blasting maxims and wounding epigrams sinking your dream boats dreamt the night before and if your shyness weren't to forever make you shut your gob, you'd let fly with your own bright and droll thoughts tersely and ingeniously expressed, which would have the fists and bottles flying in a trice. Pubs were as a bank, a chapel or a church, sacred places as if one were making some slightly sacrilegious stations of the cross, where a man's elbows hunched him over the bar and he prayed for deliverance from his own daily despair and borrowed a little peace while he hoped for better days. But indeed I exaggerate a smidgeon. There was now and again in the diatribes, as it was in Bloom's time, even a mild fondness to be found lurking among the combatants. And if the scandal mongering was good enough there were the guffaws erupting aplenty, and backslaps on the back to choke you on your beer. And an invitation to have another.

Now Bloomsday, I do believe, was inaugurated in a pub. And don't you all rise up as one to tell me I am wrong. The inventor was to best accounts Brian O'Nolan, that quiet citizen who reflectively sipping his whiskey matriculated in the interior of the Scotch House on the Quays and became more famed as Myles Na Gopaleen spoken as his name across the world. It was in taking such reverie, and pleasantly getting deeper in his cups, that Mr O'Nolan first thought of Bloom and to go step in this Joyce's character's footsteps. In going thus forth he went accompanied by the legendary poets Kavanagh and Cronin, for poets' company automatically brings you good luck. And last and most certainly not least there was John Ryan the inimitable, who was every bit the Bloom of his day, albeit an awfully affluent one.

Now it was Ryan whom one suspects paid to rent the Broughams taken on this, the very first Bloomsday. His early Dublin life was located out in Stillorgan environs living on his mother's estate and in her sumptuous house of fifteen bedrooms and as many bathrooms. John always giving gentle advice to his staying guests to enjoy the early morning ambience of pucks to eat of rashers and eggs but to be ever just that little bit cautious to stay out of the way of the mother. And approaching noonday, to achieve that, he'd always gently suggest to come with him forth in his Vauxhall along with the swarms of cycles into Dublin. Where he would make his way to his bohemian destinations each one more bizarrely unbelievable than the last, and it was to be my first ever to know of a Bloom wandering. And would be as variable as the likes of the quiet neutrality found in Kehoe's pub, to the noisy Hibernian Hotel's basement Buttery. The latter much populated by your nattily dressed and la di da accented chancers and plenty of Blooms at large among them. But always following such whole days' wanderings, past midnight would bring us to the last port of call which were the dungeons of the Catacombs where the ultimate in philosophy reigned.

These my own Bloom like peregrinations with Ryan were strange enough. But when alone, and coming as I did out of chill chambers of 38 Trinity College and looking, not for companionship but for the nearest central heating, I went straight up Dame Street and would then enter the loneliest bereft outpost Dublin has ever known. And as it would conversely be, also the most beautiful pub in all of Ireland. Tucked into the side of the old Jury's Hotel, you'd never know it was there. Admittance made up steps from the narrow darkness of Anglesea Street. Living glamour no where to be seen. But plenty of lonely gloom in the cold shadows and the fabulosity of the colourful tiles. But there to be found indeed, as if to contradict all that is Dublin, was often the one and only Gainor Stephen Crist, in meditation and holding fast as it were, at his post. And here, too, it was one strange afternoon that Crist said to me.

'Mike, even if one day you hear I'm dead, and you await patiently to be advised of further and better particulars, be prepared for later and contradictory news. For on some summer's eve when the lark is everywhere singing in the clear air, and when all but you are gone, I'll be there back in Dublin for Bloomsday. I'll be walking down to the end of Grafton Street. And if you see me thus, tell no one but believe it's me.'

And I upon this June and but one day or two ago, just returned from London, was walking on this summer eve from College Green to start up Grafton Street and was about ready to cross Suffolk when I turned to see the other side of the road passing in front of the Provost's House none other than the legendary Gainor Stephen Crist. And in his elegant dress, a tweed herring bone jacket and as always his neat grey flannel trousers. His beard and hair grey. His hands as they always did entwined twiddling in front of him. I even stopped for a moment and nearly cried out and said that bloody well looks like Crist. Till I remembered it can't be. I began to walk on but stopped again remembering his remark about Bloomsday. And said to myself in very definite words, that was Gainor Crist. And it wouldn't be the first time he's reappeared from the certain dead. And as I turned to look again I could see the upright posture of those familiar squared back shoulders pass on the granite pavement around the front of Trinity. But instead of shouting long distance for his attention I walked on. Why disturb a ghost on a pleasant summer eve. For I had many years ago a letter passed on to me from the American Vice Consul in Madrid, informing:

'Mr Crist died in Santa Cruz de Tenerife Islas Canarias on July 5th 1964 and was buried at the Cementerio de Santa Lastenia in that city.'

But now as I walked further on up Grafton Street I began to remember the curious stories reported over the years. Crist had never in fact been seen again when he disappeared as he did one day, invited aboard this strange gentleman's vessel to sail with him to South America. And this war time friend, a US Marine Major, the story was, he'd again met by accident in a Barcelona street and had not seen since the Second World War and with whom he'd previously went on a drinking spree which began in a London pub and ended up four days later in the back of a lorry full of broom sticks on the banks of the Rhine river during one of the last battles of the war, with neither gentleman, one in naval and other in military uniform, being sure as to how they got there. And as I strolled away up Grafton Street the realization came that no one who knew Gainor actually saw him dead nor, due to his landing at Tenerife, was present at the graveside to see his coffin go into the ground. But long now have I verily believed him buried, as he might be, having actually seen a photograph of his gravestone. But two years ago I smiled amused at the uncanny resemblance in surreptitiously taken photographs sent me of a cocktail gathering in Kansas City, Missouri, where a man was disporting who looked for all the world like this man Gainor Stephen Crist. And I again chortled at the photo sent me of another clone, black tied at dinner at Reid's Hotel in Madeira and but two hundred miles away by sea from his grave.

Now if I'm imagining all of this, as one does tend to do on occasionally seeing the ghost come alive in the bronze Patrick Kavanagh seated alongside the Grand Canal, I imagine, too, that there will be a reincarnation of sorts when John Ryan's statue arises somewhere suitable the top of Grafton Street. And now I know that there must also be, too, a statue commemorative of Gainor Stephen Crist to stop me imagining I'm seeing the real him. It could reign as a reminder on Bloomsday and we could go in his silver footsteps on the pavement where he walked with his nervous bird like gait. Alas the Cosmos House and the Seven Towers, two of Crist's favourite pubs where he drank, are no more. And the tiled interior once on the corner of Dame and

Anglesea Street is far away restored in Zurich. But if it's him alive passing the Provost's House or a damn good looking resemblance sporting his ghost, let me only say.

Who doth it be
Who hoots
Out of a sorrow
Cold and old
Long lain now
Believed resting in peace
Mike
Question me not
It be me
Who hoots

1994

Night Out in Dublin

There is no nicer nice person than a nice American. And he or she does not deserve to suffer. Nor be affronted by this broken tumbledown unkempt city struggling into the twentieth century as the natives emerge from their centuries old deprivation and poverty. Nor be brought to what may be the most overpriced place in Western Europe. And you, sophisticated traveller, may, like a damp pale handshake, find, as Henry James did, little here to please you.

But wait. Although the place has gone computer wild and you will jump like a scalded cat from every bill you're handed, cheap bargains are not everything in life. So don't flee just yet. The native smile will make you feel that if not your money's worth, at least the generous amount of blarney you're getting is served up at a discount. It is why I as a midlands bog trotting native, contemplating a night out in Dublin, took three nights to work up one's nerve. Terrified of prices, and the bleak prospect of scruffiness and that the music would knock my ears off and the smoke choke me.

Bravely I slot into a corner of Dublin that was once a bohemian hot bed but now houses the Westbury Hotel. This spacious lobby alone is as smoothly comfortable and as American as you could wish. I take a gastronomically agreeable French meal in the restaurant. So far so good. But soon realize in this well meant anti Irish elegance that it is no night out in Dublin. Twenty four hours later, my nerve strengthening, I attend the venerable Olympia theatre. To hear and see Billy Connolly the Scots roaming iconoclast philosopher tear Irish repression to shreds telling among other outrageous things what might hopelessly happen when an Irishman attempts to wear his condom. But again the night evaporates in chaste respectability with a trip with Billy to the King Sitric restaurant in Howth, and in these quiet confines, seafood a speciality, the night ends peacefully out on this windswept peninsula.

As another dawn comes and breakfast is taken and I begin to shrink back towards the midland bogs, a night out in Dublin now becomes remote. But I do as I intrepidly did years ago in this city and simply saunter out. For Dublin has always been a private club and old members lurk everywhere. And sure enough up an alley I meet an acquaintance, Michael Meenaghan, a polo player. Who assures me as we go for coffee at Bewley's Oriental Café that I ought not to be dismayed. The dowager lady waitress who speaks her own Irish brand of the Queen's English made one feel, ordering a coffee and spice bun, that one was being knighted in the process. And in this venerable institution with its Jersey cream, splendid coffee and cakes, my confidence creeps back that all has not been lost in this honky tonk Dublin where at least you can still listen to the priceless form of native entertainment, the blarney.

As we stroll down Grafton Street it becomes again as it used to be like the main hall in a country house. My polo playing friend has for years made it a habit to buy bouquets from the girl flower seller on the corner to give to deserving ladies. And wonders why she's absent this evening as he leads me on to the Bailey a few paces further in Duke Street. After a pint or two in this interior resembling a somewhat luxurious students' union, our pub crawl has truly begun. Warming to his task my friend in this intimate club manner of Dublin talks to anyone either side as if they'd known each other a lifetime. We cross the street to Davy Byrnes, a haunt of my own student days. Somehow Michael Meenaghan does not take to the clientele, who, although they look a perfectly acceptable bunch, perhaps seem a notch too up market and not your true denizens of a real Dublin pub. However, a drinking premises is never more than sixty seven paces away in Dublin, and you need never run out of choices. But the stale smoke and grimness of the next place drive us quickly out again and our crawl continues up Dawson Street. To enter the most astonishing confines of all. And so private is the Royal Irish Automobile Club that only one man sits in the bar remarking to nearly no one in particular except the bartender that he likes the wide marble halls in the old world hotels to remind him of the once spaciousness and graciousness of life. It's almost as if he here solitary sits in lone defiance to the awful things that have happened to this city. And in fact this is precisely what he is deliberately doing.

Ah but not all is downhill abysmal, and from singular solitude the Horseshoe Bar of the Shelbourne Hotel is suggested where Jimmy one of Ireland's most famed bartenders presides. This now being the last remaining meeting place for the socially élite. Which of course in this peasant land happily includes everybody. My polo player guide is conducting introductions and is clapping and being clapped on the back by other polo players. Queens of fashion, impresarios, horse breeders, art connoisseurs and moguls abound. Champagne bottles are dipped across the bar to pour. Cigars are puffed. And some nervously laugh as a lone tweedy defiantly Anglo Irish lady exclaims.

'If another single insufferably crass person uses that revoltingly unpleasant expression "lifestyle" again within my faint hearing I shall positively vomit.'

But to find action it's time to go two footed again out into the night. The polo player Meenaghan leads one along Baggot Street. Whose several pubs have miraculously escaped wholesale change and whose interiors are now jammed. A lady from New Jersey on her first day ever in Ireland is attempting a samba across the floor. But here inside O'Donoghue's there's only room enough to stand up straight. The music makers are seated in a circle while listeners shoulder to shoulder are packed around them. A man plays the spoons bouncing them on his knees. Elbows are in your face while the publican takes orders and

247

serves drinks standing up on the bar shouting out over the heads of the crowd. And finally, despite the pleasant music, the squeeze is just too tight.

We go dine at Dobbins down an ancient lane. Here there are rumoured to be diplomats and government cabinet ministers. Sawdust on the floor. Candles glow on the tables. And the many come here just to see and listen as the beautiful Fionnuala Monks exquisitely sings. And now with wine enough it's late enough and at last I've got nerve enough to go to a nightclub. Meenaghan guaranteeing one will not be dismayed with le Cirque. And indeed dignity is already assured by its pale blue door set in grey ashlar stone. One is signed in on a visitors' book lying open in an invitingly comfortable waiting room. Only for a moment does one think one's name might be entering a mourners' bereavement list in a funeral parlour.

And safely inside and night life ahead one thinks one encounters the strange overtones of the Adolf Loos bar in Vienna. But instead of hard shiny marble there are soft hued fabrics covering the furnishings. One sinks back in comfort savouring the fashionable people. Free of smoke, with music free of noise. Steps go down to a small temporarily empty dance floor where the coloured lights glint and blink across the shiny parquet. And I see no reason why an honest to God sophisticated American shouldn't enjoy this bijou nightclub in the city where soda water was invented. And where from now on, they tell me, human rights to pleasure without pain are going to be thoroughly observed.

1987

The Bloom of a City

It was autumn in a year following the end of the Second World War, when I first walked through the soft rain that often falls on this ancient Irish capital of Dublin. The wet glistened on the mottled greyness of the blocks of granite pavement and turf smoke rose from the chimneys and scented the streets. Trams roared by on their tracks under skies whose tumbling clouds would by evening be gently tinted in hues of pink and grey. Seagulls swooped and squawked over the slate roof tops. A bone deep cold stayed in one's feet through the night. And any pleasure one felt was mostly found in the mind.

One had already forgotten the rest of the world beyond this island when in my innocence I was invited by a charming tall Californian named James H. Leathers, with whom I shared college rooms, to go and have a cup of coffee. I was not to know that coffee in a coffee house was merely an introduction to the pubs which were jammed till closing time and that social gatherings in their spontaneous combustion could rage on through the night in this city where bitterness, backbiting and begrudgement were invented. And also that one might wake up two weeks later, miles distant from Dublin, wondering how one had got there.

Back in those days then, the modern world had little changed this Georgian metropolis gently spreading north and south from the banks of the River Liffey and reaching out into the Irish Sea around its bay. Out of teeming slums gangs of barefoot urchins then roamed the streets and black shawled women held out their hands to beg. Amid swarms of cyclists, horse carts thundered through the streets as if to guide the rattlingly old motor cars on their way. And with its worn Protestant elegance surrounded by a Catholic population, Trinity College sat a cloistered jewel in the city's centre.

And now the millennium. But for me it is coming up to forty two years when I first alighted from the green upholstered tram to go by the red brick Dental Hospital with its skylights in the roof and from which I always expected to hear screams, to enter the back gate of Trinity. And there was the university through my apprehensive eyes. With pedestrians staring at me and my black and white collegiate saddle shoes, I had come past the exotic mock Byzantine towers of what once roofed over Dublin's first steam bath. Architecture remaining, as it has long been in Dublin, a symbol of someone's abortive crumbling dreams. I had also walked by a doorway with a brass plate 'The Mission to Lepers'. And have since over the years specially travelled to stare at this doorway to wonder when it would finally disappear as so many other dignified artefacts of decency in this city have done. And I can now in this year of the millennium finally report it gone.

But Trinity College is still here with its cobbled stoned front square and its lawns still flat, green and velvet. Benches where one could sit reading, watching and wondering under the old trees when some remainder of summer was still hanging in the skies. But no longer does one hear the ringingly haughty voices of the West Brit and Anglo Irish for whom this institution was long an ancient trusted redoubt. And where once it was like crossing an empty stage upon which one might stop and declaim, my God it's all so peaceful and beautiful. Now throngs of students flow by, perhaps even healthier and happier ones, but none of whom one expects to see break down and weep in thanksgiving for all this so beloved beatific, academic grandeur.

And if now in Dublin you hanker for yesteryear and quietly strolling elegance, head up Dawson Street and keep your eye peeled. Not far away, some such folk are still emerging out of the old clubs on St Stephen's Green. They go by somehow silent and sadly grey. For there has long been contagious architectural sacrilege all over this town. And as one more unspeakable facing glares down from some new elevation, one clutches one's heart in horror and rushes down to Molesworth Street to grasp a frisson of comfort. For across from the Masonic lodge still stays affixed and gleaming on a Georgian door the brass plate of the Protestant Orphan Society, albeit nearly polished beyond legibility. And still embedded in the pavement of this street are its old coal hole covers, each one original to itself. And one gives a sigh of relief.

Ah but upon this millennium native voices have been raised against the desecration of Dublin and all the blatant paddywhack-ery. For this present celebration is by some looked upon as a hyped up effort to attract these lorry loads of visitors from across the Atlantic to what one might too hastily say is a worn jagged toothed tourist trap. And here I was myself walking up a still vaguely venerable Dawson Street and in the billowing work dust, as I stood in front of the Lord Mayor's house near the millennium candle flame, a refined Dublin gentleman said to his companion as they looked over the piles of cobble stones being installed on this forecourt in order to return it to its original eighteenth century splendour.

'By God, isn't there an awful lot of nostalgia breaking out all over the place.'

Tourist trap or not, nearly to everyone who gets there these days, Dublin's tumble down shabbiness is mystifyingly charming enough. But you might guess that it is becoming increasingly harder to tell the difference between the former ruling class and the burgeoning brand of native Irish roaming all over the place as if it belonged to them. And these days, instead of bow legged monocled Masters of Foxhounds having porters behind lugging saddlery into the Shelbourne Hotel, the shiny suited or benign Protestant Catholic might be seen. But more likely it will be a charabanc come to park to unload its American tourists. And as the weather grows warm, this swarm increases and with them

come the continental foreigners. Indeed in addition to the Book
of Kells and Abbey Theatre, Dublin might even be said to have
other genuine cultural attractions. For along with the neon
glowing leprechauns leaping out at you from behind the aspidis-
tras, lo and behold Ireland now presents to the foreigner's often
dumbfounded face, the faces of its once banned and shunned
writers. Pictures of them everywhere and written of in travel
brochures and alluded to in pubs, restaurants and nightclubs all
over the place. James Joyce on a postcard is even seen sprouting
a green pair of wings. Every gombeen man is now alert to this
phenomenon as he stands behind his counter ready to be able
to reel off at least the name of the book the man wrote. For why
hold a few ould dirty, disgusting thoughts against a genius. For
by God if there's money to be made out of literature why not
make it while their world wide reputations last out the summer.

So in the places of pleasure newly opened all over Dublin,
recognition for these once upon a time dirty minded men has
now become the rage. There's James Joyce this and Beckett that.
The Bloom this and the Wilde that. With a Molly more than
mentioned here and there. If you're heading for the airport, you
can even get a taxi driver to bring you past Brendan Behan
Court, not far from where that gentleman was born and bred,
with a sky blue plaque up on the wall to mark the place. Behan,
of course, was a true Dubliner, who gave this city its life.
Swaggering conspicuously through the streets in the terrifying
looking company of Lead Pipe Daniel the Dangerous, he would
not hesitate to shout to even the most mildly known of acquaint-
ances, me included.

'How's your hammer hanging.'

Although I didn't disappear into doorways without answering,
it wasn't for a number of years that I discovered I was misinter-
preting this. Behan, who despite his wild unkempt appearance
and explosive rhetoric, could be the epitome of indulgent reason-
ableness, explained to me that it was not in any way meant to
allude to the possible state of one's private, but was a long

established greeting sounded between professionals who worked up on scaffolds in the building and decorating trades. However, even when I had spread this acceptable news, especially among the Anglo Irish, no one with their mother or maiden aunt in tow would enter Grafton Street with Brendan Behan in sight.

But of course remember that it was in bygone days only through the written word that obscenity could reach these shores. Then came the antennae. Reaching high into the sky over nearly every Dublin roof top. They shook and shivered in the winds as the amorally nude images beamed in leaping alive in Technicolor. Now pornography is less than discreetly sold in shops over the counter in this land where once an author's manuscript branded prurient could be stolen or burnt and his books certainly banned. Ah but wait, and have it said too, that here and now things have dramatically changed. All the ills befallen these past scribblers who lurked the Dublin streets have been redressed. Authors and even obscene painters are seen contentedly strolling down Grafton Street, counting their blessings and their earnings from their works tax free. And they might stop now to listen to the new generation of street entertainer on stage in their doorways, who can actually sing and play a note and attract donations. Or smile at an earnest poet approaching who offers a sheet for sale of one of his poems.

So something is different and better in this city so long known as dear and dirty. Voices raised against gombeenism and paddywhackery. And God forbid, even the Catholic Church. And more than a tasteful thing or two can be seen as the city hurries to clean itself up. Daffodils along the new highway to the airport. The main road through Phoenix Park lined with fresh painted lampstandards gleaming with their copper caps. The surface of Grafton Street, once paved by wooden blocks on which many a cyclist skidded to their knees and long a fabled ancient thoroughfare of shopping elegance, has been torn up and replaced by a neat brick walkway. Which now, nearly at the bottom, workmen race to finish. All appropriate enough that the population can now linger here unmolested by the motor car. For once this street served as if it were the main hall of a big country house where you would see inmates wandering back and forth. They were mostly the versifying bucoliasts who had just placed a bet with their turf accountants and were repairing to one public house or another to await the race results.

And in talking of Grafton Street there is one premises which seems to have remained long after all the others have vanished. Bewley's Oriental Café. But even this venerable hold out which once sent the smell of roasted coffee beans up and down the street has finally gone the way of all progress. Its entranceway is now lined with glass cases selling exotic comestibles in the manner of a shiny delicatessen boutique and its once famed waitress service is now sadly reduced. But deeper inside some of the crimson banquettes are still there to sit on and a fire glows in at least one grate. But more important than all, one of Bewley's last elegant waitresses still plies her marvellous friendly trade. Her exquisite dignity to and fro as she gently gets for you what you want. And remembering what you had from one visit to another. Her meticulous diction as she glances out over the new pedestrian thoroughfare and remarks upon the mood of the day. And this is how this staff once presided, knowing their customers came here to more than sup and talk but also to dream.

In this recent thousand years the city has sprawled and clawed its way in all landward directions. Across the surrounds of Dublin, suburbia sprouts everywhere. And considering this is a country where not a plethora have a pot to piss in, some of the most amazingly palatial houses are to be newly seen brazenly boasting their conspicuous worth on their landscaped acres. But mostly housing and council estates creep out upon the emerald grasses. The great old mansions swallowed up, the ancient cottages and barns tumbling derelict and abandoned. The litter blows wild as the vandals and loose dogs roam. Yet on these regimented streets there are neat pretty little gardens and newly planted trees. And a social justice reigns here. For abandoned wives and the unemployed. Roofs over their heads and their children have enough to eat. And one thing is for sure in this millennium, that everyone with a new hat and presentable car is trying their damnedest to keep up with the O'Reillys and Kellys. And those handful with horses, to keep up with the Fetherstonhaughs.

God above no longer holds this city as devoutly unique. Shaking it as he has recently done with the tremors of an earthquake. Although pub rumour has it that it was a million Orangemen with their lambeg drums practising to march down here to celebrate the millennium. But somehow one feels that this shabby unloved capital may once more come to inspire and ennoble and give comfort to the spirit as it once did. There's still the smell of grass in St Stephen's Green. Ducks cruising on its ponds. Birds defiantly blasting out their song up in its leafy trees. Tulips, red, purple and yellow, burst forth from garden beds around which Dubliners stroll and children chase pigeons. There's even a tiny sylvan enclosure for the blind where they can touch copper plates of braille and read the identity of the shrubs they can sniff and feel. Amenities enough you might say. Plus a monument erected in remembrance of those who gave public service to the enfranchisement of women.

But don't go away yet. It's early afternoon, the sun out, a mild pleasant May day. Walk with me west in this city on these ancient narrow streets. Each wall, door and window I pass now the old Dublin begins to return. Bleak and shabby just as it was then. But to the Dubliner this would be Dublin. It was here where George Moore was born. It was here, too, where I would occasionally go to drink in a pub called the Bleeding Horse with a Michael Heron, my brother in law, who delightedly with his public school accent would bargain with the barrow women for his pound of tomatoes. But to stalk these streets too long would seize you up with sorrow. I made myself turn into a church. And walked up its long vestibule. Candles burning and a smell of incense. Inside further doors an organ was playing and voices singing and the pews were packed. A priest up on the altar in his braided raiment. Two friars in their brown long robes came down an aisle, both with devout humility. Here alive and living was the Dublin I once knew. These women opening their handbags in front of tiers of burning candles. Their coins clanking into the offering boxes with the terrible pagan sound of slot machines in Las Vegas. But these coins fell in prayer and gave hope and solace. This is a Dublin which had survived. With the hardship of life. As I walked out, voices made familiar greetings to one another. And I had not gone far up the street when at last a horse cart miraculously came clip clop around the corner. And through the night as I lay awake in the Shelbourne Hotel, revellers were passing. Instead of the strange defiant, inebriate shouts one might hear in yesteryear, those wandering below were singing and laughing. Proof enough that the celebration of the millennium is for real.

1988

The De Alfonce Bank

We are happy to advise that there is no need any longer to wake up scratching your head upon learning that your money has vanished in a series of dud investments or in corporate bankruptcy, not to mention the billions squandered in the treacherous financial chaos of third world countries. And the following confidential matter is disclosed for your immediate consideration.

The De Alfonce Bank is an unashamed élitist state of the art financial institution providing an impeccably discreet venue for international insider trading, tax dodging, the laundering of money and the hiding of it from unwanted seekers, the latter being a speciality. With so many arrant incompetents around these days pretending to be astute trading experts and brokers, the De Alfonce Bank will provide a unique opportunity to avoid falling prey to unscrupulous con men and in particular the financial advisers and officers of so called 'reputable' banking institutions the officers of which feel free to squander your assets without culpability.

The De Alfonce Bank is conveniently located in its own riverside building on Dublin's famed Liffey River, and is in itself an architectural marvel having its own anchorage and helicopter landing pad and with a selection of bullet proof limousines awaiting inside its bomb proof basement. Those who comprise its staff members have all been carefully chosen and are all high ranking De Alfonce players. A secretarial pool leaves nothing to be desired in the beauty and charm of such ladies all of whom are trilingual and versed in all forms of athleticism.

The De Alfonce Bank headquarters extend to seven commodious floors and provide accommodation for its clients in several lavish suites and the players will have at their twenty four hour disposal fine dining facilities, De Alfonce courts, both open and enceinte, and a computer centre directly connected to every financial trading exchange in the world. Minimum deposits required are of the magnitude of One Million Irish punts. Clients of the parent bank are limited in number to twenty five all of whom are ranking De Alfonce players.

Foreign branches of the De Alfonce Bank with De Alfonce courts are also situated in New York, Houston, Los Angeles, London, Rome, Paris, Prague, Moscow, Hong Kong, Budapest, Tokyo and Zurich and are governed by the same principles which apply to the founding bank in Dublin. Such widespread strategic access to world happenings gives a unique advantage to the parent bank's ability to strike fast and gain foot holds in special situations where the outcome is to the bank and its members' advantage, the latter who will occasionally join to exercise pressure when necessary to accomplish a desired result in such special situations. For those financiers who occasionally like to get away from it all, a special oasis branch with all the usual De Alfonce facilities and its own harem is secretly situated in the Gobi desert.

We look forward to receiving your cheque and your platinum key will be sent by return registered post.

The Honourable Founder
De Alfonce Tennis

1991

PART 8

Introductions and Reviews on Other Authors

Review of Selina Hastings's Biography of Evelyn Waugh

I write these words from a fast up and coming European country called Ireland and from a house haunted with the ghost of James Joyce, who once visited here. And also haunted, too, by other literary gentlemen who came to roam along these verdant byways of Westmeath, and one of whom was Evelyn Waugh, who while he was staying at nearby Pakenham Hall (now Tullynally Castle) actually thought of buying this house I live in, and who is the present subject of this quite marvellous biography by Selina Hastings. And a more scholarly encyclopaedic and compendious work you could not find, and one, which in revealing so much of her examinee's life, and which takes the care to transcribe her subject's eccentric spelling and punctuation, has turned one's previous idea of Waugh upside down.

Straight off sporting a dramatic photographic portrait, one is confronted by the Waugh no nonsense eyes staring at you out of the jacket cover of this extraordinary book. Immediately inside are the author Selina Hastings's two pages of acknowledgements which provide a Debrettish litany taken from the nobility of the British literary world, which formidable list alone attests to this lady biographer's splendid credentials. And reaffirmed throughout this work as she eloquently describes the phases and periods of Waugh's existence, all the way from naughty school boy, to and through university days to officer and gentleman and to finally becoming the father of a brood and the reclusive squire puffing cigars and quaffing his after dinner port on his country estate. Taken through this kaleidoscopic life, one has to adjust again and again, as emerges in each phase, a nearly new and different person in the flesh of Evelyn Waugh.

It is also pleasantly reassuring to find, as far as this gentleman's writing is concerned, that Waugh has, long past his death, remained a famed literary figure which this present work is, I'm sure, to the delight of his heirs, to amply prolong. And does so with such vividness that one feels Selina Hastings was alive and living in such scenes as she relates, at least those of the more respectable variety. And one can nearly hear Waugh's best eccentric aristocratic vowels, such being among such folk de rigueur as he insults and belittles the many he thought so deserving around him, and to a degree that one imagines the Waugh coat of arms, which he ultimately devised, proclaiming as a motto.

'I'll abbreviatedly thank you not to morally or intellectually fuck about with me, you low cur.'

From the first page this work is awingly meticulous, and even in scenes where one felt there was lots more to say, somehow Selina Hastings manages to leave nothing unsaid. Having rubbed shoulders with one or two of the protagonists in this book and stayed in some of the same houses, and exchanged words similarly deeply dipped in the deepest snobbery, one is fascinated now by the revelations of Waugh's origins and his early behaviour come to light. And being able, as the essence of the later man emerges, to see the reasons why. Juxtaposed with male friends, there are his life long platonic friendships with both highly intelligent and beautiful women as well as the elaborate documenting of public school homosexuality, the latter being done in such a subtle way as to portray Waugh as the eventual practising heterosexual he was to become.

And then, as immensely important as such things are to Europeans, every step in the awakening and honing of Waugh's life long snobberies are described, as he and Frank Pakenham, later Earl of Longford, 'climbed the slopes of London society together, to comport in patrician circles'. And in this regard, all Americans should breathe a great sigh of relief to have been born on that North American continent where the democratic use of money and rising from no account beginnings may be sung from the roof tops and matters more than a socially awesome pedigree. For here in this biography is demonstrated in both text and photographs an élitism of a kind that knows no rival. With tweeds, walking sticks, foxhunting kit and poses on the stoops of stately homes in leather boots and shiny black bowlers, along with suitable expressions on the faces to reflect the splendour of that life, to prove it.

Although Waugh took on these appurtenances of the upper crust, he was no real snob as a snob no real author can afford to be, and he did in this regard as a writer make it known 'I reserve the right to deal with the people I know best.' Which indeed to know them even better, one supposes, also involved the celebration of the self indulgent, smoking and drinking to excess, remaining unbothered to be physically unfit and delighting in the epicurean. Although missing out on serious shooting and fishing, it was clearly advantageous for Waugh to maintain a patrician bias that suited his notions of superiority, and thus he 'assumed a part that much appealed to him as that of landed country gentleman'. Waugh even maintaining that he would have liked 'to have been descended from a useless Lord'. But when he married his second wife, Laura, his in laws the Herberts found 'disturbingly vulgar his exaggerated admiration for the upper classes'.

Now then. I don't know who any more, across these good old United States, gives much of a fig in the matters of social standing and climbing but all those born and raised on the American continent may be glad they were when they read this book. Depicting as it does social snobberies galore and the agony and bitter peril encountered by those who attempt to socially step up a notch or two. And those who taste doom when they try and don't succeed. Selina Hastings makes amply clear why Waugh has attracted so much scrutiny as to his social credentials, which weren't in fact, seen from an American point of view, half bad. Damn decent in fact. However, as one has already averred, that as authors must embrace all, they can't afford to be snobs or social climbers and one might instead say that, for his practical day to day use, Waugh posed as one. In any event in Selina Hastings's biography there is more than enough evidence for the reader to form his own opinions.

Ah but then, my goodness, just as one has established Waugh's credentials as a gentleman comes an odd bomb shell as one turns a page in this work full of surprises. Waugh might, as according to his in laws, have had an exaggerated admiration for the upper classes but he could take liberties with and even be destructive and unmindful of the impression he made upon the kaleidoscopic array of your upper echelon characters of the time. As in this one instance he did with a grandiose disregard for other people's property, when Waugh, staying as a guest of his friend Alistair Graham at Barford, a country house, tore out of their big *Times Atlas* the full page of Africa. This ungenteel act would have to be regarded as not the behaviour of a gentleman and such news getting around could put paid to your social climbing for all time. As it did instantly with Graham's mother, a very proper American from Savannah, Georgia.

However, it put no stop to Waugh and somehow snobbery of some kind or another seems eternally attached to his name. And in a peculiar Irish context I'm sure Selina Hastings will forgive me in revealing a snobbery I verily believe was, according to a written observation unearthed from Texas University archives, and wielded between Waugh and a once lord paramount of London's literary world, Cyril Connolly, whom Waugh referred to as originating from a long line of Irish bog trotters, and Connolly angrily riposting that the only time his ancestors had ever trotted in an Irish bog was upon a horse or to shoot snipe.

This tome is unobtrusively packed with facts and many a lively description and recollection out of Waugh's life, done in many cases so vividly that again and again one has to remind oneself of Selina Hastings's youthful looks in her photograph to know that she could not have been there. In the stories unfolding of travel, university and his later squirearchical existence, all serve as brilliantly wonderful explanations if not an apologia for Waugh's churlishness and for the life led then. Where your once hysterically pukka vowels were the prow by which you pierced your way to succeed and alerted others to your esteem. Now they are no longer proclaimed aloud except perhaps in the dustier corners of your better clubs. Making this not so distant past enlightening to read in the light of today's American 'power' accent which, spoken, has the last word and culturally conquers all. And also Hastings's historic record is fascinating from the vantage point of a changed Britain, where one's so called upper class accents slip, drop and even mumble away their traceable identity, making it almost comforting to know from this biography and from a snob's point of view that it wasn't always like that.

Waugh has to be your genuine eccentric. Eager to get to war and then providing a strange picture flitting from place to place dining and seeing old friends, and at times it sounded as if he were doing the London season, and from Claridge's was attending Ascot, Henley and Wimbledon. Hastings gives brilliantly amusing descriptions of close combat with boredom and some of the best renditions of the one upmanship relationships among the English that can be found. And especially of Waugh, known to be brave, being perhaps the only man in military history who, often shunned by his fellow officers, was thought by his senior officers to be too rude and offensive to be allowed to go into battle. Waugh post war, even retaining his reputation in America where he spread his incivility from coast to coast. And one would have liked to have been eavesdropping when he paid his visits to Forest Lawn Memorial Park, certainly one of America's most astonishing places, and certainly by the magical account of its existence further immortalized in Waugh's *The Loved One*. Which I hope soon to hear that someone will yet make into another film. Following of course the one made of the present book.

Finally we find Waugh, his entry into the world of the landed gentry accomplished, living in the country house surrounded by your few sylvan acres but perhaps without the mile long entrance drive and the agreeable vista of parklands viewed from a stately home's mullioned windows, but nevertheless enjoying a reasonable resemblance to a lordly abode. And himself ensconced in White's, one of your better London clubs, and adding another nice social notch to his upper class existence where the members took their satisfaction on rainy days watching out the club windows at the passing damn public getting wet. And by the sound of and through Hastings's words, she must know more than a few club men, for one gets that sense of the ennobling contentment and comfort to be found in such precincts. A refuge which Waugh more and more sought and seemed deeply to enjoy in later life. And why not. Where a gent in blissfully male exclusivity could pleasantly contemplate his self esteem and where, over his second gin and tonic, had he the imagination, could let his senses merrily waft in the breeze of reverie. Ah but where I hasten to point out via Selina, Waugh did, as he sat in lonely isolation, get accused by a fellow member of looking like a stuck pig.

In his life lived, Waugh's seemed to achieve greatest contentment while still in his early thirties, and at the time of his second marriage to Laura, mother of his children. He is then described as being 'good looking, affectionate and with enormous charm, funnier than any man alive' and it's hard then to remember a just as strongly opposing view arising from a contemporary of school days, when the young Waugh is described as 'an exhibitionist with a cruel nature that cared nothing about humiliating his companions so long as he could expose them to ridicule'. However, these qualities as it happens perfectly suit the very English sport of foxhunting and prevent one from being surprised at Waugh taking it up, as he did, 'as a means of social advancement at which he was courageous and determined'.

One can at times reading this book feel alone with Waugh on his numerous travels in places like Casablanca or Marrakesh.

But in less civilized environs one wonders how Waugh, easily given to being irritated, bore 'the miseries of climate and terrain and the discomfort of the bites and itches of jiggers, fleas and ticks'. But one wonders even more, as there's no mention of such, at how he seemed miraculously protected from the constriction of anacondas, piranhas' teeth and jaws of crocodiles. But then we already know he might have been too distastefully rude to have been bitten. He also withstood without injury the abuse of devout official Catholics for his so called obscene, immoral and sacrilegious work. And one must say that Waugh with his bluntly pragmatic and confessional nature, revealing his emotions, had an enviable personality perfectly suited to being and remaining a writer. And in this, one feels through Selina's observations that Waugh owed much to the wisdom and forbearance of his literary agent, A. D. Peters. Which helped Waugh achieve to live in inconceivably lovely houses. And in business as a writer, to stand up for his prices.

This surely is a brilliant pen which wrote this tome about a writer who, now that one has read it, richly deserved to be so written about. With Selina Hastings's pertinent comments and fluently evocative lines such as one describing this era. 'Arrived in Paris, Evelyn and Laura dined off pressed duck and fraises de bois at the Tour d'Argent before boarding the night express to Rome.' And then she ends in her own words not much different from Waugh's most descriptive when saying his 'last years were bleak and wretched but his death was an unparalleled blessing, dying shriven on Easter Sunday, the most joyful day in the church's year,' which words come close to ending this astonishing book about an astonishing man who even as he lies contented in his grave still serves so well to inspire the courageously curmudgeonly in all of us.

1995

Introduction to John Ryan's
Remembering How We Stood

John Ryan was my first publisher, who presented my earliest writing, a short story, 'A Party on Saturday Afternoon', in the pages of his magazine *Envoy*. However, I knew him long before that. As an invariably polite, quiet and somewhat shy individual, who when at the bar of a pub would patiently listen to anyone's stories and if prompted sufficiently could tell splendid tales of his own. He was also a rare man in Irish life who could harbour many a secret from which, I suspect, comes much of the wisdom lurking in his words.

In Dublin, following the Second World War, there was a celebratory air and the pubs of the capital city were jammed. And in the years following, of which John Ryan writes, there was a carelessness about life with the hopeless present being made tolerable by adorning the days ahead with rosy dreams. These, for target practice, always being promptly shot down in flames by your listeners, who in a public house need have no mind for having to please a host or hostess.

Intellectual social life, rather than being conducted in the salons of Dublin and country houses, as it seemed to have been in the decades previously, was nearly entirely exercised where drink was for sale or available in one or two of the more impromptu places such as that now legendary basement redoubt, the Catacombs. Unselfconsciousness and face breaking being rampant at the time, no one knew or much cared that a so called literary period was then in the making. Comeuppance and instant amusement were all the rage and you were as good as your last fist thrown or sentence uttered. While delving into the problem of obtaining a lifetime private income, food, not for thought, but to devour was on every mind. And if little hope of that was to be had, then a drink held in your fist was the preferred substitute. The exception to all this deprivation and behaviour was John Ryan.

Courtesy a mother who was as intrepid as she was charming and who ran her considerable business of the Monument Creameries, Ryan was one of the few who personally had available to him both food and drink in plentisome quantity. With money to spare and able to elect to a degree as to what he did with his time, he could have done as nearly all did, spend his days racing and dining evenings at Jammets and the Red Bank with jodhpured cronies. However, Ryan had a distinct consciousness of the value and worth of the writers, painters and poets of the period. And he chose to be interested in his native city and the relics left by so many of its literary sons who had fled or been driven out. It was nearly as if to redress such wrong that Ryan had collected their books, music and pictures and let it be known that such banned and ridiculed things were still to be seen and heard back in the creator's native land and that there remained at least one man there who kept their names alive and held them in high esteem. For as this book reveals, Ryan was himself, as well as a publican and publisher, also a creator of painting, writing and music. And he in turn self effacingly cherished and nourished those in the same pursuit who, embattled, still remained in this land so hostile to their survival.

But Ryan was even more than a helping hand. Over the years of which he writes, he grew into a central figure to become a touchstone who was always sought out by those returning to Dublin. And when found, he would be a ready repository for news or able to report that which was soon to become news, which was usually gossip turned into a fine art. He listened to all mouths and spoke into all ears. And without snobbery he would never ignore, as many did, the awestruck gas meter readers who edged near to be in the intellectual vicinity of the greatness of poets. Nor would a deaf ear ever be turned to the 'chancers' who swarmed about him exerting their charm looking for loans or trying to launch their money making schemes. Thus, with Ryan invariably remaining imperturbably benign to and indulgent of all, did he become himself a dependable focus in a land where begrudgers abounded during a period of censorship and religious repression and when the philistine and pompous pedant held full sway, albeit with all kinds of shockingly prurient behaviour omnipresent.

As a diplomat in a Dublin where undiplomatic behaviour was invented, Ryan has no peer. The fact that he was able to keep as life long friends many of those who detested even hearing another's name mentioned is proof. But he was not to be, in the literal sense, pushed too far. He could and did, when required, mete out plenty of unpoetic justice, especially when it was required to aid a friend in battle. And unlike the slight self congratulatory slaps one might be expected to give oneself in distant reminiscence, it is amusing to read Ryan's accounts of his being constantly saved from extinction in various brawls by other hands such as those of the fair minded Gainor Stephen Crist, the patron saint of Dublin tourists and stickler for justice. It is true Crist was possessed of incredible strength and would administer punishment to the unworthy by levering them on their backs and bouncing their heads on the floor. But from my own recollection of watching Ryan's fists fly and innumerable adversaries in the briefest of seconds be poleaxed to the deck, there was never any question in my mind that here was, in spite of his well behaved diplomatic retiring nature, one of the world's all time best light heavyweights. And even now these considerable years later I can still feel the wind over my shoulder as the whoosh of his straight right fist rent the air like a thundering freight train to put manners upon some nearby vulgarian.

Perhaps because of this Ryan himself has become one of the strangest characters Dublin has ever found in its bosom. As host and friend to an astonishing array and cross section of men, including princes, criminals, revolutionaries and movie stars. For Ryan was forever in Dublin's midst. As an occasional surveying visitor to one of his mother's many shops. Or as proprietor of the Bailey restaurant and pub. Or as friend and comforter to both sides in libel actions, these so often erupting from the endlessly circulating letters and slanderous reporting of the greatest series of soap operas ever to run concurrently in the history of mankind. And as a dedicated Irish nationalist and patriot, Ryan sailed the most treacherous of these bohemian seas with the same skill he used as a mariner when navigating his yacht around the unpredictable and hostile waters of this island. Ryan survived it all. And without, as few of his contemporaries avoided doing, ever, even semi permanently, leaving these shores.

But alas, I suppose, with stories retold and in their telling added to and embellished, it's not surprising I might find, on a minor point or two, that my memory does not quite jibe with his. And I must say that I have never known Gainor Stephen Crist ever to despoil an alcoholic beverage, or to enter, sit down or drink a cup of coffee in a Dublin coffee house. Yet here it is in black and white, in *Remembering How We Stood*, and perhaps it's true, the unbelievable. Also that Crist set elaborate traps for comely females. And I reel back in surprise. And maybe that's true, too. But what I do remember is that Crist, whose compassion for and loyalty to women were a saintly obsession, was always pursued by them and himself stepped into many an elaborate ensnarement. Ah but what matter. There's plenty of time later for disputing facts if a little bit of fiction has you enthralled with the truth of entertainment said for the time being for your listening pleasure. And that is how John Ryan has always told his tales.

Now as one reads his words, dressed in their wonderful finery of irony, the world he speaks of reblossoms to be back again awhile. To see, feel and smell that Dublin of that day. Drawn from his encyclopaedic knowledge of the streets he loved and daily lived in. His erudition always used to entertain but never to impress. His savouring of language, rolled about on the tongue, tasted for its vintage and measuredly poured out into waiting ears. His words sounding with the same deft intimate solemnity which he himself uses when with a gently perceptible signal he orders a drink at a bar. Among the begrudgers, he is the least begrudging of men. And even oft accused of lacking malice in a city so noted for such. Indeed it was unknown for him to take a friend's name in vain in a Dublin where no man's name was sacred. But there could always be his nod of the head and his wry dry chuckle. Which would tell you as much as any oath of condemnation shouted from the roof tops.

In a masterpiece of reminiscence, he gives a touching tolerant account of Brendan Behan, under whose laughing vaudevillian behaviour lurked much hidden haunted suffering and whose nightmarish soul blazed its brief blasphemy in Dublin. And always between the lines of John Ryan's words, the ghosts abound, sorrow and sadness pervade. His words 'It was a bleak February in a bad year' might be, with their timeless profundity, another sub title for this book. But bleak Februaries or bad years, Ryan was always there alertly listening. To the nonsense spouting and the great bards thundering their daily complaint while all present were existentially hoping there would be no delay in the buying of another round.

We can now, before our own time comes, pick over dead men's bones with our own silver plated utensils. Sentimentally to live again in this city as it does in this book. Where the graves of the departed dead are never visited because they still live alive on our lips. If nothing else John Ryan must be said to be your true Dubliner, a man of humanity and kindness. Who will be attentive to your sorrows long after they are spoken. And if this city were ever thought to have had a king, he is and was John Ryan. Who was always one of its princes. And in the years ahead, he, who has for so many others provided memorials, is one of the very few who deserves one himself. And with the epitaph I once heard said of him.

> Ah you'd always
> Feel kind of safe
> In his presence

1987

Review of John de St Jorre's
The Good Ship Venus

As this work reveals many previously secret facts which affected one's own life and death existence for many years, I suppose one should be conscious to show restraint in one's utter fascination in reading John de St Jorre's *The Good Ship Venus: The Erotic Voyage of The Olympia Press, Paris*, which is the history of this pornography publishing enterprise and its founder, Maurice Girodias, who became one of one's greatest of lifetime enemies. And I also wonder who else will be equally fascinated to have disclosed the background workings of the supplier of erotic writings to those many bookshops of Soho who catered for furtive browsers in mackintoshes where these Paris Olympia Press green coloured tomes were for sale under the counter.

Maurice Girodias was the first publisher of *The Ginger Man* and *Lolita* and also works such as *The Sexual Life of Robinson Crusoe*, *The Whip Angels* and *White Thighs*, produced by an assorted pseudonymous team of pornographers. But lurking as well in the background of The Olympia Press and responsible for some of its more sophisticated tomes were some considerably distinguished literary figures, such as Apollinaire, Beckett, Burroughs, Miller, Durrell and the poet Christopher Logue, who when he heard I was writing *The History of the Ginger Man*, and my own account of dealings with The Olympia Press and in knowing first hand that I had much to complain about, said concerning Maurice Girodias, 'Mike you must treat him gently. Don't be too harsh on him.' And it was the sombrely sad but fond tone of Logue's voice which said it all about this man. And

John de St Jorre's marvellously vivid biography and history says all the rest.

The Good Ship Venus gives a captivatingly readable and comprehensive account of what now must be the world's most famed publishing house. De St Jorre tells of Girodias's father, Jack Kahane, who in 1932 founded and ran the Obelisk Press, the first publisher of Henry Miller. Girodias changing his name from Kahane to his mother's surname continued the tradition of publishing the exotic and erotic when founding The Olympia Press in 1953, publishing commissioned pornography which he claimed subsidized more serious work likely to be prosecuted and banned. But ironically it was from publishing the latter work that The Olympia Press and its publisher gathered praise, fame and profit.

However, as yours truly knows well in litigation over *The Ginger Man*, Girodias invariably made an enemy of his authors, not paying royalties and selling rights behind their backs and claiming editorial influence in the writing of these famed works while attempting to denigrate the author's other work he had not published. But justice intervened. For it seems that as he planned to rat he was also being ratted upon, by even bigger smarter rats. And but for the two or three books which brought world fame to both himself and the other works he published, Girodias would have died, as he did in penury, but also in well deserved pornographer's obscurity.

Ah but lo and behold, roguery would seem to have its posthumous rewards. Judging by his recent publicity Maurice Girodias may now possibly end up being the most memorably incredible publishing figure of all time. And as Christopher Logue asked me to be not unkind to his memory I may have failed a little in this, but not a most fair minded John de St Jorre. Whose marvellously aristocratic name Girodias would surely have commandeered as a pseudonym for one of his dirty books. And for anyone interested in writing and publishing, *The Good Ship Venus* is a marvellous traveller to take with you as a companion.

For here is work to fulfil Logue's request and whose charm is to be found in John de St Jorre's words, which I quote concerning the exotic voyage of The Olympia Press, and what such voyage symbolized.

> The story of the last great flowering of Paris as a crucible for creative expatriate talent, when words had power and everything was possible. When it took bravery to go into literary battle.

My own battle with The Olympia Press lasted twenty one years and ended up with my becoming owner of this Press which Girodias describes from his grave as a 'mythical entity' knowing I bought it, so forgive me if I now make it seem too full of profit and glory. But why not, I may plan to sell it.

1994

A Voyage to the Swiftian City –
an Introduction to *Gulliver's Travels*

Even now, be it winter or summer in Dublin, as the weather moves from the west, the ancient toll of its church bells and the squawk and squeal of its seagulls still echo back and forth under its morning pearl grey heavens and its evening blue pink tinted skies. The River Liffey which divides Dublin north and south remains flowing brownly by beneath the Ha'penny Bridge under which the salmon lurk darkly in the water. On the bleak pavements still sit here and there the begrimed faces of this city's faithfully poor with hand and hat held out begging. And by dint of destiny, done with an ancient dignity (for civility is all in this unique city), the chancers and cads still abound just as they did these hundreds of years past, when Jonathan Swift's pen lampooned the human condition.

This erudite gentleman resided in Dublin when its dead babies were often enough to be seen floating in the River Liffey's waters out to sea. And even as one of the major cities of Europe, its slums were reputed to rival those of Naples. Its tenement streets remained little changed up until the end of the Second World War, and there was still very little in these poverty stricken districts to be seen of pleasure, and much more of deprivation, disease and death. Escape was the tavern and entertainment was but to listen to the connivers with their conundrums, who suffering the same woes and telling and hearing stories of others' despairs, became anaesthetized over their vessels of grog. However, in your better places, there were your intellectuals and wits, each of them cautiously arriving among the assembled, hoping not to be snubbed and armed with their own words available to assail and parry the ridicule always ready to be administered by the company present. Even with Ireland having since Swift's day entered the modern world and undergoing two great revolutions in the past fifty years, and ridding itself of its social sores, much of the old Dublin is still there, and nothing changed in the Irish character.

Swift's satire has, by its own duration and recognition in the rest of the world, become sacred, but in the country where he spent most of his life, his words arising out of Ireland's writhing bowels of begrudgement, still arouse a bemused ire and awe, and his causticity of thought has remained in this country's strange conscience. His bones and epitaph anciently inciting rebellion to oppression and inspiring Ireland, a land long shackled in its own repression and held in another's subjugation, to achieve its sovereignty. But in another way the native Irish, finally becoming confident of their own destiny, and to whom Swift proposed that you can cook, boil, fry and eat babies, he has been looked upon with less than endearment until now. For the nation has at last come to cease censoring and instead to celebrate its exiled authors. And awakened, too, to the attractiveness Swift has proved to have for tourists who presently pour in their hordes into St Patrick's Cathedral where they tread, largely in-different, upon this brilliant satirist's bones resting under its cold floor.

This present edition of *Gulliver's Travels* makes for me a poignant reminder of my now long association with Ireland and Dublin. I never entered St Patrick's Cathedral till this recent day, but I a thousand times patrolled the byways which its steeple surveyed. Following other authors in their footsteps through its dear dirty, shabby streets, so long unloved but which also made this city a never forgotten place. And perhaps more ghosts such as Swift's roam Baile Atha Cliath than any other conurbation on earth, where its inmates carried as they did their dreams which, daily dismembered, left their souls adrift on its sea of despair. But even so those many who, tail between their legs, retreated, spending years away in foreign parts, always dreamt of return, and in doing so found that their only satisfaction was to be back.

My own arrival in Dublin came when Ireland had been frozen, isolated by the years of the Second World War, with most of its teeming tenements much as they must have been in Swift's time. In my sometimes nightly winter strolls through these slum streets, the front elevations of these houses were a mosaic of poverty, windows shattered and patched like missing eyes. By the cold evening's darkness, the red glow of a votive light to the Virgin Blessed or to Jesus Christ wearing his crown of thorns was the only sign of life to be seen. And passing the long terraces of Georgian mansions, their doorless entrances to the once sumptuous hallways opening to the winds and rain, rats scuttled across debris strewn floors. And descending the steps of one of these houses, one might confront a white coffin of a child borne aloft on someone's shoulders. Such scenes of sorrow in Swift's time must have provoked his sense of injustice cruel and omnipresent and aroused the scatological writings of this monumentally satiric man.

As one progresses towards the River Liffey from St Patrick's Cathedral and down the grim slope, as it was then, of Winetavern Street, one reaches the ancient hostelry of the Brazen Head, Dublin's oldest inn. It would have been one of the few such places in existence in Swift's time and one to which one can imagine someone of Swift's curious mind going to find in it a redoubt of meditation and solitariness near the river, as it was to Sebastian Dangerfield quaffing bottles of stout who made his way there, as was reflected in *The Ginger Man*.

> O the Winetavern Street
> Is the silliest
> Of the streets full of fury
> O the very, very best
> For this moo from Missouri

But there was an underlying humanity and camaraderie to the discomfort and harsh reality of the wretched poverty in Dublin which helped its surviving souls endure and in whom it bred a buoyant defiance to the grimness of its tenements choked by a dozen bodies alive to a room, with malnutrition and tuberculosis providing an ever present death. I learned of such from two of my contemporaries, Ernest Gebler* and Brendan Behan, both writers who knew this world intimately. And of the defiance found in the mouths and minds making words in the pubs, where flowed the thick and sweet 'red biddy', a drink that could stupefy the brain to the verge of insanity, or excite it to the extreme of attempting insults in their own homemade language. And if you did so inebriate yourself beyond soundness of mind onwards to death, no better place existed for mourners to mourn or to witness the solemn beauty of your remains tugged by teams of plumed black horses and followed by gleaming broughams bearing the bereaved. And if there were to be seen happy faces galore, be assured no sympathy or commiseration was lacking as they trundled to take your corpse to its final resting place, a glass or two of grog on the way, a ritual unchanged since Swift's day.

But rotund of cheeks, life for Swift would have been vastly different from the hollow faced, cowed and thwarted sea of Catholic poor and should he so choose, he could keep far distant from the lower orders of doubly shrewd connivers, twisters and shysters. For as a member of the dominating Protestant Church he would be among those who habitually dined at the great tables in the great mansions of Dublin, where music could be heard as the candles glowed and crinoline swirled and servants ministrated, and the beeves came rare upon their silver platters while crystal goblets of the best grog were put to lips. And there were many who, aware of the hordes of the hungry abroad throughout

* While most readers are undoubtedly familiar with Behan and his *Borstal Boy*, the work of his contemporary Ernest Gebler is sadly overlooked today. His book *He Had My Heart Scolded* presents a brilliant picture of the Dublin poor before the war.

the city, would take such knowledge as merely an incitement to the appetite.

However, the harsh realities of Dublin, which did not mean to be cruel and which solicited compassion, did provide where and when it could. Brendan Behan, one of the few who moved in both these worlds of the well possessed and that of the dispossessed, and was the son of its most bitter environs, often occupied for a shilling an overnight cubicle in the Iveagh Hostel, in Bride Road, merely a stone's throw from Swift's cathedral. Behan, one of Dublin's own, and later famed as poet, novelist and playwright, strode like a king in his unkempt clothes through the thoroughfares that he regarded belonged to him and he frequently talked of and quoted Swift in this Swiftian city. Met on the more fashionable streets, with the tongue of his untied shoes hanging out, he'd shout an appropriate, if not always taken as a flattering greeting, but meant as such to all those familiar he passed. Roaming everywhere he would stop and chat along the streets of Nighttown. Always exuding a universal cheerfulness, he'd know as ancient friends the whores on the quays. Up dark alleys he'd confer with gun men on the run. Greeting the passing stranger arrived anew, whom if they stopped to chat, Behan would mesmerize to follow in his wake either to a pub or the notorious Catacombs of Dublin's iconoclasts, there to live the first day of their lives changed for ever.

It was Behan who was the one and the only man I have ever heard sing Dublin's praises, reverently loving every inch of this city, and who I often heard declaim as he would from his bar stool an irreverent parody of Swift's last will and testament:

> I do hereby vouchsafe to make my last will and testicle. Not having a penny or pot to piss in I nevertheless verily do decree that there be upon the present site where I have placed what respectable parlance dictates I refer to as my buttocks, an edifice to be erected large enough for the reception of as many incurable accountants, tax collectors, bailiffs, money lenders, solicitors, barristers, judges, and hangmen and gas meter readers, and other

odiferous total bollocks as can be collected at any one time at high noon in off the streets of Dublin and without ponces, whores, eunuchs, hetero and homo sexuals galore or golden balls of malt to keep them in contentment, leave them to suffer indefinitely in their continued middle class repression.

And so, back we should go to the great ancient cathedral of St Patrick's. As it still stately sits unchanged amid a rapidly changing city. Its massive oak door opening upon its great darkness. To find revealed wolfhounds who lie crouched in their stone rigid integrity and find in the ancient grey gloom more of what is known about this man upon whose grave now march the thousands of tourists. Statues and tablets and monuments proclaim the great deeds of the departed. Words and testimonies of sincere affection carved in the stone or pressed on brass. The brightest, purest, the zealous, candid and bravely bold. None of whom ever stooped to the unworthy. And Swift. A man who loved and was loved. His and Stella's skulls lie together. He who could not be indifferent to suffering and poverty or the children's bodies floating down the Liffey.

And perhaps Swift living was not universally esteemed and perhaps dead not universally lamented. But he is not ignored. His skull upon death split open to examine his brain and later passed around the drawing rooms of Dublin. This city with another ancient church in whose tower has rung Dublin's oldest bells, tolled during stormy weather to remind citizens to pray for those at sea.

1995

A Bit More Blarney about the Emerald Isle

I live here for my sins and for my tax free status on earnings from what I presently write and have already written. Not the worst arrangement, for many of my novels occur amid the scenes and settings ancient and modern vividly described by word and photograph in many a handsome book. And this combination of strange factors will not be unfamiliar to others who have come here to reside for similar reasons. Full as Ireland is of its myths, leprechauns, blarney and blandishment. Such perhaps even verging on the mawkish as it is liberally doled out by its friendly welcoming people and the state bodies who represent them. But I still, after twenty five years, have no intention of leaving.

In spite of its literary censorship, subjugation by a neighbouring island, its famed famine and long impoverishment, no country on the face of the earth has attached to it an amount of romantic imagery as has this emerald isle. And such kept burningly alive by those escaped and exported from Ireland over the years as emigrants to other distant climes and places. Leaving well behind them the 'crut', a chronic usually celibate condition of repression known to encumber the spirit and leave its victim possessed with guilt and superstition, which in turn had long to be kept in check and disguised by respectability and a deep devotion to religion. You might even say it was a place where friendship was on the lips but not in the heart. Because if, giving vent to honesty, the truth ever got out, the gossip then spreading about the impure, defiant and disreputable thoughts you were really thinking would ruin you.

Ah but now come up to date. Forget all this old rubbish about the true nature of the Irish. The thoughts in the mind might not have changed but this is a brand new place not only for the native but for the visitor. And you would be fearfully wrong to think that any of the above guilt and superstition, impure and disreputable thoughts, had anything to do with the modern Ireland of the present, awakened as it has been from its centuries of slumber. Yet the past flavours and forecasts the future. The ghost of the two decker green upholstered tram still rumbles its way through the heart of Dublin city. There it goes now with the half dreaming poets aboard heading nowhere and everywhere and this versifier looking down at the passing citizens with a gimlet eye in case he should recognize someone and could jump down, stop them in their tracks and borrow half a crown.

Gone, too, are the shouters who from the kerbside would proclaim their theories as to the origin of the stars. And no more are the massive draught horses and drays, barrels of Guinness aboard, clip clopping upon the roadway amid a swarm of cyclists, the white gloved hands of the seven foot tall Garda Siochana raised, starting and stopping the traffic. And woe betide the infractor of a rule. He'd soon be told to mind his manners and keep his wheels where they should be. Or if on foot to take the pair of his feet and to get back up on the kerb and rejoin the alive life on the glistening granite pavements. That was the old Dublin of my university years.

But as has happened in the modern metropolis across the world, cities and towns are monitored by red and green lights and white striped pedestrian crossings. And plied by taxis, buses and crammed with motor cars. Even in Irish towns and cities, the worst has happened, the vehicle glut has dawned. But there is a difference. Crawling along you get a chance to see the architecture, not only in the buildings but also worn on the faces. Or in a taxi to be entertained by the astonishing erudition of the drivers. And no question you've got on your mind to ask will go unanswered. Indeed you might even detour and repair to a pub together to finish the discussion. But, of course, while the taxi meter outside is kept running tabulating up the fare.

Now from my unexpurgated opinions, you mustn't get the totally wrong blissful impression. As you won't. For you'll soon be reminded that the irascible, perverse and cantankerous are everywhere. And if you're a visitor, you'll be concluding that Ireland would be nearly just like the place you've just left. Except that as soon as you decided it was, you'd find out that it isn't. For out across this land there'd be plenty of conundrums. Safety of self, because it is thought to be in the hands of God, is still something many a native chooses to ignore. On wheels with a few jars of the wine of the country taken, a citizen coming around any blind bend like the hammers of hell will not in any way be mindful that you may be coming around the same bend in the opposite direction. But not to worry. Ireland has the best of ambulances to take you to the most up to date of hospitals.

But one thing can never be denied and that is the general amiability and hospitality of the people. Reinforced by the numerous signs for bed and breakfast that you will see every few yards along the road from one coast to another. And what is to be had and found even in the most humble of homes is both cheap and good. And for extra amusement you can also climb right up the social scale, motor up their mile long drive, step out on their vast apron of gravel and be greeted by the titled and once high and mighty. Who will usher you into their castle, rubbing their hands in anticipation of monetary reward, while giving a tug or two at the forelock and treating you to the best brogue you've ever heard. For keeping the silverware shined and the roofs on some of these places would bankrupt you.

Now your next phenomenon is that on foot in Dublin or in any decent town, turn in any direction and you are never more than a hundred paces from a pint of stout and every refurbished pub or hotel has a room named after gentlemen whose photo-graphs appear everywhere but in previous times had their work banned and were driven away from these shores. Three of whom are James Joyce, Samuel Beckett and Brendan Behan. And appropriate enough in the latter's case, as it must be said, he, with insults quickly leading to mayhem, wrecked plenty of these places in his time. His favourite more peaceful antic being to take 'an anointing of the spirit' as he called it by pouring a pint of porter over his head. And to then give a rendition of a British judge sentencing him to death.

No matter how well you know it, Ireland, like the bright paint slapped up everywhere, will always come to you as a surprise. Famine once writ upon the soul of this island, and long lingering in its psyche, is now nowhere to be seen or felt. Feast is the word everywhere as this nation, so long torn by troubles and adversity, has none amounting to too much at the moment. The swarm of the recent generation of children, nicely American accented from television and non believing in religion, is two fisted and footed proclaiming their independence, and living life hanging on by their finger tips. Music and dancing are everywhere. And although the famed dungeon outpost of the Catacombs of my own time is gone, and where the inebriated dispossessed cavorted and great minds conferred, there still remains a social life, with none like it anywhere else in the world. And where the definition of clarity is still remembered as that force given to a fist sent in the direction of a face that when hit had no trouble seeing stars.

As you would imagine, such dramatic changes in any nation with a past like Ireland's can cause a lot of publicity to go circulating around the world. And you guessed it, another new big surprise is in store. Word has finally reached the ears of the rich and famous who have heard news of this place on the edge of Europe with a bunch of marvellous international banks and tax advisers aplenty and these rich and famous are girding loins to make their assault. Descending out of the sky to restore the big mansions and castles with the best plumbing money can buy, mending the leaks in the roofs and reanimating the splendour that once reigned in the grand halls, drawing rooms and ball rooms. And to enjoy, if not their anonymity, at least their humility. For among the Irish you can wash off and shed your celebrity and be as natural and normal as other natural and normal human beings. As in Ireland, far away from the tumult and torture of crowded places, no one matters more than you do and no better place exists on earth to be with your own decent fair minded self wrapped up in solitude.

And now what more can I say than the best words I ever said about Ireland which were the last words said in *The Ginger Man.* Come here till I tell you. Where is the sea high and the winds soft and moist and warm, sometimes stained with sun, with peace so wild for wishing where all is told and telling. On a winter night I heard horses on a country road, beating sparks out of the stones. I knew they were running away and would be crossing the fields where the pounding would come up into my ears. And I said they are running out to death which is with some soul and their eyes are mad and teeth out.

> God's mercy
> On the wild
> Ginger Man
> And on Ireland

1996

PART 9

Ireland, Then and Now

The Water of Life

As here be nectar sweet upon the air, it's time to talk of Irish whiskey. For by God, the congenerics thereby occasioned by this distillate lets you soon know that its golden liquid is there nearby resting in its glass ready to be drunk. For there is no drink pervades the elemental ether nor enters the nostril as do the lovingly condensed vapours which produce the aromatically rare blissful bouquet of Irish whiskey. And many are the malty soft and honeyed varieties to choose from.

Now then. Think of it. Whiskey is a drink that can be made wherever it is wanted yet is capable of elegant distinction reflecting the natural conditions from which it originates. And it is produced from barley of the grass family, one of the most ancient of all cultivated crops, originating with a plump and mellow seed 5000 BC in Egypt. Of all the grains, it is one of the most adaptable to climate, ripening in the shortest time and needing less warmth. Now think of Ireland. Wouldn't you know that in the winter winds of monastic times the drink whiskey was invented here. And being that this grain barely is the basic ingredient in the process of malting, and is alive and growing well across these many counties, the grand tradition continues, which in these fast passing recent years has made Ireland that rare parkland paradise at the western tip of Europe.

And this aromatic distillate first came to my attention when my good old ancient friend, Gainor Stephen Crist, now rumoured everywhere to have been the model for *The Ginger Man*'s Sebastian Dangerfield, would approach in his ambassadorial manner and ceremoniously rap the edge of his half crown upon the mahogany of a Dublin public house and in his own inimitable way say to the bartender, 'A large Three Swallows Powers Gold Label, when you're ready.' And I'd always stop and think at these words, 'when you're ready' as if it were possible that a Dublin bartender, the best in the world, would ever not be ready. Or whether the swallows mentioned were those meant to fly or winglessly go goldenly down the throat. In the case of Crist, from Dayton, Ohio, they went down the throat.

Crist was a stickler for purity and would always remind that the grain which provided his drink had been nourished by the clean soft moist winds from the Atlantic. And even I had known from an early age in America and through my own mother that every good thing came out of Ireland. That with her oats and grain burgeoning fresh and green up out of the mist moist loamy landscape, you were at the source of your good health and which ingredients I remember were indeed imported for my Bronx growing up well being. And if Gainor Crist stood in front of his pint of plain, which as Myles Na Gopaleen said was your only man, always next to it nearby Crist's elbow was his large trusty ball of malt waiting to be sent down a slaked throat, an inspiration, as he said, for the soul to soar and for the gizzard to reblood the veins.

Now for longer years than most people can remember your Irish whiskey has been an exotic aristocrat of drinks and an important national product of Ireland that the natives who know their spirits have always relied upon to be drinking ready on their sideboards. And the scholars have come to help you if it's more knowledge you're looking for, you can grab a copy of Jim Murray's scholarly almanac on the subject, or Andrew Bielenberg's actually vivid portrait of Locke's Distillery. And in a trice you can be a connoisseur of this whiskey, distilled three times and left in the pot sometimes for as long as ten, twelve or fifteen years. And names you'll soon be learning to reel off. Bushmills, Coleraine, Jameson, Kilbeggan, Locke's, Middleton, Murphy's, Paddy, Powers, Tullamore and, last but not least of the rare flowers, the Tyrconnell single malt. If you can't get all these in Dublin, and your thirst is still getting the better of you, and for you who can't wait to taste the best, then go on your way on the autobahn or better on the train to Mullingar. For right now on a shelf there is a limited edition Dungourney 1964 Special Reserve Irish malt whiskey in a nice wooden box containing a fifty year old malt at the knock down price of two hundred and twenty five Irish punts and offered for sale at the Old Stand in this now Joycean famed town.

Ah but meantime in the meanwhile Ireland has gone jumping mad to be giving publicity to its great literary figures of the past, few of whom did not take their literary elixir of Irish whiskey and down a couple of large ones every day. And one such who bent his farmer's elbow in this manner was the great poet Patrick Kavanagh, who, always a man he said for the great purity, be it either in the soul or in the whiskey, having come from his turf accountants and having placed his bet for the first day's race, would growl across the bar.

'While this ould nag is running with the brakes off, I'll have a big one of Jameson to keep me in optimistic company.'

And another such great taster of the malt was himself Brendan Behan, a man always exploding with generosity, but a scourge to respectable social life in the capital and terror most terrible to the middle classes. He loved referring to where the clergy got their own special brew of whiskey from the midland's Locke's Distillery, at Kilbeggan. With their now graciously blended brands and the growing fame of their Tyrconnell. And you'll be pleased to hear all is under the able aegis of a former foxhunting gentleman, Brian Quinn, who, a perfectionist, is as elegant as is his whiskey, and presides over this marvellous restoration of this fabled distillery which in fact can show you the very barrels to which Behan referred and from which the clergy religiously took their brew.

And a word more about this poet, playwright and novelist whose blazing presence was often heralded by his shuffling approaching footsteps as one did hear him come into McDaid's

293

pub on Dublin's Harry Street, sockless in his shoes without laces and so far down at heel that Behan walked with permanently sprained ankles. And one would perk one's ears to hear said beside me in his slightly quavering and stammering voice one of the most fervent requests for the native Irish whiskey refreshment ever given at any bar in drinking history.

'Verily now Paddy O'Brien or you Jim Gallagher, me old friend, as I am with a beseechment, an hosanna and an hallelujah having just now strayed absent mindedly and wandered more than was good for me and left as I was so marooned with me sobriety overcoming me that with me taste buds in ferment I'm here in a hurry to continue to be in my mild and enjoyable state of previous inebriation. Standing before you in some solemnity, as I've done more than once in the dock before the British courts where dropping me in a hangman's noose they were planning to constrict me fatally by the neck which predicament put me firmly amind of that Epiphany said by all good Protestants, that I know that my redeemer liveth. And as you can see my neck is not yet broken and allows me to render the present request, that would you, ever Paddy or you Jim, plonk down upon the mahogany a genuine bottle from Locke's Distillery and pour out of it a large whiskey, and thus shall my eyes be pleasantly bedazzled with its anciently grand liquid golden gleam yielding on the palate its superb spiciness and gentle fruitiness and with the aromatics of it hurrying up me nose the sweet malty honeyed velvetyness, it would be informing me belly, which is with the thirst, screaming that me throat is cut. And whiskey taken internally.

Is every bit
As good
For bowels
As
It is good for
Lust

1995

The Second Revolution –
the Modern Enthral of the New Ireland

Following the TV antennae flying their masts over Dublin, and beaming in the nonchalant amorality of the BBC, the Second Revolution has now dawned. The cattle dealers' lunch has all but disappeared. Even the gossip is modernized. It's now who is in the shiny blue BMW, revving his or her way down the intimacy of Dawson Street, and has the crates of fresh chilled champagne delivered each dawn like the milk to the front door.

The last of the diehard cynics, the once conscience of the nation, lurking out there behind their suburban shrubberies from Dollymount to Dalkey, are saying little and less as their days creep closer to the crematorium. This last tradition shattering innovation to be imported said to be faster to send you to heaven.

I tell you all that because now I tell you that Ireland is ready to bask in her blaze of glory. An ancient green nation known alive to the world afar for dancing Gaelic hell out of all the competition. Them nearby British themselves, too, God bless them, are coming along likewise, winning their battles here and there. And they must be good at a fight, for as the saying goes they beat the Germans and didn't they come as close as damn it to nearly beating the Irish as well.

Their eminently intelligent Prince of Wales has come to make friends. But then indeed it need not be reminded to anybody that Ireland is truly the land of the welcomes. And glad to see him were most, for the Prince, horticulturalist extraordinary that he is, knows there are few places in the world that can grow a blade of grass faster or bigger than on the emerald isle and no where can grow a blade more nutritious.

Now then. What I have already had to say is said in even louder words by the brave British pound, for so long supreme, it has at last finally succumbed to the Irish punt. The latter nation, too, having had so many saints, has increased another value, with new saints for the tourists to adore. Never mind Yeats and Joyce and forget old Gogarty and his ivory Martello tower.

The recent ready to be sanctified and to go down singing in history are Hume and Haughey and Adams, with the spectrum widening to President Robinson, herself admired by the world. These outstanding citizens emerging in an Ireland modern and new, bursting from its long bondage of isolation, ready now to outdo the Danes and Dutch in freedoms of the flesh. Excel the French in the quality of cheese. And noblest and best of all, to out do the Swiss in banking. But of course thoroughly wised up to this, haven't them foreign financial institutions in their dozens been glad to elbow in upon the gravy and join the other guzzling snouts at the trough.

And so the cornucopia has come. Nicely now refilled to overflowing by the European Union. Millions stacked up in the vaults. And why not, this is the land where the gombeen man was invented who was once the little village banker with his book of credit and his shelves full of food. And he especially goeth as Ireland goeth and Ireland goeth well. And ask where he doth now be found. He now be found, as he always was, behind his counter in every village and down the side streets of every town.

And these days he's blossomed in a supermarket in his neat light blue suit behind his accountant's cash register and in the thickening files of his solicitors as he accumulates more gold. He'd be behind the big building boom, behind the new pub and nightclub availing of this new freedom of making a monster profit. And not a thing is wrong with that because it has been a long time coming. For Ireland needs its millionaires. For no one is better to splash the optimism in a country's reputation around the globe.

But just to put things a little bit more in perspective, while the brogue is beginning to reverberate all over the Internet. Didn't the dawn of the Protestant Catholic come without a sound of hyperbole and to be found proliferating in your better golf and tennis clubs.

And Reverend Ian Paisley himself would be amazed if not amused to see them taking tea with the international set as they populate these rural parkland palaces across the country that would make you think you were in your first earthly paradise. But the Reverend Ian Paisley maybe was pleased when the first chink or crack in the carapace of the great Church of Rome came when meat was no longer forbidden on Friday, leaving the long devout population, who hated fish all their lives, up standing shaking their fists back at Rome for the past penitent needlessness of it all.

And pleased, too, should Reverend Paisley be as Protestantism, too, is also infiltrating other great Romanish traditions threatening to fall asunder, as they are now out, by God, even to ban the last spiritual glory left among the Catholic clergy, their celibacy.

Ireland may not have put a mouse on the moon yet, but the whole country is firmly pledged to get up and go with the great and the good. And few would be left not predicting better times ahead. The wrong pipes attached to the right pipes and the days of having to go up to the bedroom to turn the lights off in the kitchen are gone.

All the modern medicines and gentle techniques for toying with intestines are here. The good native doctor is now better than your previous foreign imported edition and knows every blessed thing about your better health. With a mere peek at you he'd be able to diagnose and tell you to eat more garlic and chew your carrots well.

As for the taste of food, the French are here in droves, no longer complaining about the cooking. And no longer complaining about the complacency and inefficiency of the natives, the Germans are becoming natives themselves.

A new morality most profound and cataclysmic is fermenting in the revolution. The young are in rebellion voting for people instead of politics. Traditional parents are changing, authority diminished. Politicians especially those up loudest howling on their hind legs are not always believed and perhaps never were.

The homosexual of old is gone when once it was a stigma that would drive you out of the country or you could seek the refuge of the church. The pregnant single girl no longer has to leave for foreign more permissive parts. Welfare is everywhere keeping the wolf from many a door. Again it's the cornucopia of the EU and its plenitude which pours out plenty for bypasses around them rustic little towns so you won't be wasting time getting to Dublin or Galway and back. And who can't say that isn't progress.

But with the nation in its modern enthral, one might ask, just to be romantic for a moment, are there any of the old Anglo Irish left. And you'd have to say that only merely a few are in a mansion here and there, still hanging on quietly to their after dinner port and British vowels. Ah but bravely in their place has come a new aristocracy replacing those who with generations of land, wealth and so called good breeding gave a vision of poise and beauty.

Their places now taken by Kitty, Edna, Maeve, Bridget and Dymphna who were once found behind the village chemist's counter and there they are now, it's cocktail time. Radiantly engowned atop the grand stairs. Having read Joyce and Beckett, Heaney and Hughes cover to cover, and with their own tiaras sparkling upon their hair. And himself isn't doing badly either in black tie and sporting your long Havana Bolivar cigar.

The news, too, is seeping into the Republic that God did not invent us. But never mind that rumour for a moment. No longer are there droves emigrating out into the far off world to become pagans. The Bishops are still given headlines for their opinions to inform what the Catholic Church thinks. But it angers the young minds of Ireland for now they think what they think. As the golf courses, hotels and tourists multiply, there are the nightclubs till dawn, cocaine, hashish and ecstasy.

Murder victims are to be found under the floor boards and in the boots of cars. And in a land so expensive it's a relief to know that the cheapest thing in Ireland still remains these days the company and conversation of the people. And listen a moment as I harp back to the good bad old days.

It only seems but a micro second ago that of a Dublin evening when the late dark of June had descended, I ventured down that fashionable street of Grafton that walks its way through so many Dubliners' lives. My eye spotting the shadow of a crane rising high in the sky, I turned east into Duke Street and I knew instantly that another great step forward in progress was in the making.

Massive lorries, flood lights and roaring machinery all over the place. I knew the crow bar bending Irish held the world record in the time it took to beat a concert grand piano to a pulp and pieces but I wasn't ready for this. The Bailey, that old hostelry of Yeats, Joyce and Beckett, was gone. Turned into a massive hole in the ground. And not a single sign of any anti blood sport folk, nor a single chanting voice nor torch light procession of protesting architectural preserving purists to be seen.

Nor an echo left of all the blazing afternoons and nights of rhetoric preached from the poets and out of mouths that lost a week's wages on the last race with mouths to feed at home. Drowning their sorrow in more sorrow. And lonely was I to realize that the old times of *The Ginger Man* were finally vanished for their second hand worth into a bunch of old books and pub signs.

But then one can turn to go back into the new of the old Ireland. And fashionable Grafton Street still with its flow of pedestrians in many colours of skin and every colour and shape of cloth. Where mummers and mimes did tip toe past in frozen poses. Where the perfume of a roasted coffee hovered, as a poet stood guard at the gates of Bewley's Oriental Café. Reminding still of the country where the songs born out of pain go singing. Religion has been diminished, prejudices nearly abolished.

A revolution has raged, everything turned on its head. And in this land where they are adored, the voices of children echo. Where the brooding heavens carry their veils of rain to hide all her sins and keep her safe in her graces. And where above all your self importance can still achieve the heights.

1995

A Book of Irish Quotations

I was being interviewed not that long ago in New York City by an attractive young lady journalist who said she'd just returned from attending at a conference of Irish publishers and in seeing nothing anywhere referring to me at this, she asked what about J. P. Donleavy, doesn't he live in Ireland and write books. The reply she got was, 'Oh him, he's nothing but a black mark on Irish publishing.'

How nice it is then to pick up a book, fresh from the O'Brien Press, which in every way is a credit to Irish publishing. The fine book has now become a native reality. And this present volume has a tasteful attractive design by Jacques Teljeur, photograph by Pieterse Davison and quotations edited by Sean McMahon. Ireland is standing up on its hind legs these days and getting as go ahead modern as any place on earth. Even Mullingar, out here beyond the Bog of Allen, could once boast of its own publishing house, the Lilliput Press, now moved to Dublin. And there is a rampant rumour that John Betjeman was first published with a poem in our own local newspaper, the *Westmeath Examiner*. And indeed another rumour is that a young James Joyce trod in the halls of this very house where I write. This Mullingar association may also be why the astonishing life sized wax effigy of Mr Joyce is in the lobby of a local hotel.

Ah but that's not all. Here, too, in Ireland was born the most astonishing legislation in the history of nations, an antidote to the previous kicking of authors and poets in the teeth, the destruction of manuscripts, the insult and ridicule, the banning of books and paintings and where now by the grace of Charles Haughey, father of such, artists may live with the fruit of their

301

work, tax free. And if the proof of the pudding be in its immediate reading, ah then you can imagine what is said in the present volume concerning such an enlightened man. And here straight away may we aptly quote from Conor Cruise O'Brien, who clearly is an incisive commentator: 'If I saw Mr Haughey buried at midnight at a cross-roads, with a stake driven through his heart – politically speaking – I should continue to wear a clove of garlic round my neck just in case.'

But surely, in spite of Mr O'Brien's words, this man Charles Haughey must be destined to become, when his time is nigh, canonized and ultimately the patron saint of Ireland's Painters, Poets, Composers, Sculptors and Writers, all of whom will quote only words of praise for this political gentleman in the next edition of this work.

Here, too, in this volume are the stunning insights of many an Irish author like Flann O'Brien, Patrick Kavanagh and George Bernard Shaw. And there is no doubt whatever that being Irish or even merely being in Ireland, when it comes to putting a word out of a mouth or on a page, gives you a knife edged head start over the rest of the world, in seeking to cut gems fashioned in the infinities of philosophy. Taking, as can be done in the Irish vernacular, grand leaps through the imagination. That invariably would leave you landing in a conclusion that would amount to as near next to nothing as made no difference. If you follow my version of Erse jargon.

Now there is no where on the face of the earth where a turn of phrase is more admired and, if admired, repeated than in Ireland. Even I myself, the black mark on Irish publishing, am quoted. Although I don't see any of my better ones, especially when I had Ireland particularly in mind, such as, 'Will God ever forgive the Catholics.' Never mind. This book has Beckett, Behan, Betjeman, right on to Honor Lilbush Wingfield Tracy, the latter by God has for many a year been employing her brilliant marksmanship with bull's eyes galore upon the natives.

Even here are the words of the Rev. Ian Paisley, staunch

fighter for Protestant freedom, who has for so many long years faithfully sung the song of the Orange Man with such honest fervour that were he ever to stroll the length of central Dublin from the Rotunda to St Stephen's Green, he would be a pied piper cheered and followed by every devout Catholic who could walk a Dublin street, worshipped as he secretly is south of the border. And none of your smart remarks are invited here as to where would you ever find a devout Catholic in Dublin.

This book at the least is a major insight into Ireland, that country that, if it could ever be understood at all, would only be more misunderstood as a result. Leaving the understander forever in frustration but with knowing as much as one can ever know about this race. For whom the joy of disagreement has always been an Irish tradition and blessing, an Irishman always willing to see both sides of an argument provided it can result in a fight. And you can quote me on that.

1984

The Boy is Back in Town

Taking one on a merry ride, this is a story, with Desmond Guinness as its instigator, which is a long time in the making and much devoid of the principle of socialism and equal shares for all. In this pursuit I was this while back on an optimistic day hurrying up to Dublin hoping the rattles and whines one hears in one's car are not about to express themselves further by sending all four wheels spinning off in all directions. Parking my motor machine in one venerable club I walked but a mere few paces to another and there within at one of its large Georgian windows overlooking the trees and shrubs across in St Stephen's Green, I took a glass of Guinness in the beautiful company of the famed lady Rachel Murray, who has a wonderfully eccentric savvy in matters aesthetic and over whom Desmond Guinness sighs with awe.

It is five thirty precisely on this fine Dublin afternoon. And in no city in the world could you be feeling more contented. Out of the blue a fax arrives to say the Loyko Trio is playing that very night at Whelan's Pub in Wexford Street and where Desmond Guinness will be, and urges me to be, at 9.00 p.m. Meanwhile, as it does in Dublin, another engagement intervenes. Caught in immense traffic, Rachel and I slowly motor out through streets where both Brendan Behan and Jonathan Swift once sported about, and along the central avenue of Phoenix Park to ply the tricky roads this way and that till we reach the walled parklands and the splendour of Luttrellstown Castle. And wouldn't you know by the style of the people arriving there and the grand samplings of furniture to be seen that there was no shortage in Ireland of the well fixed

304

in this world or the champagne flowing to keep their thirst slaked.

Now it's been a long time since I've been in Dublin. But from the midlands these days, and on the new bypasses, one can hurry across the Bog of Allen and up to town in a trice. To let the senses get stimulated again by the teeming civilization. And if the state of the capital is anything to go by you could get soon stimulated out of your mind, so swept has the city been with its dramatic changes. Duke Street, half down, is half up again. The thoroughfares all about are flowing full with your fancy motor vehicles. Folk sublimating their road rage are looking out over their steering wheels and down their bonnets at any of youse who's got a conspicuous licence plate announcing the advanced in years state of your chariot. And with land prices and house prices flying into the sky, and with the watchword 'Forward with the Rich' being whispered loud and clear from Ballsbridge to Blackrock, you'd ask where is all the money coming from. And best keep that a mystery.

Meanwhile the night's festivities are not yet over. And from Luttrellstown, holding on to one's hat, it was back with Rachel in her exquisite flowing robes to Dublin for Sancerre and poached salmon, pudding, Armagnac and coffee, amid the silver trophies and under the great chandeliers of this pleasantly dignified club. Then off to attend the playing of the Loyko Trio in Whelan's Pub of Wexford Street and to see if we could confront Desmond Guinness of the impeccable manners and the laser blue eyes. And we were too late for Desmond but my goodness there was no shortage of less handsome, but equally enthusiastic people. And it was as if one were in a pre-war Berlin or post-war Hamburg cellar. Your musical aficionados cheek by jowl at their tables covered in glasses full of your diverse potables. And there on the small stage, this astonishing Loyko Trio producing their music from three voices, two violins and a guitar. And never ever have one's ears heard such acoustically joyous, and exquisitely high or funereally low, notes coaxed from such stringed instruments. Which at times even turned into spine shivering sounds of the human voice.

And so it came to pass that upon such exquisite octaves, and with the opportunity of hearing them again, do we come to the next part of our chronicle. And to the unparagoned Desmond Guinness and his lovely lady, Penny, and Leixlip Castle. And to where nearby did first get invented the brew that makes much of this tale possible and has over the many literary years nourished the best imaginations of Ireland. So, too, may we take comfort that as Dublin grows and creeps beyond itself to inevitably surround the antique and serene, and as the mini palaces of the gombeen rich erupt well meaning but fatally architecturally half assed across the Irish countryside, this great ancient edifice of Leixlip Castle stands, still there triumphant upon its sylvan hill. And along with its master, an outpost staunch against the philistine and reassured by the babble and gurgle of the Liffey beneath its massive grey cut stone elevations. On the roadway below, its great gates opening as if by magic, and in fact by telecommunicated computer, allowing you to enter upon an unforgettable oasis. And if your feel good factor thermometer hasn't risen a few notches as you motor upwards over the driveway cobblestones. Then there's something bloody well wrong with you.

All that's next is to get up a few massive granite steps and in through that white knobless door. And if luckily inside you get, (and by God it's not everybody who does) you are by any aesthetic measure able to witness one of the most supremely unique magnificences in the world. In an interior which holds itself firm against all that is commonplace, nothing is to be found so shocking to the eye as to be new or unused. The vast chambers providing a spacious comfort to both body and soul, and collectively, not only giving shelter but keeping at a decent distance the woes of life. And now you guessed it. What a bloody great place for a party. And if a dinner goes with it all the better. It's fresh vegetables from Penny's garden and other viands which come delicious from Eileen's kitchen. And if visitors come who make a bit of a stir on the world scene of celebrity, why not. It altogether adds to the good taste of things. And the more, the merrier.

And the first due to come is Jerry Hall, guest of honour. But she's delayed, and instead her quietly disposed and eminently courteous husband Mr Jagger is there. Now forget reminiscing about them great old unexpurgated obscene days down in the Catacombs. Where deep down in the spiritual dungeons of Dublin's Fitzwilliam Place, Lead Pipe Daniel the Dangerous once roamed, and between scribbling his poems, and his great bulk looming through the shadows, could be heard to accost with his heed those wretched of demeanour.

'Cheer up or I'll break your face.'

For let me tell you, the faces appearing here at a damn sight more tranquil Leixlip Castle, you'd rather kiss. The first of whom is Ruby Wax of television fame, whom I confront in the kitchen. And why not. This is Ireland. Where the kitchen is as sacred as any parlour and tends to relieve you of your airs and graces. Now in the flesh of real life, Miss Wax's mere presence knocks your socks right off. Her visage composed, intelligence written upon her face, she is quite a stunning beauty. She's exactly what America needs to be let loose on their somnambulant awareness and to disturb them out of their couch potato trance of indifference. And, too, in tribal company with Ruby Wax, there is another strange and austere beauty. Carrie Fisher from Hollywood, famed actress, famed daughter, famed author and both these ladies are mothers. Opinions flow from rapid fire lips. Making one's ear alive to stories and tales to be minted anew in the mind. And learning all you ever wanted to know about women's verities.

But this night, your eye cast in any direction, other legendary emerge. Marianne Faithfull, who carries her wonderful mystique as if straight from the cellars of pre-war Berlin. For indeed she does, having just recorded songs which reigned then and which she has now brought exquisitely back to life to soon celebrate on compact disc. And within the frame of the great chimney pieces the fires blaze. As always, our host Desmond Guinness, effortlessly being himself, has no trouble reassuring you that you're managing well enough in your own desperate effort to be liked. This man, celebrator of architectural follies, and brilliant with his pen that describes some of the utterly beautiful architectural treasures of this land, has long been a symbol to encourage the seeking out and preservation of the neglected beauty of Ireland. He is also equally brilliant at spotting talent of all sorts and variety in other arts. And this is why he has just converted his old coach house to provide this venue for Loyko Trio to be admired. So more of the same can happen again.

Meanwhile the next generation of beauty arises on long willowy legs. The old hat men delighted. And Van Morrison of the amazing voice sits contented under his hat. The sound of four letter words lets you know there's youth about. And nobody is in awe of anybody. Away at the corner of a table the thoughtful titan of the pop world, Paul MacGuinness, sits sipping wine with his charming wife. There's the gentle benignity of the beautifully spoken Gareth Brown, who behaves with a courtesy of another age as an Emperor might without being imperious. Flashed before the eye goes the elegantly and perennially beautiful couple the Knight and Madam Glin. But away in a corner, a quiet gentleman sits strumming a guitar, as if waiting for his loved one, and he is. For it's Mr Jagger waiting for the absentee Jerry Hall.

But there is another figure who moves quietly and effectively behind the glories within Leixlip Castle. Whose magic hands tend every tiny corner of this vast castle and wondrous gardens and where the flowers and vegetables in their neat rows grow with a beauty all of their own. As no one is allowed to suffer a discontent around her whose eyes watch for another's loneliness that it be quickly ended. I find her because I've stepped out into the darkness of the bleakness. And there she is, in the softness of the chill rain, Penny Guinness, alone. And trying to coax a chauffeur in out of the cold and wet of the night and into the comfort of the castle. And would that such thoughtful charity be more prevalent in the world.

Next morn, vetting the city again, didn't I confront a living docile cow chewing its cud and standing in front of Buswell's Hotel in Molesworth Street. To remind me of the great Dublin pranksters of yesteryear and my faith in the bygone Dublin is restored. Nothing serious has changed. Up the Republic!

1996

Pasha of Heartbreak House Seeks Companion

Slightly reclusive but anxious to get out more, gracefully older fit man, still capable of eight and a half successive deep knee bends, nine sit ups, and five and a half push ups, and with minor public status, requires pleasantly attractive younger lady of principle with a bent for flower arranging and entertaining and who, in also being ambitious, wants some of her own public attention to enable her quickly if not so quietly to move on after eighteen months to better things, but meanwhile before flying the coop, can adapt to country life in modest mansion set in parklands by large lake where staff are kept. Remuneration modest, food and wine plentiful. An interest in the out of doors, architecture, restoration, and horses an advantage. Excellent for hunting near by for the brave and bloodthirsty. But the lady must see to her own equine grooming and mucking out. However no gardening or ditch or indeed grave digging should the Pasha fall from his perch, in which latter case a five star hotel suite will be provided for the pleasantly attractive younger lady of principle, expenses paid, to comfortably live out remainder of agreement.

1997